Imaginaries of Connectivity

Global Epistemics Series
In Partnership with the Centre for Global Knowledge Studies (*gloknos*)

Founding Editor:
Inanna Hamati-Ataya (University of Cambridge)

Editorial Assistants:
Felix Anderl and Matthew Holmes (University of Cambridge)

Editorial Review Board:
Rigas Arvanitis (Institut de Recherche pour le Développement) | Jana Bacevic (University of Cambridge) | Patrick Baert (University of Cambridge) | Shadi Bartsch-Zimmer (University of Chicago) | Maria Birnbaum (University of Bern) | Avital Bloch (Universidad de Colima) | Jenny Boulboullé (Utrecht University) | Jordan Branch (Brown University) | Sonja Brentjes (Max Planck Institute for the History of Science) | Karine Chemla (Centre National de la Recherche Scientifique & Université de Paris) | David Christian (Macquarie University) | James H. Collier (Virginia Tech) | Steven Connor (University of Cambridge) | Helen Anne Curry (University of Cambridge) | Shinjini Das (University of East Anglia) | Sven Dupré (Utrecht University) | David Edgerton (King's College London) | Juan Manuel Garrido Wainer (Universidad Alberto Hurtado) | Simon Goldhill (University of Cambridge) | Anna Grasskamp (Hong Kong Baptist University) | Clare Griffin (Nazarbayev University) | Marieke Hendriksen (Utrecht University) | Dag Herbjørnsrud (Senter for global og komparativ idéhistorie) | Noboru Ishikawa (Kyoto University) | Christian Jacob (Ecole des Hautes Etudes en Sciences Sociales) | Martin Jones (University of Cambridge) | Katarzyna Kaczmarska (University of Edinburgh) | Isaac A. Kamola (Trinity College, Connecticut) | Tuba Kocaturk (Deakin University) | Pablo Kreimer (Universidad Nacional de Quilmes) | Michèle Lamont (Harvard University) | Helen Lauer (University of Dar es Salaam) | G. E. R. Lloyd (University of Cambridge) | Carlos López-Beltrán (National Autonomous University of Mexico) | Eric Lybeck (University of Manchester) | Christos Lynteris (University of St Andrews) | Amanda Machin (Witten-Herdecke University) | Tara Mahfoud (King's College London) | Maximilian Mayer (University of Nottingham Ningbo) | Willard McCarty (King's College London) | Atsuro Morita (Osaka University) | Iwan Morus (Aberystwyth University) | David Nally (University of Cambridge) | John Naughton (University of Cambridge) | Helga Nowotny (ETH Zurich) | Johan Östling (Lund University) | Ingrid Paoletti (Politecnico di Milano) | V. Spike Peterson (University of Arizona) | Helle Porsdam (University of Copenhagen) | David Pretel (The College of Mexico) | Dhruv Raina (Jawaharlal Nehru University) | Amanda Rees (University of York) | Hans-Jörg Rheinberger (Max Planck Institute for the History of Science) | Sarah de Rijcke (Leiden University) | Francesca Rochberg (University of California at Berkeley) | Alexander Ruser (University of Agder) | Anne Salmond (University of Auckland) | Karen Sayer (Leeds Trinity University) | James C. Scott (Yale University) | Elisabeth Simbürger (Universidad de Valparaíso) | Daniel Lord Smail (Harvard University) | Fred Spier (University of Amsterdam) | Jomo Sundaram (Khazanah Research Institute) | Swen Steinberg (Queen's University) | Tereza Stöckelová (Czech Academy of Sciences) | Liba Taub (University of Cambridge) | Daniel Tramaiolo (University of Hong Kong) | Corinna Unger (European University Institute) | Matteo Valleriani (Max Planck Institute for the History of Science) | Stéphane Van Damme (European University Institute) | Andrés Vélez Posada (Universidad EAFIT) | Aparecida Vilaça (National Museum, Brazil) | Simon Werrett (University College London) | Helen Yitah (University of Ghana) | Longxi Zhang (City University of Hong Kong)
tinyurl.com/GlobalEpistemics | tinyurl.com/RLIgloknos

Title in the Series:
Imaginaries of Connectivity: The Creation of Novel Spaces of Governance
Edited by Luis Lobo-Guerrero, Suvi Alt and Maarten Meijer

Imaginaries of Connectivity

The Creation of Novel Spaces of Governance

Edited by Luis Lobo-Guerrero, Suvi Alt
and Maarten Meijer

**ROWMAN &
LITTLEFIELD**
──────── INTERNATIONAL
London • New York

Published by Rowman & Littlefield International Ltd.
6 Tinworth Street, London, SE11 5AL, United Kingdom
www.rowmaninternational.com

Rowman & Littlefield International Ltd. is an affiliate of Rowman & Littlefield
4501 Forbes Boulevard, Suite 200, Lanham, Maryland 20706, USA
With additional offices in Boulder, New York, Toronto (Canada), and Plymouth (UK)
www.rowman.com

Selection and editorial matter © 2020 by Luis Lobo-Guerrero, Suvi Alt and Maarten Meijer

Copyright in individual chapters is held by the respective chapter authors.

All rights reserved. No part of this book may be reproduced in any form or by any electronic or mechanical means, including information storage and retrieval systems, without written permission from the publisher, except by a reviewer who may quote passages in a review.

British Library Cataloguing in Publication Data
A catalogue record for this book is available from the British Library

ISBN: HB 978-1-78661-137-6
 PB 978-1-1-5381-7408-1

Library of Congress Cataloging-in-Publication Data Is Available

ISBN 978-1-78661-137-6 (cloth)
ISBN 978-1-1-5381-7408-1 (pbk)
ISBN 978-1-78661-138-3 (electronic)

Contents

	List of Images	vii
	Series Editor's Note	ix
	Introduction *Luis Lobo-Guerrero, Suvi Alt and Maarten Meijer*	1
Chapter 1	Novelty and the Creation of the New World in Sixteenth-Century Spain *Luis Lobo-Guerrero*	13
Chapter 2	Faciality and the Digital Politics of Identity: At Face Value *Carina Huessy*	39
Chapter 3	After Ports Were Linked: Paradoxes of Transpacific Connectivity in the Nineteenth Century *Sujin Eom*	67
Chapter 4	Zones at Sea and the Properties of Connectivity: (A)roundness, (Imm)unity and Liquidity *Barry J. Ryan*	89
Chapter 5	From *Tian Xia* to Sovereignty: The Shift of the Chinese Imaginary of Connectivity in the Nineteenth Century *Ariel Shangguan*	109

Chapter 6	'Making up Germans': Colonialism, Cartography and Imaginaries of 'Germandom' *Zeynep Gülsah Çapan and Filipe dos Reis*	127
Chapter 7	Friedrich's 'Germany': Landscape Painting as Imaginary and Experience of Connectivity *Benjamin Tallis*	153
Chapter 8	Cultivating Disconnection: Imaginaries of Rurality in the Catalan Pyrenees *Camila del Mármol*	177
Chapter 9	Organisms, Nodes and Networks *Paolo Palladino*	199
Chapter 10	Conclusions *Luis Lobo-Guerrero, Suvi Alt and Maarten Meijer*	219
Epilogue	Only Connect *Peter Adey*	235
	Index	243
	About the Editors and Contributors	251

List of Images

Chapter 6

Figure 6.1	Map of 'The Dissemination of Germans All over the World' in *Deutscher Kolonial-Atlas, Justus Perthes Gotha*, 1897	138
Figure 6.2	Statistics of 'The German Metropoles of the World' in *Alldeutscher Atlas, Justus Perthes Gotha*, 1900	142
Figure 6.3	Auxiliary Map of 'The German Empire and Its Inhabitants Then and Now' in *Alldeutscher Atlas, Justus Perthes Gotha*, 1900	144
Figure 6.4	Map of 'Central Europe' from Joseph Partsch's *Mitteleuropa, Justus Perthes Gotha*, 1904	145
Figure 6.5	Statistical Graph on 'Nationalities of Central Europe' from Joseph Partsch's *Mitteleuropa, Justus Perthes Gotha*, 1904	146

Chapter 8

Figure 8.1	La vall de la Vansa i Fórnols, Alt Urgell, 2016	184
Figure 8.2	Josa de Cadí, Alt Urgell, 2014	191

Chapter 9

Figure 9.1	Jean Luc Cornec, "TribuT," 1991	201

Series Editor's Note

It is a great pleasure for me to inaugurate the *Global Epistemics* series and to do so with a volume that reflects so well the series' ambition to communicate advanced as well as exploratory research on knowledge across traditional disciplinary boundaries.

Imaginaries of Connectivity illuminates the many ways in which connections, connectivity and connectivities are imagined, translated, embodied, materialised and made meaningful and efficient within and across particular temporalities, regimes of meaning, modes of reasoning and spatialities. The range of contributions not only highlights the ubiquitous character of connectivity as idea and reality but also brings forth the many ways in which it shapes and informs self-perceptions, social interactions and projects of societal control. The volume will speak to readers interested in historical epistemologies and their materialisation in technologies of knowledge, power and governance as well as those exploring the interfaces and convergences between modes of knowing and modes of being and (inter)acting.

By highlighting the processes through which connections are imagined and performed within and upon spaces of social action, (re)production and innovation, the volume itself enacts its subject matter in a way that reflects the *Global Epistemics* series' core ethos and objective, namely to embrace and promote the connected and connective character of human knowledges beyond the institutional and vocational divisions of labour that shape our everyday engagement with them as scholars, academics and scientists.

Imaginaries of Connectivity is the first volume of a trilogy of collaborative projects in historical epistemology that I very much look forward to introducing to our readers in the next months. In the meantime, I invite colleagues sharing the series' commitment to opening up the space of transdisciplinary research and communication around the richness of human and non-human knowledges to contribute to this new initiative and help us connect those spaces of thought and epistemic praxis that have unnecessarily been segregated for too long.

Inanna Hamati-Ataya
(Cambridge, 16 July 2019)

Introduction

Luis Lobo-Guerrero, Suvi Alt and Maarten Meijer

Connectivity is ubiquitous and lies at the core of human interaction with the world. Power, knowledge, scarcity, order, language, experience, culture, materiality, spatiality, vitality, intellect, spirituality and expression are all dimensions of existence that depend on forms of interaction. Connected cells create molecules, individuals connect with each other giving rise to communities and societies, ideas connect into theories and paradigms, satellites connect with earth sensors to relate location and data, language enables communication, rationalities and logics allow for the abstraction of thought and art connects being with expression.

Connectivity has been and remains a central phenomenon with observable manifestations through which the articulation and sustenance of forms of life can be explored. Ancient cultures, for example, developed systems for weaving fibres to make baskets and accounting systems to link and govern productive processes and assembled wood, cloth and rope into vessels for navigation. Urban centres emerged as part of wider interconnected structures involving religious beliefs and practices, political systems and economic activities. Empires have operated on their capacity to connect cultures, economies and forms of governance. Economies operate on the possibility to connect supplies with demands. Technologies connect aspirations of efficiency with physical and intellectual capacity. Life itself is the result of incalculable connectivities of all orders.

Connectivity, as the state or capacity of being connected or interconnected (OED 2018), is a noun of adjectival origin expressing a tendency, disposition or function to connect. As such, connectivity constitutes a phenomenon that relates to a condition or expectation of being connected. Its substantial meaning relates to what is being connected, the processes through which connections are made possible and the ideas, practices, beliefs and material conditions that need to be in place for a particular form of connection to take place. Due to its relational character, however, connectivity as phenomenon does not figure prominently in scholarly thought in the humanities and the social sciences (Tellmann, Opitz and Staeheli 2012, 209–10). Yet, it is frequently claimed that the world is now more connected than ever before. The interconnectedness of life under globalisation is discussed as if it were a reality so self-evident that it requires little thought on its conditions of possibility (cf. Tellmann et al. 2012; Tsing 2005). Ideas of the globe are constantly invoked as interconnected wholes such as the environment, so much so that it even seems a rather unnecessary exercise to inquire how the globe has ever come to appear this way (e.g., Flyverbom 2012, 295–96; Sampson 2012; Staeheli 2012, 233–34).

Imaginaries of Connectivity

If connectivity is ubiquitous and the interconnectedness of life under globalisation is assumed as fact, why is it that connectivity has not deserved much detailed attention in social sciences and humanities scholarship? Part of the problem of preparing connectivity as an area of research in the social sciences and the humanities has had to do with the difficulty of conceptualising it. Connectivity, for example, does not lend itself to a Kantian style of transcendental conceptualisation where quantity, quality, relation and modality operate as *a priori* categories of understanding (Kant 1965, A70/B95–A93/B109). Connectivity is not aprioristic in the sense that what makes it possible is an experience of connecting, which leads to saying that its being is always contingent on the assemblages that make it possible. In this respect, connectivity always constitutes unique phenomena which resist the deductive form of reasoning that supports grand strands of Western theory formation. While it has been presented as a quasi-transcendental that allows for understanding specific forms of life that rely on their capacity to connect (Dillon and Lobo-Guerrero 2009), such a way of understanding does not allow for generalisations and constitutes an obstacle for theory formation. Rather than seeking to provide a strategy through which to conceptualise connectivity as phenomena, an alternative intellectual route is to think of it through the imaginaries that make it possible.

The imaginary is a key idea in contemporary social and political theory which is often used but its meaning is rarely explicitly reflected on. In common normative parlance, the imaginary is opposed to the real and distrusted as irrational (Fourastié and Joron 2016, 53). Its role, however, has figured prominently in making sense of core ideas around which political community is articulated. Benedict Anderson argued, for example, that the nation is a socially constructed community, a cultural artefact which is imagined by people who perceive themselves as members of that group (Anderson 2016, 6–7). Charles Taylor defined the social imaginary as 'the ways in which people imagine their social existence, how they fit together with others, how things go on between them and their fellows, the expectations that are normally met, and the deeper notions and images that underlie these expectations' (2004, 23). In both perspectives, how people imagine is not predetermined but constitutes a field for intervention subject to structural historical changes (such as what Anderson called 'print capitalism') and is also subject to contingent interventions through media, education, religious faiths and ideologies.

Thinking about the imaginary is much more mundane than it might appear. It relates to the fundamental role of the imagination in all human action, a reflection which draws inspiration from Spinoza's theory of the mind. In his thought, 'An imagining [*imaginatio*] is an idea whereby the mind regards a thing as present . . . but which indicates the dis-position of the human body rather than the nature of the external thing' (Spinoza 1982, 160). A political imaginary in this respect is connected to the human ability to create images, and politics as understood by Spinoza is characterised as a field of the immanent movement and confrontation of imaginative forces (Saar 2015, 116). As explained by Saar, politics, as mediated through images, is made *through* the imaginary (ibid.).

The imaginary, however, is not simply about images as correlates of reality. Cornelius Castoriadis, through his work on the institution of society, advanced an understanding of the imaginary that helps interrogate the making of the rational, as a mode of reasoning, and the real as a field of formation, which is central to the strategy of this book. As put by him,

> The imaginary does not come from the image in the mirror or from the gaze of the other. Instead, the 'mirror' itself and its possibility, and the other as mirror, are the works of the imaginary, which is creation *ex nihilo* [out of nothing]. Those who speak of 'imaginary', understanding by this the 'specular', the reflection of the 'fictive', do no more than repeat, usually without realizing it, the affirmation which has for all time chained them to the underground of

the famous cave: it is necessary that this world be an image of something. The imaginary of which I am speaking is not an image of. It is the unceasing and essentially undetermined (social-historical and psychical) creation of figures/forms/images, on the basis of which alone there can ever be a question of 'something'. What we call 'reality' and 'rationality' are its works. (Castoriadis 1998, 7)

Castoriadis' reflection contributes to exploring the imaginary, not as reflecting a real but as an empirical space where the terms under which the real is constituted can be interrogated. This understanding of the imaginary as 'an ontopolitical specification of the nature of being, as such, construed in terms of the problematic of government and rule' (Dillon and Lobo-Guerrero 2009, 2), allows for intellectual challenges to ready-made expectations of what imaginaries represent. In this respect, rather than assuming connectivity as given, imaginaries can be approached as empirical spaces from which to observe the creative processes productive of connectivity. In turn, these processes can be interrogated through the ideas, practices, beliefs and material objects and conditions that combined in specific ways to give rise to novel specifications of orders interpreted as constituting reality. In other words, imaginaries can be used to reveal the novel terms that are to constitute the ground for political decision and action.

To say that connectivity as such has not been the object of scholarly reflection in the humanities and the social sciences does not mean that imaginaries of connectivity have not been theorised. Prominent within these have been systems analysis, complexity theory, non-linear thinking, assemblage theory, actor–network theory, and world systems theory. A brief survey of these theoretical articulations of different imaginaries of connectivity demonstrates the need for carefully scrutinizing, to paraphrase Castoriadis, the different mirrors with which these theories describe and analyse the connections that characterise reality. Economists and international relations (IR) scholars since the 1950s onwards have described the behaviour of consumers, firms and states in relation to the markets or anarchic international systems in which they operate (e.g., Wallerstein 2004; Waltz 2010). System analysis, in its various guises, operates on an imaginary that envisions the connectivity of units in relation to the overarching structure of which they are a part. More recently, interest in complexity and non-linearity has sought to refine traditional system analysis by adding a historical or evolutionary dimension to the connection between units and structures (e.g., Mainzer 2007; Root 2013). Other approaches such as assemblage thinking and actor–network theory have been motivated to think beyond or rather beneath the problematique of structure and agency by carefully describing the connections between heterogeneous (i.e., discursive and non-discursive, human and nonhuman) elements involved in the production of a particular order, phenomenon or action (e.g., Acuto and Curtis 2014; Latour 2005).

What these theories have in common is an endeavour to detail how the terms under which what is being connected; the processes through which connections are made possible; and the ideas, practices and beliefs and material conditions that need to be in place for a particular form of connection to take place produce a specific order. Such order is an expectation of the representation of reality. Their limitation, however, is that through a theoretical construct they operate the role of the image that Castoriadis criticised. In so doing, they lend themselves as platforms of the real on which to make decisions and exercise action (e.g., MacKenzie 2006).

Thinking beyond such influential perspectives, however difficult it might appear given their overwhelming intellectual influence in the West, this volume proposes that imaginaries are approached as empirical spaces from which to explore what is assumed as foundational in understandings of order, power and governance. As empirical spaces, imaginaries of connectivity have the potential, if explored creatively, to reveal the novelty involved in what could have otherwise been taken for granted in the process of employing theoretical frameworks.

Novelty refers here, following Blumenberg, to the human ability 'to introduce absolute beginnings into reality' (Blumenberg 1985, 169). Whereas, as observed by Arendt, the strange pathos of novelty has been 'the almost violent insistence of nearly all the great authors, scientists, and philosophers since the seventeenth century that they saw things never seen before, thought thoughts never thought before' (1998, 248–49), claims to novelty will never be exhausted. They can, and should, be understood as the foundation of emerging orders. Claims such as North's, that novelty lies at the heart of modernity and that the question of how novelty comes into the world is a typically modern question (North 2013, 15), can thereby be challenged. Novelty, as observed by Lobo-Guerrero in this volume, has not been the monopoly of modernity. Modernity has been articulated around a specific understanding (problematisation) of novelty, namely that of discovery. How novelty comes into the world is not a magical phenomenon but a result of human intellectual creativity that takes place in the realm of the imaginary and is heavily influenced through experience. In this sense, every imaginary of connectivity has been the site of introduction of absolute beginnings, and it is the role of the intellectual to explore how so, its conditions of possibility and its implications – in our case, in terms of governance and rule.

By interrogating the novelty implied in imaginaries of connectivity, one is engaging with the very creative foundations of order manifest in perceptions of reality and practices of governance. In examining the creation of novel spaces of governance, the chapters in this book are concerned with the ways in which various forms of connectivity constitute new objects of knowledge through experience.

The Structure of the Book

Connectivity has been imagined and practiced in various ways and to varying political effects in different historical and geographical contexts. Drawing on a range of case studies from the sixteenth century, to the nineteenth century, to the present, and from Spain, to the Maritime Alps, to Germany, to China, to East Asia, the chapters of this book address the problem of how the creation of novel spaces of governance relates to imaginaries of connectivity in time. More specifically, the chapters respond to the following questions: What are the terms under which things are made to connect? How are they connected? What is the effect of those connections? The historical and geographical variety of the cases serves to highlight the diversity of the meaning and function of connectivity in the constitution of novel spaces of governance.

The contributors to this book engage with such imaginaries of connectivity through two registers. On the one hand, they explore and problematise different images of (dis)connectivity – that is, different ways of perceiving and representing (dis)connected spaces. On the other hand, imaginaries of connectivity are explored on the level of onto-political principle. Here, images are underpinned by more complex historical ontologies of (dis)connection. Imaginaries produce and affect the way we connect with spaces, but connectivities also affect, subvert and generate spatial images. The chapters show that the conditions of possibility of particular imaginaries of connectivity range from advances in technologies to changes in governmental policies, to exchanges of ideas, to transformations of social practices, to historical narratives. The imaginaries of connectivities, in turn, have the effect of justifying particular policies whether in terms of the production of commercial value, the governing of unwanted bodies, imperialism or the acceptance of international regulation.

Although the chapters are ordered by way of partially overlapping themes, some of which will be briefly noted below, there are many ways in which their discussions resonate beyond the preceding and succeeding chapters alone. We therefore invite the reader to explore the various connections and tensions between individual chapters, as they explore novel spaces of governance and the particular imaginaries of connectivity and disconnectivity that give rise to them.

Globality, empire and the international are examples of such novel spaces of governance that emerged through distinct forms of connectivity that constituted them as new objects of knowledge and governance. Luis Lobo-Guerrero (chapter 1) explores the emergence of early modern Spanish understandings of novelty. By engaging with discussions around the claim made by Spanish mariners in the late 1490s that they were the first moderns since their exposure to constellations unknown to the ancients allowed them to explore a new world in experimental terms, he analyses the situated experience and the knowledge practices that contributed towards the formation of the New World as a space of governance. Drawing on the work of Jose Antonio Maravall, Lobo-Guerrero situates the early modern Spanish notion of novelty in opposition to earlier ideas of invention as bringing into knowledge something that already existed. Moving away from such notions of the new inherited from the ancients, the Spanish began to understand themselves as creating and developing something that had not existed before.

Carina Huessy (chapter 2) discusses the idea of the human face as a site and sight of connectivity and novelty in digital surveillance technologies. Functioning within state apparatuses of everyday security and border control, digital facial recognition technologies claim to be able to not only identify persons but also use facial cues to detect lies and uncover hidden intentions. In doing so, these biometric technologies generate novel governmental orders in which the face becomes a networked space in which the border between inside and outside, civil and criminal, can be drawn and surveilled. Huessy shows a Janusian twofold character of the face where its biophysicality becomes a novel site and sight of biopolitical strategies of securitisation and as a surface where resistance to order takes place. In doing so, her chapter draws out the order(s) generated by facial recognition technologies and prepares the ground for recognising the face as source for understanding novelty and freedom.

Similarly concerned with the interaction between technology and bordering practices, Sujin Eom (chapter 3) demonstrates how the increasing international migration and maritime transportation through the opening up of ports in East Asia in the nineteenth century gave rise to novel urban spaces. These new urban forms – particularly the invention of the idea of Chinatown – created the division of residential areas along racial lines and a highly structured system of urban mobility between them. In the spatial imaginaries of the time, the 'traits' of different racial groups became seen as intimately intertwined with the characteristics of the built environment of their residential areas. The governing of specific groups of people was interwoven with the governing of urban space.

Barry Ryan (chapter 4), in turn, develops a systematic understanding of maritime space in relation to connectivity by exploring the historical emergence of maritime zones through the conceptual framework of Lacanian psychoanalysis. Employing the properties of zones through the registers of the imaginary, the symbolic and the real, Ryan provides us with a rich layered understanding of maritime spaces that are respectively composed of human experience, governmental ordering practices and nonhuman *Umwelts*. It is through their properties of aroundedness, immunity and liquidity that maritime zones gain their particular connective capacities, and it is through their unique interconnected character that maritime zones need to be understood.

Ariel Shangguan (chapter 5) is interested in the emergence of an international imaginary in the nineteenth century. Her chapter examines how an idea of the international began to appear in Chinese political thought in response to its violent encounters with European powers. In contrast to ideas about sovereignty operating in international law, earlier Chinese political imaginaries premised on the concept of *tian xia* or 'all under heaven' did not understand political space as bordered or state-based. Drawing on discussions among and writings of prominent Chinese intellectuals and diplomats in the nineteenth and early twentieth century, Shangguan traces the shift in political imaginary from *tian xia* to the international and explores its relation to racialized worldviews exposed by advocates of Western learning in China.

Zeynep Gülsah Çapan and Filipe dos Reis (chapter 6) focus on the imaginary of German spatiality in the late nineteenth century. They argue that understanding the emergence of Germandom, as a desired spatial imaginary at the time, requires paying attention to the role of colonialism and empire in the constitution of imaginations of space located outside Europe and also within it. Çapan and dos Reis show how ethnonationalist ideas were transposed to the mapping techniques developed by the private publishing house *Justus Perthes* in their maps of Eastern Europe as well as non-European spaces. The effect of this cartographic imaginary was to provide justification for German imperialism towards the east.

Likewise concerned with the production of Germans and Germany, Benjamin Tallis (chapter 7) argues that landscape painting, such as that of Caspar David Friedrich, can be understood as an imaginary of connectivity that brings about spaces and subjects of governance. Challenging instrumentalist readings of art that conceive of artworks solely as representations of nationalist or other political projects, Tallis seeks to revise the reading of Friedrich's paintings as mere correlates of Nazi politics. He identifies in Friedrich's paintings an imaginary of connectivity that links German territories and produces subjects connected to those territories. Yet, Tallis argues that this imaginary does not necessarily lead to authoritarian or imperialist nationalism but can equally well function as the basis for liberal subjectivity and governance.

Developing a different approach to local and national heritage, Camila del Mármol (chapter 8) points towards the conceptualisation of space in terms of *disconnection* by analysing imaginaries of rural space. She examines the way in which local heritage is used in the Catalan Pyrenees to cultivate imaginaries of disconnection. Regardless of the various representations of remoteness, del Mármol shows that the Catalan Pyrenees also harbour a complex history of political, economic and symbolic connectivity that is often concealed by the touristic imaginary of disconnection. Imaginaries of disconnectivity can thus function to produce value and particular orders of connectivity – as in the case of rural tourism.

Similarly, Paolo Palladino (chapter 9) foregrounds the importance of disconnection to the understanding of connectivity. He extends the focus on connectivity in rural space by examining the relations between node, organism and network in the context of the economic regeneration of rural communities in the Maritime Alps and the Catalan Pyrenees. Drawing on contemporary post-humanist theory, Palladino argues that meaning emerges from the connectivity of networks, but disconnection is nevertheless the condition of possibility of the constitution of such networks. Palladino seeks to articulate the imaginary of a particular kind of connectivity, namely 'touch', as presupposing a particular notion of being disconnected. Here, ontologically speaking, disconnection is the condition of possibility for connectivity to exist in the first place. Therefore, imaginaries of connectivity presuppose a sense of separation that allows us to conceive of specific forms of connectivity as novel. Similarly, our ability to perceive novelty is premised on the designation of the old.

While variously situated historically and spatially, all the chapters highlight the importance of connectivity as an idea and a practice underpinning the emergence and development of modernity. New technologies from seafaring to cartography gave rise to forms of connectivity that made possible not only the governing of novel geographical spaces but also the governing of the people inhabiting them. The emergence of digital technologies has pushed these developments even further. Furthermore, the novel spaces of governance are as much ideational as they are physical. Connectivity is always premised on the existence of singularity and difference, the recognition of which also reminds us of the need to probe the social, political and economic consequences of the ways in which connectivity is made sense of. Hence, some of the important political and ethical questions that arise when claims to novelty and connectivity are made concern precisely the ways in which the relation between connection and disconnection, novelty and tradition, is rendered.

Bibliography

Acuto, Michele, and Simon Curtis, eds. 2014. *Reassembling International Theory: Assemblage Thinking and International Relations*. Basingstoke: Palgrave Macmillan.

Anderson, Benedict. 2016. *Imagined Communities: Reflections on the Origins and Spread of Nationalism*. Revised edition. London: Verso.

Arendt, Hannah. 1998. *The Human Condition*. Chicago, IL: University of Chicago Press.

Blumenberg, Hans. 1985. *The Legitimacy of the Modern Age*. Translated by Robert M. Wallace. Cambridge, MA: MIT Press.

Castoriadis, Cornelius. 1998. *The Imaginary Institution of Society*. Translated by Kathleen Blamey. Cambridge, MA: MIT Press.

Dillon, Michael, and Luis Lobo-Guerrero. 2009. 'The Biopolitical Imaginary of Species Being'. *Theory Culture Society* 26(1): 1–23.

Flyverbom, Mikkel. 2012. 'Globalization as It Happens: On Globalizing Assemblages in Tax Planning'. *Distinktion: Scandinavian Journal of Social Theory* 13(3): 295–309.

Fourastié, Brigitte, and Philippe Joron. 2016. 'The Imaginary as a Sociological Perspective'. *Current Sociology* 41(2): 53–58.

Kant, Immanuel. 1965. *Critique of Pure Reason*. Translated by Norman Kemp Smith. New York: St. Martin's Press.

Latour, Bruno. 2005. *Reassembling the Social: An Introduction to Actor-Network-Theory*. Oxford: Oxford University Press.

Mackenzie, Donald A. 2006. *An Engine, Not a Camera: How Financial Models Shape Markets*. Cambridge, MA: MIT Press.

Mainzer, Klaus. 2007. *Thinking in Complexity: The Computational Dynamics of Matter, Mind, and Mankind*. 5th revised and enlarged edition. Berlin: Springer.

North, Michael. 2013. *Novelty: A History of the New*. Chicago, IL: University of Chicago Press.

Oxford University Press. March 2018. 'Connectivity'. *Oxford English Dictionary Online*. Accessed 25 April 2018. http://www.oed.com/view/Entry/39340?.

Root, Hilton L. 2013. *Dynamics among Nations: The Evolution of Legitimacy and Development in Modern States*. Cambridge, MA: MIT Press.

Saar, Martin. 2015. 'Spinoza and the Political Imaginary'. Translated by William Callison and Anne Gräfe. *Qui Parle: Critical Humanities and Social Sciences* 23(2): 115–33.

Sampson, Tony D. 2012. 'Tarde's Phantom Takes a Deadly Line of Flight – From Obama's Girl to the Assassination of Osama Bin Laden'. *Distinktion: Scandinavian Journal of Social Theory* 13(3): 354–66.

Spinoza, Baruch. 1982. *The Ethics and Selected Letters*. Translated by Samuel Shirley. Edited by Seymour Friedman. Highlighting Edition. Indianapolis, IN: Hackett.

Staeheli, Urs. 2012. 'Listing the Global: Dis/Connectivity beyond Representation?' *Distinktion: Scandinavian Journal of Social Theory* 13(3): 233–46.

Taylor, Charles. 2004. *Modern Social Imaginaries*. Durham, NC: Duke University Press.

Tellmann, Ute, Sven Opitz, and Urs Staeheli. 2012. 'Operations of the Global: Explorations of Connectivity'. *Distinktion: Scandinavian Journal of Social Theory* 13(3): 209–14.

Tsing, Anna Lowenhaupt. 2005. *Friction: An Ethnography of Global Connection*. Princeton, NJ: Princeton University Press.

Wallerstein, Immanuel. 2004. *World-Systems Analysis: An Introduction*. Durham, NC: Duke University Press.

Waltz, Kenneth N. 2010. *Theory of International Politics*. Long Grove, IL: Waveland Press.

CHAPTER ONE

Novelty and the Creation of the New World in Sixteenth-Century Spain

Luis Lobo-Guerrero

Between 1488 and 1492, the years in which Bartolomeu Dias reached the Cape of Good Hope in Africa and Christopher Columbus reached what was years later called America, the 'European' cosmographic imaginary of the world ventured beyond the Greco-Roman Occidental limits of Ptolemy's *Geographia* (second century A.D.). Dias's African expedition challenged the southern limits of Ptolemy's *oikoumene* and provided the possibility of sailing eastwards and northwards opening up a connection with the Indian Ocean and the Orient. Columbus' 'discoveries' were followed twenty-seven years later by Magellan/Elcano's circumnavigation of the planet and exposed European sailors to phenomena for which ancient cosmography and Western knowledge had no explanation. The 1,200-year Ptolemaic cosmological order was suddenly disrupted by exposure to different latitudes and longitudes, new sea currents and wind systems, special climates, unknown fauna and flora, unfamiliar illnesses and different cultures. The challenge was met at times by the adaptation of known techniques and knowledge but mostly by the development of new ones to tackle emerging realities. Not only were Western understandings of experience and knowledge insufficient, so were the knowledge and belief systems on which European people and organisations operated. The doctrine of Christianity, considered at times as the pivot that supported the connection between the old and newly discovered worlds, proved short in providing explanations for emerging phenomena and had to be adapted to recognise and cater for the problem of novelty.

As an intellectual problem, novelty relates to an explicit intervention in the ways in which order is conceived in whatever understanding of the real one might have. Novelty, however, does not simply happen. It is the complex result of the interaction between intervening (epistemic) agents with their modes of reasoning and systems of thought and beliefs, the (epistemic) communities of knowledge with which they interrelate and an audience that is informed and discusses/employs the new 'findings'. Novelty, in sum, constitutes a social epistemological phenomenon that lends itself as an intellectual space from which to observe the careful, complex and precarious character of emerging knowledge formations.

Novelty disrupts order. Because of its disrupting character, it exposes the fallibility of pre-existing ways of knowing, thinking and being. It betrays the operation of particular ways of experiencing the world that are always imbued with specific forms of power relations, forms of subjectivity and systems of rule. Observing novelty and the ways in which it emerges, always in precise historical moments, allows for an understanding of the conditions under which something is deemed possible and real. Its usefulness transcends the anecdotic and relates to the possibility of introducing new ways of labelling the outcome of experience, of creating new narratives and grammars for describing what had not yet been encountered or thought, of reflecting about a real without recourse to the strictures of theory and dogma, of creating new markets for ideas and products and, as explored through this book, of creating spaces of governance.

Novelty, as the chapters in this book attest to, is embedded in imaginaries of connectivity, which, as noted in the introduction, relate to the *terms* under which things connect or disconnect. Imaginaries are understood here as the plethora of beliefs, rationalities, traditions and feelings about what a real is about. Different from being opposed to reality and treated as irrational, as common normative parlance would have it (Fourastié and Joron 1993, 53), imaginaries are intellectual domains where commonality of spirit, of understanding and of practice operate (Taylor 2004, 23). It is within imaginaries, as sites of political intervention, where novelty takes place.

How, then, should imaginaries be approached as the sites of and for novelty? This empirical question constitutes a major challenge within the history and theory of international relations and the humanities at large. Whereas there is no single imaginary in time, and there can be multiple, overlapping imaginaries in relation to given events, the intellectual effort should aim, not at providing a meta-narrative that explains how imaginaries come about but in developing the capacity to understand the singularities of specific knowledge formations and their connectivity with wider claims to the real and to order within imaginaries. Such aims have immediate resonance with Foucaultian (e.g., 2002, 1998), Veynian (Veyne 1984, 1988, 2008), Derridean (1996, 2005) and Deleuzian-Guatarian (Deleuze 1990; Guattari 2015) intellectual efforts, as they do with older Spinozan (1982) and Nietzschean (2000, 2007) contributions. They differ, however, from efforts within international relations aimed at discussing and stabilising the methodological scientific inquiry (e.g., Jackson 2010; Lebow and Lichbach 2007), in distinguishing between ontology and epistemology (Hollis and Smith 1991, 1994, 1996) and in understanding the structure and role of narratives in the study of international relations events (Suganami 2008). The aim is therefore the constitution of imaginaries as empirical sites for interrogating novelty and its role in questioning the ontological basis of central intellectual constructs such as order and governance. Invocations of novelty can be taken as invitation to wonder about the lofty convictions on which our disciplinary and intellectual foundations operate.

This chapter engages with a very particular moment in the history of a Western experience of knowing life, space and governance. It explores claims to novelty in sixteenth-century Spain in the context of the Columbian trips of discovery and the early conquest of America. It does so by exploring the seminal contribution made by José Antonio Maravall, a Spanish historian of culture and mentalities, to the understanding of the problem of novelty through what he considers to be its three conditions of possibility: (i) the pretension of originality, (ii) the interest for the invention and (iii) the curiosity for the strange.

In what follows, the chapter introduces Maravall's work and continues with a discussion on how the problem of novelty, as an empirical fact, opens up the possibility of engaging with practices of discovery and creation, not as political strategies but as fertile spaces from which to learn about *empirical acts*, *empirical spaces* and *empirical dexterity*. Some writings by Pedro Mártir, Bartolomé de las Casas and José de Acosta are used towards the end as empirical cases.

Committing Empirical Acts and the Pretension of Originality

José Antonio Maravall (1911–1986), working in the 1950s and 1960s, explored the problem of novelty in relation to claims to modernity made by various authors in the late fifteenth and sixteenth centuries in the context of the Columbian trips of discovery. In a work widely unknown within Anglo-Saxon academic circles, Maravall made the claim that it was in the Iberian Peninsula, and particularly Spain, where intellectuals first developed a sense that the moderns had superseded the ancients. Such sense, as will be explored below, resulted from empirical observations that motivated reflections on the foundations of knowledge and truth on which imaginaries of the time operated. The following quote is but an opening of what Maravall explored in his work in relation to empirical spaces where novelty became the norm.

> The discovery of hitherto unknown patterns of oceanic wind currents, the development of new vessels, and the mastery by sailors of new techniques to find their bearings in the open sea led in the fifteenth century to a growing realisation that the cosmographies inherited from the ancients were wrong. (Maravall 1966, 14)[1]

Maravall is considered one of the pioneers in the history of culture and of mentalities in Spanish historiography. A student of José Ortega y Gasset, he obtained a PhD in 1944 at the University of Madrid with a thesis on the Spanish theory of state in the seventeenth century and was subsequently appointed professor of Political Law and Theory of Society at the Universidad de La Laguna (1946). Between 1949 and 1955, he was director of the Collège d'Espagne in Paris where he came closer to the intellectual lines of the Annales School. By 1955, he was appointed chair of Political and Social History of Spain at the University of Madrid, a top academic position in the country.

In his work, widely described as a history of mentalities in medieval and early modern Spain, he adopts a comparative approach where he actively explores Castilian as well as Aragonese sources, an uncommon practice at the time, in relation to their European intellectual context. In his book *Antiguos y Modernos: la idea del progreso en el dessarrollo inicial de una sociedad* [Ancients and Moderns: The Idea of Progress in the Initial Development of a Society] (1966), one of his lesser known works, he builds on previous contributions and rejects the fracture between Middle Ages and Spanish Renaissance prevalent at the time and challenges the Italic-centric perspective on the latter. His wider contributions to the theory of historiography came through his book *Teoría del Saber Histórico* [Theory on Historical Knowledge] (1958), which provides an early historical epistemological analysis on the role of the scientific revolutions, their impact on how history is thought of and the struggles it created with forms of representation. Perhaps related

---

[1] All translations in this chapter are my own.

to the place, period and politics in which he wrote, his works have not as yet attracted much attention from the English-speaking world and remain to be translated.² In spite of the importance of his work on the study of historical epistemologies in the early modern period, his political sympathies with the early Franco regime during his youth have cast a shadow in his intellectual brightness (see Fresán-Cuenca 2003 and his son's book *Dictatorship and Political Dissent*: Maravall 1978).

To prepare the ground for understanding the importance of Maravall's conditions for novelty, I would like to begin by recognising the idea of originality as taking place within a community of knowledge, an epistemic community imbued by what Lorraine Daston referred to as moral economies (cf. Antoniades 2003; Daston 1995; Lobo-Guerrero 2012; Haas 1992). A pretension of originality takes place within the context of a community that would recognise and authorise, through its beliefs, traditions and practices, something as 'novel'. It requires, therefore, the agency of an author (Foucault 1980), a public or an audience (Rayner 1993) and an imaginary, where an intervention takes place.

A pretension of originality, Maravall's first condition, relates to an understanding of novelty as an urge for original creation. Such creation, not to be confused with Christian Creation, presupposes the development of an individual conscience, which in turn reveals the role of a subject who is aware that innovation results from creative practices and attitudes. This subject is not ready-made and is not the logical outcome of (preceding) systems of rationality. It is one that emerges out of the experience of encountering unknown circumstances, of dealing with problems for which no recorded knowledge lent its value and the need to resort to new narratives and vocabularies to make sense of reality. Epistemologically speaking, this conscience, or as put by Maravall, the 'vigorous development of individual conscience' that took place in the intellectual crisis of the fifteenth and sixteenth centuries (1966, 56), corresponds to the emergence of what could be called 'senses of the new' – a term used by Maravall – a categorical and not simply an incremental matter. The distinction here is important, since, as explained by Bergson (1992, 206), differences in degree (increments) refer to intensities in a known or related experience; differences in kind (categories) give rise or are the result of 'new' experience. Contemplating the emergence of senses of the new as

---

2 With the exceptions of *Culture of the Baroque: Analysis of a Historical Structure* (Minneapolis: University of Minnesota Press, 1986) and *Utopia and Counterutopia in the Quixote* (Detroit, MI: Wayne State University Press, 1991).

constitutive of an individual conscience exposes the idea of novelty to a categorical dimension where creation or emergence, rather than evolution or Creation (cf. North 2013), sets the empirical space for epistemological interrogation. Creation and emergence acquire an ontological role.

In Maravall's understanding, such mode of reasoning clashed starkly in the late fifteenth and sixteenth centuries with the humanist thought of the classics, where, quite prominently, Horace and Cicero, drawing on old Platonic ideas, exalted the attitude of not being admired by anything as the characteristic of the happy man, the 'wise man' (1966, 73). Horace's often quoted lines from one of his poems in *Epistles 1*, 'Marvel at nothing, Numicius. This is the only rule to follow / That can make and keep you happy' (Horace 1.6. 1–2), has repeatedly been taken as evidence of such an attitude (e.g., Mayer 2010). Cicero's initial dialogue in *De Republica*, which Maravall reads as 'not intended to bring any novelty or offer any innovation but to expose what others, more learned and wiser, had said on the matter' (1966, 47; see Fowler 2009, 261), is another often cited passage on the prevalence of classical reasoning on the medieval imaginary which anchors order on authorised knowledge and claims that the authorisation of such thought resulted from tradition.

The work of the classics, assumed to be 'the general object of knowledge for the man of the Middle Ages (1966, 50)' is, however, an idea that has been challenged time and again. Understanding of order in the Middle Ages was not a matter restricted to the study of the classics, or of theology, but a problem that attracted interest from very diverse fields. Evidence of interest in innovations in medieval governance, finance, trade, urban life, social organisation and arrangements and aspects of the personality and goals of the individual have now been carefully documented (see, e.g., Dear 2018; Jordan, McNab, and Ruiz 2015). Innovation in thinking and practicing navigation (e.g., Bacci and Rohde 2014; Hourani 1995; Pryor 1992), in cartography and the charting of space (e.g., Baumgärtner, Debby, and Kogman-Appel 2019; Dekker 2012; Pinet 2016), in making sense of the cosmos and its reordering (Sacrobosco 2018), and in making sense of wonder and nature (Daston and Park 1997) are just some examples of how the complexity of order attracted the work of medieval scholars whose writings as a whole demonstrate that there was no awareness of the operation of a stable episteme (cf. Foucault 1989).

Maravall, the empiricist, was well aware that even if they had not been the subject of medieval scholarly study, cultural practices could be taken to express forms of creativity that were not anchored on tradition but rather, on experience. In *Antiguos y Modernos*, he notes, for example, how *trovas*, the lyric poetry of the troubadours of the high middle ages, were narrations of the artists' personal experience in relation to problems of life. Trovas, as cultural expressions, depicted the work of an author that was presented to others in musical form and exposed pride of what an author had reached through their own effort. As such, trovas were creations that intervened in the popular imaginary.

He also notes how the very recognition of the existence of 'marvels' played important roles in classical imagination with clear representations in medieval texts. Marvels, as Daston and Park have shown (1998), were recognised in scholarly practice and popular culture and, as phenomena, give away the possibility of empirically recognising difference in nature and of understanding the idea of an event for which no narrative existed in the imaginary. The very recognition of difference, however, presented what we could today refer to as an epistemological shortcoming, that of confusing the marvellous with the fabulous. Maravall argues that 'without doubt, throughout the Middle Ages, compilations of lapidary inscriptions and bestiaries, in circulation until quite late an age, were evidence of how artists and authors were attracted to the marvellous'. However, he adds, 'without a precise technique with which to know and dominate the empirical world, they confused the marvellous with the fabulous' (1966, 78).

Such a refinement was to be achieved in the Renaissance through the emergence of the senses of the new that would admit for the understanding of phenomena as real and present, regardless of lack of knowledge that would reveal its existence and character. The senses of the new would allow for the acknowledgement and acceptance of ignorance in the presence of fact, however controversial this term is (see Poovey 1998), and such acknowledgement was to play a central role in the constitution of an individual conscience. An individual conscience will allow the renascent scholar the possibility of moving away from a classic idea of invention, understood as bringing into knowledge something that already existed in the imaginary (an intervention *through* the imaginary), to an idea of invention as the creation of something with no prior existence (an intervention *in* the imaginary). An invention for the renascent scholar is understood as a categorical creation by an author who employs his or her talents in producing an unprecedented account of an experience in the world. In Maravall's words,

> To invent was, etymologically, to bring into knowledge something that already existed. It was nothing different than a discovery. Now, the term will assume a new meaning, deeper, more radical. To invent is to build into reality something that did not exist, the personal work of its author, even if articulating data from experience. (Maravall 1966, 60)

The epistemological shortcoming of confusing the marvellous with the fabulous begins to fade in the new (renascent) man who starts to develop an attitude towards the marvellous, within a marvelling conscience, that not only recognises difference but also starts to recognise novelty by inventing (creating) ways of exploring nature. By the mid-fifteenth century, 'a new sense of nature, and to its service, a new science of natural things, allows for giving the marvellous a concrete reality and to render it as strange, in recognising strangeness in the new things that are discovered' (Maravall 1966, 78).

In the link between innovation and invention (creation),[3] an epistemological move that allows for transforming the marvellous into an event can begin to be recognised. It denotes a shift with its prior mode of reasoning – not in time but in practice – where the strangeness of the marvel begins to be constituted as a new empirical norm and authorship becomes coupled with legitimisation. The norm performs a role of authorisation where the author, the artist, the explorer, becomes an experimenter for as long as it marvels with what is not known. The practice of marvelling with the unknown legitimises practices of knowledge in as much as it embraces phenomena. In this shift, from the marvellous/fabulous to the marvellous/novel, the attitude of those who marvel reveals a new individual conscience that begins to share the focus of recognition of novelty from the object to the subject. Novelty here, Maravall tells us,

> is not only on things seen but on the eyes that see them, in the spirit that precedes the seeing. In the language of XVI and XVII C. an interesting semantic displacement takes place. The word 'novelty' does not only refer to a condition of things when they appear to someone for the first time. It also expresses the internal impression such things produce in the observer. To 'cause novelty' is a more frequent expression of admiration in this epoch. (Maravall 1966, 81)

The very idea of novelty as the result of experience, that which requires the marvelling attitude and the marvelling conscience, clashes with scholarly traditions represented through Horace and Cicero and, most significantly, with the Platonic paradox posed in *Meno*. As put by Michael North, the paradox can be expressed as a problem of recollection expressed in terms of, how can I be able to 'find out what I want to know unless I already know it well enough to identify it?' (2013, 8–9). Such problem explores the production of knowledge through practices of recollection that require erudition

---

3 I use henceforth the term 'invention' (creation) to distinguish it from the medieval understanding of invention, as mentioned in the Maravall's quote above.

from history and the experience of others. The logical corollary, drawing on North (2013, 8–9), is the foreclosure of the possibility of novelty and, I would add, of the possibility of *creating* knowledge through experience.

North provides what he calls a basic history of the conceptual models for thinking novelty which originate before Plato and have not changed much since (North 2013, 7). He argues that recurrence, as noted above, and recombination, as offering unlimited novelty 'but only if unprecedented relations between existing elements can be considered truly new entities', constitute the two foundational models on which past and contemporary conceptions of the term operate. When in dialogue with Maravall's claim on the emergence of the senses of the new as a defining characteristic of the renascent man of experience, North's models do not allow for an understanding of the myriad empirical practices of discovery and invention that took place in the fifteenth and sixteenth centuries of which I will say more below. For North, the science that results from the modern, mostly referring to the late seventeenth- to eighteenth-century enlightened man, is one premised on methodological protocols of recombination, which prescribe the object of analysis, and allows for its development but does not cater for the so-called revolutions that Kuhn wrote about. The very idea of revolution denotes an interruption/disruption, in this case of an intellectual order, an order of knowing and an order of reasoning about phenomena. It is required when an alternative order of knowledge, substantiated through evidence and logic of reasoning, emerges as an alternative to understand given phenomena. The very necessity of the idea of revolution in the history and philosophy of science reveals the incapacity of a method-driven approach to knowledge to cater for creation and invention. This moment when knowledge begins to be assimilated as and by science must not veil the very exciting possibilities that resulted from the premise of experience in constituting the knowing subject.

By the time of the 'discovery' and 'conquest' of the 'New World', classical thinking and models of thought (North's model of recurrence) did not offer Iberian/European writers much on which to make sense of the mundane reality they were experiencing. Neither could they afford not to be admired by the exotic phenomena exposed to them. What they saw and experienced demanded either to invent (create) new terms resorting to verbal and visual domains or to resort to the writings of their contemporaries whenever they recognised categorical differences with what they had previously known. They could no longer do what their contemporary writer, Niccolo Machiavelli, did when using the classics to speak of the Germans instead of using the contemporary description provided by Eneas Silvio (Pope Pius II) in his work *Germania* (Maravall 1966, 435). Whereas Machiavelli's sense of time was premised on that of the classics, those involved in the 'discovery' and 'conquest' had the opportunity to sense for their contemporary selves. Their creation of new phenomena through novel descriptions based on their experience can be analysed as constituting *empirical acts*. By committing empirical acts, renascent authors, artists, explorers and writers built their confidence to make claims such as being the first true moderns and of presenting new issues as problems worthy of discussion and solution.

Creating Empirical Spaces and the Interest for the Invention

By the time of the renascent humanism of the sixteenth century, Maravall tells us, 'statements of originality are presented with an insistence that appears at times fastidious and on occasions, unfounded' (1966, 51). Such are the cases in which claims to originality arise from treating a subject for the first time in a specific language: the first work to speak of agriculture in Castilian, of painting in Portuguese, for example. These claims relate to the urge to constitute an audience on which to impress a novelty and which would recognise the validity of the claim.

Statements of originality, of course, require responses that express a positive interest in what is formulated as novel.

> What is most interesting, historically, in relation to the spirit of the epoch [Maravall argues], is the case of those who demanded recognition that their deeds represented full innovation which bore no resemblance to anything done before, revealing a state of conscience that make them believe, at least in their area, superior to all, including most explicitly the ancients whom they argued did not reach what the author presently offered. (Maravall 1966, 52)

Maravall provides the example of Juan Luis Vives who criticised authors of the then recent philosophical studies on the soul for not adding anything to the thought of the ancients and for falling into their mistakes. Such is the base of the claim for novelty in his treatise *De Anima* as the first to penetrate on that aspect of psychology (Maravall 1966, 52–53).

The Renascent urge to invent and to be recognised through claims to novelty reveals for Maravall the emergence of the new figure of the modern man for whom 'the world reveals to him as a space for manipulation' (Maravall 1966, 59). Manipulation is understood here as an intervention in an established order so as to reset the terms under which subsequent order is to operate. The possibility to manipulate depends on the capacity to innovate, and to innovate one must invent – an invention is work (cf. Arendt 1998). As put by Maravall in the context of the intellectual crisis of the late fifteenth and sixteenth centuries,

> To be original is to invent, and to invent is one of the faculties that characterise man and that provides a higher quality, above all, to his work. The inventing passion of 'homo faber', in all aspects of production, from a sonnet to a technical apparatus, is an unquestionable mark of the renascent man. (Maravall 1966, 60)

The interest for the invention, which Maravall considered to be the second condition for novelty, reveals again his claim on the individual conscience of the new (renascent) man that he demonstrates in the character of some of the works produced at the time. 'Esteem for individual work prevails over the forces of established traditions' (Maravall 1966, 64). Maravall invokes, for instance, the writing of Pedro Ciruelo, a well-known writer on logic in the first half of the sixteenth century 'who does not resort to the authority of Aristotle to legitimise his work, as medieval tradition demanded, but highlighted his own novel contributions to the analysis: *Novus sed preclarissimus in Posteriora analytica Aristotelis Commentarius* (Alcala, 1529)' (1966, 64). He also mentions the work of Miguel Sabuco, medic and philosopher author of *Nueva filosofía de la naturaleza del hombre, no conocida ni alcanzada de los grandes filósofos antiguos, la cual mejora la vida y salud humana* [New natural philosophy of man, not known or reached by ancient philosophers, which improves human life and health] (Sabuco y Álvarez 1728). As examples of a well-established logical tradition that countered late medieval scholasticism, Maravall compares it with Bacon's later claims in his *Novum Organum* of 1620 which makes a claim of having introduced an approach that countered the old ways of syllogisms as a system of knowledge production. What these mid-to-late sixteenth-century writings demonstrate, counter Bacon, is work that challenges scholasticism based on an author's invention and the result of his personal efforts – labour. Such inventions operate within a general esteem for originality and innovation which creates a readership and what we would today call a market (Maravall 1966, 65).

As a second example invoked by Maravall to sustain his claim was the polemic on neologisms that took place in Spain in the second half of the sixteenth century which he uses as an illustration of the social, cultural and political relevance of the problem of novelty. The polemic reveals the creative and inventive capacity of what he calls the human, of its receptiveness towards innovation and its willingness to accommodate descriptive language to prescriptive norms. It must be borne in mind the context under which this 'polemic' (note the scholastic tone) takes place. In 1492 Antonio de Nebrija published his Castillian *Grammatica*, the first printed book on the study of the rules of a romance language. Nebrija takes pronunciation as the basis for setting the rules on orthography, the instrument through which commonality in writing and speech should be achieved in the Castilian speaking regions (see de Nebrija 2006). The book, highly criticised at its time since it assumed many Andalusian words as the basis of pronunciation, evidences the political struggles behind uniformising the language of what was then a nascent empire which had in Seville one of its strongest economic, cultural and political centres (see, e.g., Alconchel 1995; Perez 1993).

If the imposition of a prescriptive linguistic view was problematic, the introduction of neologisms into practice or form was also so. For example, in Martin Cortes's *Breve Compendio de la Sphera y de la Arte de Navegar* of 1556, Maravall notices a comment on how reticent Spaniards were to new and foreign words. Decades later, in contrast, due to what he refers to as the 'trivialisation of the appearance of the new' evident in fashion, entertainment, literature, architecture, art and politics (see Maravall 1966, 68–70), new French and Italian terms start gaining acceptance. In a curious way that deserves investigation and criticism beyond this chapter, Maravall argues, based on Heckscher's work (Heckscher 1994), that a possible reason for this was the interest of mercantilism as an economic doctrine towards technical inventions.[4]

Empirical Dexterity and the Curiosity for the Strange

Maravall tells about the 'huge resonance the adjective "new" was to acquire in the conscience of contemporary men when applied nothing else than to refer to a world until then ignored' (1966, 434). 'From this historical situation the belief in the superiority of the epoch and of those who lived through it, where novelty without comparison could be lived, arose and became a systematic issue' (1966, 435–36).

It is not surprising that Maravall's reflections on novelty revolve especially around the context provided by the 'discovery', 'invention' and thinking of

---

4 Maravall makes an observation, almost as a cause for what he calls the 'trivalisation of the appearance of the new' which relates to Spain's immature mercantilism of the sixteenth century (Maravall 1966, 69–70). His observation is subsumed into a mercantilist logic, which, in my opinion, is anachronistic given that the term was not in use at the time and refers to a particular way of understanding economic practice reflecting on particular historiographies. It would be worth exploring what the terms of such logic would have been in contrast to a tendency towards a globalisation manifest, for example, in the use of Mexican silver as currency by the Ming dynasty by the 1600s.

the New World. The very idea of the New World was a renascent formation where all things novel could flourish. Speaking of and relating to the New World involved enormous dexterity in creating novel spatial, cultural, economic and social spaces, which did not directly correspond to a preconceived order. The understanding of novelty involved in these processes, however, was far from stable and definitely not simple. As will be shown below, the initial experience of discovery and conquest very quickly came to coexist with an experience of creation of the new, of invention. Empirical acts of knowing provided the experience required for creating empirical spaces, not least the idea of a new continent. Not wishing to simplify a complex and rich phenomenon, it can broadly be argued that the period between the first Columbian trip (1492) and the time in which the Magellan-Elcano expedition returned from its circumnavigation of the globe (1522) witnessed a transformation and concurrence of epistemological orders, between one of discovery and one of invention (creation), both fuelled by a voracious empirical dexterity by those involved. In a period of thirty years, the world ceased to be that of the Ptolemaic *oikoumene* to become a global political space of interaction and contestation, not simply characterised by a geopolitical partition of the globe through the treaties of Tordesillas and Zaragoza and the growing imperial opposition to, and competition with, that order but mainly by an openness to the strange, a capacity to marvel and an extraordinary empirical resourcefulness in action and thought.

Columbus died in 1506. A year later, Martin Waldseemüller referred in his 1507 map for the first time to the geographical space of the New World using the name of America. Waldseemüller's map was built on a, by then, current imaginary that considered the New World to be a continent, as had been depicted as early as 1500 in the map of Juan de la Cosa (see Lobo-Guerrero 2018). Empirical confirmation of this idea only came later and mainly after the 1519–1522 Magellan/Elcano circumnavigation. The name America was quickly adopted and Copernicus already mentioned it in his 1543 *De Revolutionibus Orbium Caelestium* (Copernicus 1543, Bk. I, Ch. 3, 2). As an empirical and intellectual space with no precedent in classical thought, America became a site for intense experimentation where empirical acts gave rise to new empirical spaces, all of which required empirical dexterity and true empirical craftsmanship based on experience.

Maravall refers to three authors whose writings reflect the transition, and in parts coincidence, of the two epistemologies of novelty of discovery and invention: Pedro Mártir, a priest who acted as *Cronista de India*s between 1492 and 1525; Bartolomé de las Casas, a Dominican, first Protector of the Indians under appointment by King Charles V; and the Jesuit José de Acosta, author of the most prominent treatise of natural philosophy published in Seville in 1590 and translated into English in 1604. The work of all three marvelled Maravall as depicting an individual conscience of experiencing strangeness and novelty regardless of their classical education and strong attachment to the Castilian and Catholic establishment. All three were clerics with close links with the Crown, the Court, the *Consejo de Indias* (an administrative entity in charge of all American business) and the Vatican.[5] This interplay between discovery and invention (creation) will be explored in what follows through the works of Mártir, de las Casas and de Acosta.

Pedro Mártir, an Italian humanist and courtesan at the service of the Catholic Kings, addressed his protector, Count Juan de Borromeo, a letter dated 14 May 1493, just a month after Columbus returned from his first trip, to announce the arrival of a Cristobal Colon from the antipodes region loaded with gold and precious stones (Maravall 1966, 436). The use of the image of gold and precious stones is revealing given that it was regularly used in traditional cosmography to refer to exotic regions (Maravall 1966, 436).[6] Exoticism, as Gilbert Chinard argued in the early twentieth century, is a quality used to refer to a desire to escape from one's own time and the environment that surrounds it (Chinard 1918, v). It was actively used in the context of Ptolemaic cosmography to refer to the frontier of the *oikoumene* as a limit that liberated the constraints of being in the known world. As put by Lestringant, one might 'have recourse to the notion of "exoticism" in order to gauge the evolution, at the progressively enlarged fringes of the *oikoumene*, of marvellous realities bequeathed by earlier ages and gradually idealised or allegorised in new myths' (Lestringant 2016, 1). Mártir's reference to the antipodes in the same passage reinforces this idea of the liminal character of an emerging imaginary of novelty. Antipodes are an area geographically located opposite to one's position, and their invocation is revealing of the geographical imaginary in which Mártir operated. It reveals the spherical character of the globe and of the existence of an unknown land. Most importantly, it reveals a conscious engagement with a cultural frontier constitutive of his identity. As Beilharz noted, the antipodean can be understood as reflecting a metropolitan culture, as a relational idea that betrays a relationship of identity (Beilharz 2002, 97). The antipode 'is not a place', it is not

---

5 For a good description and analysis of the systems of power and the institutions in place in early sixteenth-century Spain, see Brendecke (2016).

6 On the role of exoticism in defining the identity of Europe in the final third of the seventeenth century, see Schmidt (2015).

anywhere (Beilharz 2002, 97), it is always in relation to whoever thinks and uses the term, rhetorically, to relate to a cultural frontier.

Mártir's marvel with Columbus' trip is revealed further through another letter, this time to Íñigo López de Mendoza, Count of Tendilla, and Hernando de Talavera, Archbishop of Granada, in which he triumphantly announces the return of Columbus with the expression 'Lift your spirits, dear elder friends, listen to the new discovery' (Maravall 1966, 436, footnote 15). López de Mendoza and Talavera represented the epitome of the establishment of the Catholic Monarchy, the first being a hero in expelling the caliph from Granada and a military bastion of the Crown in command of the newly conquered Iberian land, the second representing the advance of Catholicism over Islam. Mártir's use of language that commands them to lift their spirit and listen demonstrates his character, confidence and belonging to the governing Castilian elite. Later in the letter, he demonstrates his intellectual authority by adding that if there is a possible relation between the found lands with what the ancients might have written on islands adjacent to the Indies, he does not share that view (1966, 436). As Maravall tells us, in subsequent letters,

> Mártir continues to insist to his [very powerful] friends that Columbus's admirable feat lies on the surprising, extreme novelty and strangeness of the things discovered. The taste of modern men for the strangeness of the unknown is revealed when Mártir confesses his tears of joy with the news of Discovery ever since there is nothing more pleasant to a high spirit than to quench the thirst of novelty that will lead him to insatiably interrogate those who arrive from the New World. (1966, 436, footnote 17)

The use of the term 'discovery' in Mártir's letters constitutes, in my analysis, an empirical act that betrays an individual conscience of having found something novel. Whereas O'Gorman's reflection in the late 1950s, published in his *The Invention of America*, on the logical absurdity of anyone discovering something that was come upon by chance (O'Gorman 1961), Mártir's use of the term makes reference to having found something that was being sought. The very imaginary of the Columbian trip was built on the belief that the world was a globe and that there was an antipode to be found when sailing west. This is evident, if only, in the 'Erdapfel', the oldest surviving European terrestrial globe produced between 1490 and 1492 by Martin Behaim, before Columbus returned from his first trip.

Mártir's understanding of the novelty of the New World experiences a quick change as the years pass. On a letter dated 9 August 1496, addressed to another key figure of the establishment, Cardinal Bernardino de Carvajal, Spanish ambassador to Pope Alexander VI, he states

> that although he recognises the classical references to Aristotle and Seneca to unknown lands, he reveals that what interests him in spite of his humanist profession, is the modern feat and the news brought by those arriving from the other side of the Ocean, through their own experience. 'The Admiral [Columbus] – he says – prides himself of having given humankind this land, because having been hidden, he has discovered it with his labour and industry'. (1966, 437, footnote 18)

Reference to 'his labour and industry' refers to an agency that begins to believe in human creation that construes a reality as a result of its experience of it, through empirical acts. You will recall Maravall's statement earlier in the chapter where he refers to the emergence of the figure of the modern man for whom 'the world reveals to him as a space for manipulation'. Mártir's approach of the novel character of the New World and his contemporaries' appreciation of it is quickly approaching an idea of invention where the recurrence to the classics has almost disappeared. The following letter addressed to Pomponio Leto, an Italian humanist and professor at the University of Rome, this time of 1 September 1497, is revealing in this concern.

> What more exquisite thing could I present than to notify you about what Nature has hidden until the times we were born? It soothes us with smooth foods, with sweet delicacies of which Antiquity, if not completely fasting, really famelic, filled the course of its days. (1966, 437, footnote 19)

As noted by Maravall, for 'a humanist carved according to the orthodox patron of Italian classicism, allow[ing] himself to call Antiquity famelic and to consider his contemporaries as moderns above those of all ages' (1966, 437) is clear evidence of an individual conscience and of a daring sense of the strange that begins to characterise the senses of the new. His mention of Nature, not God, as hiding something to be found, betrays an anthropocentric character where experience, not revelation, becomes a vehicle for knowledge. By now it is no longer a matter of discovery but of knowing and of developing the means for doing so.

The second writer that impresses Maravall with his sense of individual conscience and curiosity for the strange was Bartolomé de las Casas. De las Casas was not a simple priest. His father, a merchant, had sailed with Columbus on his second trip and brought back a slave which he gave to Bartolomé as servant (Borges and Morán 1990, 22). He then allegedly used him to study his language and beliefs until he was returned home after Queen Isabel forbade the enslaving of Indians (ibid.). Bartolomé completed studies at the University of Salamanca and in 1502 sailed to Santo Domingo where his father had been granted an *encomienda* (hold of land with the right to employ and govern native labour). Having fought against rebel natives in La Hispaniola he was himself rewarded with an *encomienda*, which he exploited until 1506 when he returned to Seville to receive minor religious orders and was subsequently ordained in Rome a year later. In 1508, at his return to La Hispaniola, he combined his role of *encomendero* with that of *doctrinero* (parish priest among Indians) and played an important role in the conquest and Christianisation of Cuba for which he was rewarded with another *encomienda* for the exploitation of gold. After experiencing a radical transformation, he became in 1515 defendant of Indian rights, renounced his *encomiendas*, travelled to Spain to advocate for the Indians, joined the Dominican order and was granted by the King the new and influential role of Protector of Indians. It is mainly under that office that his work became known and that he could exercise the kind of influence that led to the adoption of the New Laws of the Indies for the Preservation of the Indians of 1542. These, which drew on the earlier 1512 Leyes de Burgos that sought to regulate relations between Indians and colonists and are recognised as the first humanitarian laws in the New world, abolished the system of *encomiendas* in which de las Casas had participated and set the basis for the establishment of the subsequent *hacienda* system.[7]

Presenting him as a sixteenth-century thinker who anticipated the thought of Rousseau, albeit from within a Christian tradition, Maravall admired the comparisons de las Casas made on the feats and civilization of the savages with those of Antiquity. For de las Casas, Indians 'believed in living according to nature, in the native goodness of men, in the good savage, in the liberty and equality of nature, in the virtues of primitive society, in the natural ways of education' (Maravall 1966, 447). His argumentative sense was based on the conviction that 'the ancients had many vices and defects regardless of the esteem granted to them, while the men in natural state that populate the Indies possess many more virtues and values, reason for which they deserve greater esteem than cultured people' (Maravall 1966, 447).

According to de las Casas [Maravall tells us], the historical process of civilization . . . is based on two ideas:

---

7 All references to de las Casa's biography are taken from Borges and Morán (1990).

a) all nations were equally feral in their beginnings and then reached a heightened level of civilization; b) there is no need to marvel in the backwardness of some civilizations and the perfection of others since this situation changes and can even be inverted. Therefore, we would have to conclude that a historical vision cannot be based on a definitive appreciation of peoples but as a circumstantial and relative valuation. (Maravall 1966, 447–48)

Maravall's appreciation of de las Casas's ideas might surprise many who still believe, following Francis Bacon's *Novum Organum*, in the backwardness of scholastic thinking and the state of Iberian science in the early sixteenth century (see Slater and López-Terrada 2017; cf. Barrera Osorio 2006; Cañizares-Esguerra 2002, 2006). De las Casas actively rejected any classicist heritage from which to make sense of the reality he was experiencing, and to use North's term, he rejected recurrence as a mode of reasoning. His empirical dexterity consisted of developing arguments, based on scholastic logic and informed by personal experience, to produce some of the most influential writings on human rights until today. His writings between 1515 and 1561 provide an account of what he considered to be wrongdoings in the treatment, administration and rights of the Indians, not according to European customs and traditions but based on an experiential account of local indigenous cosmologies and traditions. The legitimacy of his empirical acts, such as the writing, address and publication of his *Brevísima relación de la destrucción de las Indias* [A Short Account of the Destruction of the Indies] in 1542, was underwritten by his authority in political, commercial and religious circles and his personal experience with problems of governance in the New World. Combining his empirical knowledge of indigenous people, with that of trade and of politics, and his classical education obtained at Salamanca and Rome, de las Casas was in a privileged position to query against those who, supported by Aristotelian ideas prominent then, argued on the slave nature of Indians on the basis of them being rude and barbarian people. Whereas de las Casas' Salamanca was not yet the one of Vitoria, De Soto, Azpilcueta, Mercado and Suarez, the so-called School of Salamanca that questioned the legitimacy of conquest and developed the law of the people and a doctrine of just war, it was nonetheless the bedrock of scholastic thinking. It was there where he acquired expertise in scholastic reasoning and its logic of argumentation that allowed him to advance a claim on the novelty of the category of 'savagery' employed to refer to the nature of the Indians, as compared to that of the 'barbarian' category employed by the classics.

This idea links importantly with a prominent role of de las Casas's empirical acts as Protector of Indians. Apart from the well-known regulations influenced by his writings recognising the humanity and rights of Indians, his texts constituted the base for the works of Vitoria, de Soto and other scholars of Salamanca for the creation of humanitarianism as an empirical space of governance. Humanitarianism materialised as a legal space which created an imaginary that connected the lives, cosmologies and ways of life of indigenous people in the New World with an emerging European nomos, a spatial-economic-religious order of governance, which was to lend legitimacy to subsequent European acts of conquest and colonisation in America, Europe and beyond (cf. Brunstetter and Zartner 2011). Such nomos was not thinkable within classical canons of power and cultural hierarchies such as those professed by Aristotle as these did not allow for an encompassing of an other as part of a whole, which was at least politically achieved in the Spanish case through the Laws of the Indies which turned Indians into subjects of the King. The struggle on the subsequent implementation of these laws, and indeed the wars with colonists in America in the sixteenth century – which do not figure prominently in the historical imaginary of contemporary Europeans – can be interpreted as one between the newly created order of governance versus the rights of colonisation derived from the prior order. Given that Indians were under law considered vassals of the King, and that the newly created entities in America constituted kingdoms under the Spanish crown, it is historically inaccurate to speak of Spanish America as a colonial space, at least until the Bourbonic reforms of the eighteenth century.

Maravall finishes his analysis of contributors to the idea of novelty and modernity in the Spanish sixteenth century with the work of the Jesuit priest José de Acosta. Acosta, just like Mártir and de las Casas, was deeply involved in the introduction of novelty in knowing about the New World particularly in relation to the natural sciences and geography. He contributed the first systematic treatise on the study on the natural and geographical history of the Americas, *Historia natural y moral de las Indias* [Natural and Moral History of the Indies], published in Spanish in Seville in 1590 and translated into Latin and Italian in 1595, French in 1598, English in 1608 and German in 1617 (Acosta 1894, iv). All versions had the approval of the Church regardless of Acosta's rejection of the ancients' ideas on the heavens, the distribution of waters and lands, the conditions of the Torrid Zone, the limits and the figure of the world as globe, the existence of other lands and the origin of Indians, among other topics. His work revised Aristotelian premises for the understanding of nature and natural sciences and, very importantly, found a way to reconcile the problem of Creation as read in the Sacred Scriptures with the creation of knowledge through personal experience and observation (Acosta 1590; see also Caraccioli 2017). To do so he argued that it 'suffices to know that in the Divine Scriptures we must not follow the letter that kills, but the spirit that grants life, as stated by Saint Paul' (Acosta 1894, 21).

Acosta's education and background is revealing about the context in which he intervened and the claims he made on the understanding of nature and science. Born in 1540, his education was the result of the recently established Society of Jesus that emphasised the joint study of letters, philosophy and theology aimed at preparing students to become teachers and establish schools (Pavur 2016). After his novitiate, he furthered his studies in philosophy, theology and natural sciences at the University of Alcala de Henares (1659 and 1657), by then a well-recognised, if recently created, centre of humanism with a privileged collection of natural sciences books (Acosta and del Pino-Diaz 2008, xx–xxi). Cardinal Cisneros, a Franciscan who was then Archbishop of Toledo and therefore second to the Queen in the Castilian power structure, founded the university based on the existing *Studium Generale* dating from 1293. Cisneros was key to the monarch's ecclesiastical reform that standardised religious practice in Spain and subordinated the Spanish Church structure to the monarchy by *de facto* allowing it to nominate bishops to the Vatican (see Oro 1971). The University's role was to form secular and regular clergy in charge of consolidating the ecclesiastical reform and to educate the new crown officers and clerks required by the Kingdom in the peninsula and the New World (see Gordejuela, Nieto and Sandoval 2002).

By 1570 Acosta travelled to Lima, Viceroyalty of Peru, to join six fellow Jesuits in their evangelising mission. Diverting slightly from the Jesuit goals and methods in Europe that focused on the production of knowledge at schools and universities, Jesuits in Peru concentrated on their missionary ministry, which implied different goals for the study of nature. Whereas European colleagues produced texts at universities seeking the patronage of nobles and princes, Jesuits in Peru travelled extensively and recorded their observations for later analysis (Prieto 2011, 4). Those involved in these missions had first-hand empirical experience in all practical and theoretical things related to the New World, including navigation, people, geography, governance and, of course, nature. Dealing with and reflecting on them demanded an active intellectual engagement in transforming them into subjects for action and study, and great resourcefulness and creativity, empirical dexterity, for making practical and theoretical sense of them.

Acosta's *Historia Natural y Moral de las Indias* can be interpreted as an empirical act that presents a novel programme of investigation that transcends philosophical attempts to rationally explain natural phenomena, reconciles the study of nature with the Holy Scriptures and sets the grounds for what was to become from 1599 onwards the field for Jesuit Science as expressed in the *Ratio Studiorum*, the basic structure for Jesuit education until our days (see Prieto 2011, 146). Its empirical action was also aimed at attracting attention from powerful patrons. Written in Spanish, it was addressed to a courtly readership with the hope of attracting support for the Jesuit mission in Peru (Prieto 2011, 149), but also, as stated in its dedicatory note to the *infanta*, it noted one of its benefits in the following terms:

> Besides that every one can obtain some fruit for himself, for no matter how lowly the subject, the wise man gets for himself wisdom, and from the vilest and smallest animals derives a very lofty consideration and the most useful philosophy. (58)

Such a statement reveals Acosta's marvelling attitude in a way that breaks apart hierarchies of (scientific) knowledge and transforms nature into an empirical space open to scrutiny to whoever decides to engage with it.

Novelty, Epistemology and the Creation of Spaces of Governance

The work of Maravall on the problem of novelty and the above-mentioned scholars helps understand that the experience of discovery and creation of America can and should be transformed into an empirical space from which to learn about the constitution of categories order, power and governance. Practices of discovery can be interpreted as empirical acts where spaces are created and invented to suit very particular problems (e.g., the governance of landmasses, of people, of nature). Empirical acts have as their effect the constitution of empirical spaces, sites where human intervention proceeds through the force of belief, knowledge, tradition and imagination. And the constitution of empirical spaces and their governance denotes empirical dexterity that can be interrogated to learn from it the resourcefulness and creativity of those involved.

In the introduction to this chapter, the question of how should imaginaries be approached as the sites of and for novelty was posed. Ideas of discovery and of conquest have traditionally been approached as imaginaries where political strategies and narratives of victors and oppressed are depicted, with almost linear outcomes of imperial making and colonial exploitation. What this chapter shows is how a historical epistemological interrogation of ideas such as discovery can be explored to reveal claims to novelty, which in turn can be analysed as worlds in the making. The making of such worlds is an empirical endeavour where doing and thinking are its constitutive practices, both practices that leave traces and can be interrogated. The nature of the interrogation is one that seeks to explore how those involved marvelled upon realities which they were not equipped to understand, how they resorted to claims to novelty as a way to legitimise their newly authored descriptions, accounts and theorisations of a real that revealed as emergent to them. By engaging with those actions and thoughts as empirical deeds, it is possible to transform narratives of discovery and conquest into empirical spaces from which to understand the creation of spaces of governance.

Bibliography

Acosta, José de. 1590. *Historia Natural y Moral de Las Indias*. Sevilla: en casa de Iuan de Leon.

———. 1894. *Historia Natural y Moral de Las Indias*. Madrid: Ramón Anglés.

Alconchel, José Luis Girón. 1995. 'Nebrija Y Las Gramáticas Del Español En El Siglo De Oro'. *Historiographia Linguistica* 22(1): 1–26. https://doi.org/10.1075/hl.22.1-2.02alc.

Antoniades, Andreas. 2003. 'Epistemic Communities, Epistemes and the Construction of (World) Politics'. *Global Society* 17: 21–38.

Arendt, Hannah. 1998. *The Human Condition*. Chicago, IL: University of Chicago Press.

Bacci, Michele, and Martin Rohde. 2014. *The Holy Portolano: The Sacred Geography of Navigation in the Middle Ages*. 1st edition. Boston, MA: De Gruyter.

Barrera-Osorio, Antonio. 2010. *Experiencing Nature: The Spanish American Empire and the Early Scientific Revolution*. Austin: University of Texas Press.

Baumgärtner, Ingrid, Nirit Ben-Aryeh Debby and Katrin Kogman-Appel. 2019. *Maps and Travel in the Middle Ages and the Early Modern Period: Knowledge, Imagination, and Visual Culture*. 1st edition. Boston, MA: De Gruyter.

Beilharz, Peter. 2002. *Imagining the Antipodes: Culture, Theory and the Visual in the Work of Bernard Smith*. Cambridge: Cambridge University Press.

Bergson, Henri Louis. 1992. *The Creative Mind: An Introduction to Metaphysics*. New York: Citadel Press.

Borges, Pedro, and Pedro Borges Morán. 1990. *Quién era Bartolomé de las Casas*. Madrid: Ediciones Rialp.

Brendecke, Arndt. 2012. *Imperio e información. Funciones del saber en el dominio colonial español.: Funciones del saber en el dominio colonial español*. 1st edition. Madrid: Iberoamericana Editorial Vervuert.

———. 2016. *The Empirical Empire: Spanish Colonial Rule and the Politics of Knowledge*. Berlin: Walter de Gruyter.

Brunstetter, Daniel R., and Dana Zartner. 2011. 'Just War against Barbarians: Revisiting the Valladolid Debates between Sepúlveda and Las Casas'. *Political Studies* 59(3): 733–52. https://doi.org/10.1111/j.1467-9248.2010.00857.x.

Canizares-Esguerra, Jorge. 2002. *How to Write the History of the New World: Histories, Epistemologies, and Identities in the Eighteenth-Century Atlantic World*. 1st edition. Stanford, CA: Stanford University Press.

———. 2006. *Nature, Empire, and Nation: Explorations of the History of Science in the Iberian World*. 1st edition. Stanford, CA: Stanford University Press.

Caraccioli, M. J. 2017. 'The Learned Man of Good Judgment: Nature, Narrative and Wonder in Jose de Acosta's Natural Philosophy'. *History of Political Thought* 38(1): 44–63.

Chinard, Gilbert. 1918. *L'exotisme américain dans l'œuvre de Chateaubriand*. Paris: Hachette et cie.

Copernicus, Nicolaus. 1543. *De Revolutionibus Orbium Coelestium*. Nuremburg: apud Ioh. Petreium. http://ads.harvard.edu/books/1543droc.book/.

Daston, Lorraine. 1995. 'The Moral Economy of Science'. *Osiris* 10(1): 2–24.

Daston, Lorraine J., and Katharine Park. 1997. *Wonders and the Order of Nature, 1150–1750*. New York: Zone Books.

———. 1998. *Wonders and the Order of Nature, 1150–1750*. New York: Zone Books.

Dear, Peter. 2018. *Scientific Practices in European History, 1200–1800*. London: Routledge. https://www.amazon.de/Scientific-Practices-European-History-1200-1800/dp/1138656410/ref=sr_1_1?keywords=scientific+practices+in+european+history&qid=1553682940&s=books-intl-de&sr=1-1-catcorr.

Dekker, Elly. 2012. *Illustrating the Phaenomena: Celestial Cartography in Antiquity and the Middle Ages*. Oxford: Oxford University Press.

Deleuze, Gilles. 1990. *The Logic of Sense*. Translated by Charles Stivale. London: Athlone Press.

Fermin del Pino-Diaz. 2008. 'Estudio Introductorio'. In de Acosta, José, *Historia natural y moral de las Indias*, XVII–LVI. Madrid: Editorial CSIC.

Derrida, Jacques. 1996. *Archive Fever: A Freudian Impression*. Chicago, IL: University of Chicago Press.

———. 2005. *Rogues: Two Essays on Reason*. Meridian, Crossing Aesthetics. Stanford, CA: Stanford University Press.

Foucault, Michel. 1980. 'What Is an Author?' In *Language, Counter-Memory, Practice: Selected Essays and Interviews by Michel Foucault*, edited by Donald F. Bouchard, 113–38. Ithaca, NY: Cornell University Press.

———. 1989. *The Order of Things*. London: Routledge.

———. 1998. *The History of Sexuality Vol. 1: The Will to Knowledge*. London: Penguin.

———. 2002. *The Archaeology of Knowledge*. London: Routledge.

Fourastié, Brigitte, and Philippe Joron. 1993. 'The Imaginary as a Sociological Perspective'. *Current Sociology* 41(2): 53–58. https://doi.org/10.1177/001139293041002007.

Fowler, Don. 2009. 'Horace and the Aesthetics of Politics'. In *Horace: Odes and Epodes*, edited by Michele Lowrie, 247–70. Oxford: Oxford University Press.

Fresán-Cuenca, F. J. (Francisco Javier). 2003. 'Un ideólogo olvidado: el joven José Antonio Maravall y la defensa del Estado Nacionalsindicalista. Su colaboración en Arriba, órgano oficial de FET y de las JONS. 1939–1941'. *Memoria y Civilizacion* 6(1): 153–87.

Gordejuela, José Javier Etayo, Francisco Galino Nieto and Francisco Portela Sandoval. 2002. *Universidad Complutense de Madrid: de la edad media al III milenio*. Madrid: Editorial Complutense.

Guattari, Felix. 2015. *Lines of Flight: For Another World of Possibilities*. Translated by Andrew Goffey. London: Bloomsbury Academic.

Haas, Peter M. 1992. 'Introduction: Epistemic Communities and International Policy Coordination'. *International Organization* 46: 1–35. https://doi.org/10.1017/S0020818300001442.

Heckscher, Eli F. 1994. *Mercantilism*. 1st edition. London: Routledge.

Hollis, Martin, and Steve Smith. 1991. *Explaining and Understanding International Relations*. 1st edition. Oxford: Clarendon Press.

———. 1994. 'Two Stories about Structure and Agency'. *Review of International Studies* 20(3): 241–51. https://doi.org/10.1017/S0260210500118054.

———. 1996. 'A Response: Why Epistemology Matters in International Theory'. *Review of International Studies* 22(1): 111–16. https://doi.org/10.1017/S0260210500118492.

Hourani, George F. 1995. *Arab Seafaring: In the Indian Ocean in Ancient and Early Medieval Times – Expanded Edition*. Revised edition. Princeton, NJ: Princeton University Press.

Jackson, Patrick Thaddeus. 2010. *The Conduct of Inquiry in International Relations: Philosophy of Science and Its Implications for the Study of World Politics*. London: Routledge. https://doi.org/10.4324/9780203843321.

Jordan, William Chester, Bruce McNab and Teofilo F. Ruiz. 2015. *Order and Innovation in the Middle Ages: Essays in Honor of Joseph R. Strayer*. Princeton, NJ: Princeton University Press.

Lebow, Richard Ned, and Mark Lichbach, eds. 2007. *Theory and Evidence in Comparative Politics and International Relations*. Basingstoke: Palgrave Macmillan.

Lestringant, Frank. 2016. *Mapping the Renaissance World: The Geographical Imagination in the Age of Discovery*. London: John Wiley & Sons.

Lobo-Guerrero, Luis. 2012. 'Lloyd's and the Moral Economy of Insuring against Piracy'. *Journal of Cultural Economy* 5(1): 67–83. https://doi.org/10.1080/17530350.2012.640555.

———. 2018. 'On the Epistemology of Maps and Mapping: De La Cosa, Mercator, and the Making of Spatial Imaginaries'. In *Mapping and Politics in a Digital Age*, edited by Pol Bargués-Pedreny, David Chandler and Elena Simon. London: Routledge.

Maravall, Jose Antonio. 1966. *Antiguos y Modernos: La Idea de Progreso En El Desarrollo Inicial de Una Sociedad*. Madrid: Sociedad de Estudios y Publicaciones.

Maravall, José María. 1978. *Dictatorship and Political Dissent: Workers and Students in Franco's Spain*. London: Tavistock.

Mayer, Roland. 2010. *Horace Epistles Book I*. Cambridge: Cambridge University Press.

Nebrija, Antonio de. 2006. 'On Language and Empire: The Prologue to Grammar of the Castilian Language (1492)'. In *On the Wings of Time: Rome, the Incas, Spain, and Peru*, edited by Sabine MacCormack. Princeton, NJ: Princeton University Press.

Nietzsche, Fredrich. 2000. 'On the Genealogy of Morals'. In *Basic Writings of Nietzsche*, edited by Peter Gay. New York: The Modern Library.

———. 2007. *On the Use and Abuse of History for Life*. Sioux Falls, SD: NuVision.

North, Michael. 2013. *Novelty: A History of the New*. New edition. Chicago, IL: University of Chicago Press.

O'Gorman, Edmundo. 1961. *The Invention of America: An Inquiry into the Historical Nature of the New World and the Meaning of Its History*. Presumed 1st edition. Bloomington: Indiana University Press.

Oro, José GARCIA. 1971. *Cisneros y la Reforma del Clero Espanol en el Tiempo de los Reyes Catolicos*. Madrid: CSIC.

Pavur, Claude, N. 2016. 'The Historiography of Jesuit Pedagogy'. *Jesuit Historiography Online*. https://referenceworks.brillonline.com/entries/jesuit-historiography-online/*-COM_194129. Accessed: 2 April 2019.

Perez, Pedro Ruiz. 1993. *Gramatica y humanismo. perspectivas del renacimiento español*. Madrid: Libertarias, Ediciones.

Pinet, Simone. 2016. *The Task of the Cleric: Cartography, Translation, and Economics in Thirteenth-Century Iberia*. 1st edition. Toronto: University of Toronto Press.

Poovey, Mary. 1998. *A History of the Modern Fact: Problems of Knowledge in the Sciences of Wealth and Society*. Chicago, IL: University of Chicago Press.

Prieto, Andres I. 2011. *Missionary Scientists: Jesuit Science in Spanish South America, 1570–1810*. Nashville, TN: Vanderbilt University Press.

Pryor, John H. 1992. *Geography, Technology, and War: Studies in the Maritime History of the Mediterranean, 649–1571*. Paperback edition. Cambridge: Cambridge University Press.

Rayner, Alice. Spring 1993. 'The Audience: Subjectivity, Community and the Ethics of Listening'. *Journal of Dramatic Theory and Criticism*, Vol. 7:2 3–24.

Sabuco y Álvarez, Miguel. 1728. *Nueva filosofia de la naturaleza del hombre, no conocida ni alcanzada de los grandes filosofos antiguos : la qual mejora la vida, y salud humana : con las adicciones de la segunda impression*. Madrid: Domingo Fernandez.

Sacrobosco, Johannes de. 2018. *Sphaera Mundi*. London: Forgotten Books.

Schmidt, Benjamin. 2015. *Inventing Exoticism: Geography, Globalism, and Europe's Early Modern World*. Philadelphia: University of Pennsylvania Press.

Slater, John, and Maríaluz López-Terrada. 2017. 'Being Beyond: The Black Legend and How We Got over It'. *History of Science. An Annual Review of Literature, Research and Teaching* 55(2): 148–66. https://doi.org/10.1177/0073275317694897.

Spinoza, Benedict. 1982. *The Ethics and Selected Letters*. Indianapolis, IN: Hackett.

Suganami, Hidemi. 2008. 'Narrative Explanation and International Relations: Back to Basics'. *Millennium* 37(2): 327–56. https://doi.org/10.1177/0305829808097643.

Taylor, Charles. 2004. *Modern Social Imaginaries*. Durham, NC: Duke University Press.

Veyne, Paul. 1984. *Writing History: Essay on Epistemology*. Translated by Mina Moore-Rinvolucri. 1st Wesleyan edition. Middletown, CT: Wesleyan University Press.

———. 1988. *Did the Greeks Believe in Their Myths?: An Essay on the Constitutive Imagination*. First printing edition. Chicago, IL: University of Chicago Press.

———. 2008. *Foucault: His Thought, His Character*. Cambridge: Polity.

CHAPTER TWO

Faciality and the Digital Politics of Identity

At Face Value

Carina Huessy

Janus, the two-faced god of Roman antiquity, was the god of beginnings, transitions, time, duality, passages, and endings—a god of change and time whose symbolisms resonate with imaginaries, novelty, and connectivities. Reflected in his two-faced visage looking both to the future and the past, as god of transitions between war and peace, Janus presided over the beginning and ending of conflict as well as birth, journeys and exchange, travelling, trade, harbors, and shipping. Spatial transitions, too, through doors, city gates, and boundaries were Janus' domain.

The ubiquity of connectivity is matched by that of borders and bordering practices. So too, the question of the face, as one of both singularity and ubiquity, has been widely taken for granted. Recognizing the face to be inherently political and focusing on the realm of digital connectivity, this chapter situates the site/sight of the face within the latitudes of connectivities and borders. Critically, taking the face as site and sight of an experience of connecting leads to the phenomena of affect. What assemblages make these connectivities possible, and what fields of intervention are invoked and exercised through particular political imaginaries of the real? What is the dimension of "real time" in such securitizing, bordering, and affective connectivities? The face relates a topological[1] suspension of tensions between the "inner" control of individuals

---

1 The meaning of topology is defined as follows:
  (a) Ecology: Topology is the study of patterns of interconnections in a network system.

and "outer" forces of governing practices. This discussion engages two interconnected terrains of the face as site/sight of connectivity—biometric and behavioral facial profiling—to consider the political imageries that inform these practices. The face, as connectivity, constitutes a field for intervention "subject to historical changes" (Lobo-Guerrero, Alt, and Meijer 2019), in this case the collaboration of liberal capitalism, digitalization, and securitization. Imaginaries of time (as real) are deeply enmeshed in these imaginaries and the structural and liquefied practices they entertain and function through. Thinking about the face as a particular field of forces or force field, Janus-like, of immanent movement and confrontation of imaginative forces (Saar 2015, 116), runs as connecting thread throughout. How this space is created and the connectivities that engender it are its central questions.

First, briefly sketching the development of the face in Western imaginaries, the discussion is brought to present-day politics of the face, exploring faciality[2] in light of contemporary bordering, securitizing, and governing practices. Following an overview of the spatial-temporal, globalized, and securitized context of post-9/11 imaginaries and digital facial profiling techniques, the IARPA's "Janus" facial recognition program is taken as an example of emerging biometric profiling practices. Next, the links between liberal capitalism and the commercialization of security in relation to the face as a novel sight/site of governance in Amazon's "Rekognition" software are described. Third, I look at the (dis)connectivities of the digitalized face as border site in the cases of border control systems in Australia, the EU, and the United States. A theoretical analysis of the relationalities between governance and the face as biopolitical connectivity follows. In a concluding section, the realm of affect, the novel dynamics and dimensions of algorithmic assemblages of facial profiling devices, and the political and ethical implications such technologies of governance and security raise are engaged.

Imaginaries: From Image to Profile

The (novel) openings of biblical *Genesis* pronounce Man as "created in God's own image."[3] The etymological groundings of the term "face" as

---

(b) Mathematics: In topology and related branches of mathematics, a topological space is defined as a set of points, along with a set of neighborhoods for each point, satisfying a set of axioms relating points and neighborhoods. The definition of a topological space relies only upon set theory. It is the most general notion of a mathematical space allowing the definition of concepts such as continuity, connectedness, and convergence.

2 The term "faciality" is used here following Deleuze and Guattari's account in Deleuze and Guattari (1987).

3 *Genesis* 1:27. 1999. *The Holy Bible, King James Version*. New York: American Bible Society.

"image" in Western modes of thought may be traced in significant part to these theological imaginations. The figure of Man, as image, thus always already contains a mirroring aspect, a dynamic of reflection that, following Cornelius Castoriadis, engenders the creation of particular imaginaries (Castoriadis 1998). Through imaginaries of connectivity understanding Man as created, created *in* the image of God, we can approach the face not as given but as a certain empirical space. What makes connectivity possible, as highlighted in this book's introduction, is connecting as an experience contingent on the assemblages through which it is enabled (Lobo-Guerrero, Alt, and Meijer 2019). Decisively, in similar fashion to the structural historical changes of Anderson's "print capitalism" (Anderson 1983, 52) previously, the parallel revolutions in digitalization and molecular science since have transitioned modernity to an era characterized by highly fluid, networked and contingent, and digitalized fields of intervention (Dillon and Reid, 2009). In the twenty-first century, "real-time" biometric and behavioral profiling practices illustrate and enact a very different imaginary premised on the digitalized connectivities of the profile. Here too, the face is (re)created as an empirical space, one that requires sighting, securing, and governing.

As enquiry into the contemporary political era, this analysis considers the dominant liberal political imaginary to be framed and exercised in terms of a post-9/11 world, a global space. The primary temporal marker of this spatial terrain, the terrorist attacks on September 11, 2001, in the United States, redefined political, social, and military boundaries and imaginaries. The event redrew previous categories of threat as primarily external—civilians from combatants; peacetime from wartime. It drastically heightened transport, mobility, and the nodes and networks of circulation as focal points of security (Lyon 2007/2009). It also zoomed security's focus on the space of populations as networked, mobile, and contingent. The need to surveil and separate good life from dangerous life at these junctures of mobility and in real time became extrapolated.[4] As the very connectivities of global circulations (transport, finance, information, ideologies) created and delivered radically asymmetrical, networked warfare, logics of prediction and preemption became paramount to strategies, apparatuses, and imaginaries of security (Amoore and De Goede 2008).[5] The border, as I go on to explore,

---

4 The U.S. Department of Homeland Security Report, 'Implementing 9/11 Commission Recommendations', *Progress Report 2011*, provides a good example of this security emphasis post-9/11. Available at: https://www.dhs.gov/xlibrary/assets/implementing-9-11-commission-report-progress-2011.pdf.

5 For further analysis of such securitizing practices, see Amoore and De Goede (2008).

itself becomes mobile and mobilized. Post-9/11, the blurring of inside/outside distinctions bordering space became increasingly also their correlate and inverse. Discerning the border itself *as* space, characterized by contingency and porosity, and equally the face in terms of this interstitial spatial bordering, is fundamental to the analysis I draw out below. These borders embody, inscribe, and deploy the contingencies and connectivities of Janus' mythological powers. The terrain of security and warfare has changed; so too has the face of war—and its borders.

Senior CIA RAND analyst Bruce Berkowitz's explanation of how information has revolutionized warfare, "The New Face of War," articulates these political-military imaginaries clearly. "The ability to collect, communicate, process, and protect information," he declared in 2003, "is the most important factor defining military power"[6] (Berkowitz 2003). The elimination of the concept of a front, believed Berkowitz, would be information's most transformative effect on warfare. Informational connectivity has, through the digital revolution, redrawn the face of war. As this chapter will unfold, the face of warfare and the face of politics become, resembling Janus, two sides of the same coin.[7] Foucault's inversion of Clausewitz's dictum describing politics as the continuation of warfare by other means (Foucault 2003) is flipped again, reimagining the contingent frontline of the face as profile(d) in real time. Playing here on Saars, the face becomes, literally, a force field of information and imagination.

The face as indicator of identity has been used throughout human history. Face recognition technology measures and matches unique characteristics for the purposes of identification or authentication. Increasingly widespread, the use of biometric facial recognition systems by security agencies has become extensive (Lynch 2018). Biometric recognition refers to the automatic recognition of individuals based on their physiological and/or behavioral characteristics through mathematically mapping facial features. Frequently employing a digital or connected camera, facial recognition begins with extracting the coordinates of features such as the mouth, cheekbones, jawbone, chin, nose, eyes, and pupils. These details are subsequently converted into a mathematical representation and compared to data on other faces previously collected and stored in a face recognition

---

6 Berkowitz, Bruce. Cited in Haseltine, Eric. 2007. "Book Review: The New Face of War: How War Will Be Fought in the 21st Century." Center for the Study of Intelligence, CSI Publications, *Intelligence in Recent Public Literature* 48: 4.

7 Janus' two-faced image featured on early Romans coins. The first coin of the liberal series, the *as*, bears his effigy.

database. This facial data are often termed a "face template" or "faceprint," designed to contain only particular details used to differentiate one face from another. An individual's identity is verified through software using so-called deep learning algorithms to compare a live capture or digital image to the stored faceprint. Rather than positively identifying an unknown person, many face recognition systems are designed to calculate a probability match score between the unknown person and specific face templates stored in a database. These systems provide several potential matches, ranked in order of likelihood of correct identification. The FBI's system, for example, functions in this way.

The Janus Program: Face Recognition in the Wild

> The goal of the Janus program is to enable dramatic improvements in unconstrained face recognition . . . to develop novel representations to encode the shape, texture, and dynamics of a face. (IARPA BAA-13-07 2013)

The Intelligence Advanced Research Projects Activity (IARPA) is an organization within the Office of the Director of National Intelligence in charge of leading research in tackling challenges faced by the U.S. Intelligence Community. Its "Janus" program, announced in 2013, seeks to improve face recognition performance in massive video collections through "novel approaches capable of leveraging the rich spatial and temporal information" provided by multiple views captured in unconstrained video by today's "media in the wild" (IARPA 2013).

"Janus" addresses both the vast data volumes, the scale of connectivities, involved in establishing individual identity, and the inherent unpredictability of the face, *its ability to change*. Rather than a problem, data volume is to become an elemental part of the solution.

Enabling recognition from various angles, poses, lighting conditions, and movement, addressing the "uncertainties" (IARPA 2013, 5) arising when working with possibly incomplete, inaccurate, and ambiguous data is key. During daily activities, the program announcement reads, "People laugh, smile, frown, yawn, and morph their faces into a broad variety of expressions" (IARPA 2013, 6). Formed from unique skeletal and musculature features, these expressions are individual to each face, remaining similar throughout the individual's lifespan. The Janus program's representations will exploit the "full morphological dynamics of the face" to facilitate better and faster matching and retrieval (IARPA 2013, 6). The biological uniqueness of an individual's facial features enables identification, representation, and encoding. Facial mobility and its morphological dynamics that generate its unpredictability and contingency require new forms of capture, calculation, and recognition.

"Janus" aims to reduce these uncertainties by expanding biometric facial recognition capabilities using automated machine learning to process data. Moving beyond existing two-dimensional image matching methods, the program seeks to develop more model-based matching capable of fusing all views provided by available stills and videos. The fields of pattern recognition and machine learning, computer vision and image processing, mathematical statistics and modelling, and data visualization and analytics are relevant areas of research. Central is developing algorithms to tackle an ongoing problem for research bodies and security forces: Current facial recognition algorithms operate well in controlled settings; the "Janus" algorithms target unconstrained situations where "people are just naturally going about their everyday activities" (IARPA 2018). These algorithms are able to capture the face's everyday presence and then to recognize that face. The program's importance, its proponents state, is first helping operational partners "identify bad guys" (terrorists, criminals, sex offenders). Second, the advances made in deep learning and convolutional neural networks hold broad applicability for other applications within and beyond national security.

Reducing uncertainty in the everyday space of "the wild" and the dynamic morphologies of the face as topological space is the "Janus" program's essential objective. The inherent contingencies of the environment and the face itself, the unpredictability of everyday life, are its primary focus. Probabilities generated by algorithmic calculations are informationalized connectivities enabling automatic recognition of mobile populations, bodies, and faces. Strikingly, convolutional neural networks, inspired by the connectivity patterns of biological processes between neurons, are a type of deep, feedforward artificial neural network most commonly utilized in analyzing visual imagery. Even as the face as mobile threshold becomes a networked space to be surveilled, the neurological connections beyond its exterior surface are mirrored in the very technologies that seek to capture and fix its (biological) biometric identity. The digitalized networks spawned through this research are imagined as connectivities circulating across the spectrum of life itself.

Rekognition: The Novel Face

It's a smart city, they have cameras all over the city. (Ranju Das, Rekogition Head, 2018)

It started its commercial journey as a bookseller, digitally connecting readers to books. Expanding into a global retail giant, the online company Amazon now sells everything from flowers to fashion, electronics to groceries; products for births, weddings, and funerals; beginnings, transitions, and endings. It now also sells facial recognition technology; it sells surveillance.

In November 2016, Amazon Web Services (AWS), a subsidiary that sells cloud computing services, launched Amazon Rekognition, an easy-to-use facial recognition service. Amazon's Rekognition Image lets customers "easily build powerful applications to search, verify, and organize millions of images" (AWS Website, 2018). Rekognition Video allows users to extract motion-based context from stored or live stream videos and assists in their analysis. Its image recognition service detects objects, scenes, and faces, as well performing searches and facial comparisons.

Amazon's customers are, however, not just private individuals—it is now marketing Rekognition in the United States for government surveillance. In May 2018 the American Civil Liberties Union of Northern California (ACLU) released public records describing how Amazon has been marketing and selling facial recognition software to law enforcement agencies (Cagle and Ozer 2018). Pitching its product as a law enforcement service, Rekognition can, Amazon claims, monitor "all faces in group photos, crowded events, and public places such as airports" (AWS Website 2017). Moreover, it is assisting governments in the software's deployment. Put to use by police departments in Florida and Oregon, in May 2018 Rekognition face surveillance began operating across Orlando in real time. The Washington County Sheriff's Office's use of Rekognition has, senior information system analyst Chris Adzima states, reduced the identification time of reported suspects "from 2–3 days down to minutes" (Adzima 2017). Within a week of using the new system, according to Amazon's website, their first suspect had been apprehended.[8] Using Rekognition in real-time conjunction with police body cameras has also been promoted in Amazon marketing—embodying, embedding and entwining corporeal and digital connectivities and borders.

The (dis)connectivities of Amazon's technology, however, have been shown to misidentify. In a trial run by the ACLU, the software incorrectly

---

8 For a description of Amazon Rekognition software's use by law enforcement forces and the digital "indexing" of faces, in a guest post by Chris Adzima, Senior Information Systems Analyst for the Washington County Sheriff's Office, on the AWS website, see Adzima (2017).

matched 28 members of Congress from a database of 25,000 mugshots, identifying them as other people who have been arrested for a crime (Snow 2018). Moreover, incorrect matches were disproportionately of people of color, including six members of the Congressional Black Caucus. Revelations that Amazon employees met with officials from Immigration and Customs Enforcement (ICE) during the summer of 2018 as part of a continued attempt to sell its facial recognition technology indicate its potential further application in governing the circulations and spaces of external borders.

Manifesting both singularity and ubiquity, faces inhabit the space of the public and the everyday. According to a report published by Georgetown Law's Center for Privacy and Technology in 2016, the facial images of one in two American adults are held in a law enforcement face recognition network (Bedoya, Garvie, and Frankle 2016). Critically, the increasing use of these systems has disproportionately impacted nonwhite citizens.[9] Biometric facial recognition, enabling remote, covert, and mass capture and identification of images and the continuous linking of networks of surveillance (Lyon 2009), is a technology that reconfigures both the public realm and the face as new spaces of governance. Algorithms, not humans, create this perpetual "virtual line-up" (Bedoya, Garvie, and Frankle 2016) of suspects, a digitalized identification process that will disproportionately affect nonwhite Americans.

In the Face of Uncertainty: Avatars at the Border

The god Janus was the deity of gateways and thresholds, entrances, exits, and passageways. Emerging technologies now herald the face as novel passport. Australia's Department of Home Affairs, for example, has installed smart border control technology. "Your face will be your passport and your boarding pass at every step of the process," declared Geoff Culbert, Sydney Airport CEO (Culbert 2018). In 2007, SmartGates were introduced at eight international airports, extending to departure terminals in 2015. Passengers scan an ePassport holding name, nationality, and a digital facial photograph stored on an embedded microchip and then undergo a face scan measuring biometric data to verify identity. These systems are now the primary method

---

9 For the disproportionate impact of facial recognition systems on nonwhite persons and women, see Buolamwini and Gebru (2018).

for processing travelers across Australia's major international airports.[10] The purpose is to increase both flow and security.

The (dis)connectivities of digitalization have developed substantially further. "Contactless traveller" technology, originally known as Cloud Passports, that eliminates showing any form of passport or paper travel documents was announced in 2015 by Australia's Department of Foreign Affairs and Trade Department. This involves scanning a passenger's face and biometrically matching a person's image to one held in Australia's Department of Home Affairs' databases. In 2017, Australia trialed the world's first "contactless" immigration technology, a passport-free facial recognition system. Termed "contactless" because of the *lack* of contact passengers have with border control officials, it signifies a new kind of (dis) connectivity.

Your face, however, is becoming imagined as something significantly more than simply your identity or even passport. Behavioral profiling focusing on facial expressions is emerging as a novel field of security. The analysis of facial expressions is in itself not new. The development of digitalized technologies of behavioral profiling focusing on facial connectivities as indicators of potential threat, however, is a radical transition in ways of knowing, securing, and governing life. The development of so-called "intelligent control systems" by EU border management authorities is one such novel example.

Technology that analyzes facial expressions employing digital, computer-animated border guards using artificial intelligence (AI) lie detector technologies to interrogate travelers at EU borders is being trialed in Hungary, Greece, and Latvia. Its aims, according to the European Commission, are efficiency and security, to "speed up traffic" and "ramp up security," identifying illegal immigrants and preventing crime and terrorism while increasing the flow of legitimate, productive travel (EU Commission 2018).[11] Dubbed "iBorderCtrl," this automated border-control system is part of a six-month pilot led by the EU and Hungarian National Police. First demonstrated in October 2018 at the Manchester Science Festival, it is proposed to

---

10 Other countries have since adopted similar systems. The U.S. Department of Homeland Security uses the Automated Passport Control system; the EU's Smart Borders system processes travelers from Schengen member states.

11 Cited in: "Smart Lie-Detection System to Tighten EU's Busy Borders." European Commission website. Published: October 24, 2018. http://ec.europa.eu/research/infocentre/article_en.cfm?artid=49726.

be used alongside biometrics and other recognition systems, such as checking travel documents and face recognition using passport photos.

In an initial "pre-screening step," after uploading pictures of passports, visas, and proof of funds via an online application form, passengers answer questions from a computer-animated border guard using a webcam that is personalized to the traveler's gender, ethnicity, and language. The travelers' "micro-expressions" are analyzed using this "deception detection" system to discern whether the interview is telling the truth or lying (European Commission 2018). Those travelers deemed as "high-risk" then encounter a more thorough check by border officials. Using a handheld device that automatically cross-checks information, facial images captured during the prescreening stage are compared to passports and photos taken on previous border crossings. Leveraging software and hardware technologies, multiple technologies check travelers' authenticity and validity. The collected data are encrypted, transferred, and analyzed in real time, providing an automated decision support system for border control officers. "We're employing existing and proven technologies—as well as novel ones—to empower border agents to increase the accuracy and efficiency of border checks," said the project's coordinator, George Boultadakis. The system, he asserts, will collect data that will "move beyond biometrics and on to biomarkers of deceit" (Boultadakis 2018).

The rationales behind such technology are fundamental to understanding the imaginaries that create these (dis)connectivities. "Micro-expressions" such as pupil dilation, eye direction, voice changes, and patterns that are undetectable to a human interrogator are believed to reveal deceptive intent. These "non-verbal behaviours" or "micro-gestures" are combined with a risk score to determine the level of potential risk: "It does not make a full automated decision; it provides a risk score," Keeley Crockett of Manchester Metropolitan University explains in a promotional video (Crockett 2018).

Similar virtual border agent kiosks have been tested by the United States, Canada, and the European Union. The University of Arizona's BORDERS program, funded by the U.S. Department of Homeland Security, has developed the Automated Virtual Agent for Truth Assessments in Real-Time (AVATAR) screening system. Envisioned to increase risk assessment capacities and tested at the U.S.–Mexico border, the research team proposes that AVATAR technology could be used at ports of entry and detention centers and for processing citizenship, asylum, and refugee status applications.[12]

---

12 See the research report: Nunamaker et al. (n.d.).

The kiosk-like system uses automatic screening systems and "virtual conversational agents" to conduct interviews designed to assess credibility "automatically and independently . . . detecting potential anomalous behaviour" via analysis of data streams from "noninvasive sensors" such as cameras, microphones, and eye tracking systems (BORDERS 5). This information is routed through an analytical algorithm producing almost instantaneous results: Green clears the subject to pass; yellow alerts to issues to be investigated; and red indicates serious issues requiring deeper investigation. Like biometric facial recognition systems, these new technologies map the encoded face using automated, digitalized systems. They go beyond biometrics, however, in seeking to establish "biomarkers" of affect. Apparatuses of truth-telling, the connectivities they analyze aim to distinguish not identity but truths.

Connecting the Dots: The Face as Sight/Site

Relationalities of governance to space are pivotal; spatial transitions are key. The eighteenth century, Michel Foucault perceived, saw the emergence of forms of government that, operating through strategies of making life live, took populations as a vital theater of intervention and control (Foucault 1977–1978). The biological framing of "species," rather than those of a people or peoples, heralded a transformative shift whereby political power became exerted over life as species, recognized in terms of biological mass sharing biological characteristics. Notable here is the shift from Man as image of God to Man in terms of species life, whereby population and its circulations—its connectivities—became novel spaces of governance. Foucault's account of governing practices illuminates specific governing technologies in terms of "biopolitics" (Foucault 1978). Central to biopolitics was the realization of certain ways of knowing life imbuing power apparatuses with technicalities of control over life, promulgated through power/knowledge discourses establishing and operating particular regimes of truth.

Biopolitical relations between power, governance, and freedom are interconnections of governmental rationality (Burchell et al. 1991). For Foucault, the activity of government could relate to relations between self and self as well as interpersonal relations, relations within social institutions, and those exercising political sovereignty. "Biopower" describes certain modes of power exercised over persons imagined as living beings (Foucault 1978). Fundamental to this, Foucault showed, is the nature of power as other than mere physical force or violence, as that concerned with and exercised over individuals who are in some way free to act.

This understanding of power functioning not as fixed or closed regime but operating in terms of an open, unceasing strategic game holds particular relevance in considering the ways power relations are exercised in, over and through the (digitalized) face. Profoundly connected to how biopower operates as "actions upon others' actions," the agency of subjects is essential to the very way power operates:

> At the very heart of the power relationship, and constantly provoking it, are the recalcitrance of the will and the intransigence of freedom. Rather than speaking of an essential freedom, it would be better to speak of an "agonism"—of a relationship which is at the same time reciprocal incitation and struggle; less of a face-to-face confrontation which paralyzes both sides than a permanent provocation. (Foucault 1982, 221–22)

This "agonism" is played out at the very site/sight of the face; the liberal alignment of biopower with freedom functions at the crux of the interfaces of power relations today. And it is at this juncture that digitalization instigates a novel role.

Visualizations of facial profiling technologies overwhelmingly present the face as mapped through a series of points, points connected by lines—a facial map, a constellation.[13] Integral to the connectivities that render the face as novel space of governance is the imagining of the face as site/sight. Following Foucault, the site is "defined by relations of proximity between points or elements." His analysis of siting in terms of demography in "Of Other Spaces: Utopias and Heterotopias" (1967) distinguishes this idea further:

> This problem of the human site or living space is . . . also that of knowing what relations of propinquity, what type of storage, circulation, marking, and classification of human elements should be adopted in a given situation in order to achieve a given end. (Foucault 1967)

"Our epoch," Foucault goes on to say, "is one in which *space* takes for us the form of *relations* among sites" (Foucault 1967). Sites are elements of connectivities, their very definition predicated by relations between points. With this observation of the spatial and demographic character of relationality,

---

13 For example, the facial personality technology company "Faception" (https://www.faception.com/) and the intelligence technology company "Athena" (http://www.athenaiss.com/index.html).

taking the face as site, we see how imaginaries of connectivity in and through facial recognition create novel spaces of governance in the form of *(in)visible relations* among sites. Digitalization, biometrics, and algorithmic calculations initiate these relations: The topology of the digitalized face becomes visualized as interface, an interconnected site/sight. Point by point, its biometric and behavioral coordinates are detected, quantified, and matched. Thus connected, the biometric faceprint provides a profile establishing identity—and constellations of risk.

Profile, etymologically traced, is both boundary and thread. Border and connectivity, its meaning is interwoven with a certain dynamic of interstitiality. As securitizing technology, facial profiling interlaces both an inside and an outside, a past and future. Analytically mapping the contours of the human face, profiling digitally biographs these details. It does so through algorithmically counting and discounting and through processes of (dis)connectivity. Captured and fixed, the profile is contained through its very fluidity as digitalized connectivity.[14] Intrinsically related to its correlates of territorial continence and containment on a global, (bio)geographical, and temporal scale, the face becomes, as the cases above illustrate, a virtual border site. The face has become a topological field of information but also its correlations of recognition and, most pivotally, of precognition. More than simply a site/sight of exposure, we might understand the face as a site of disclosure. A pivot upon which the faces of Janus, god of gateways, are (digitally) hinged.

Face Value: The Face as (Ex)change

1: the value indicated on the face (as of a postage stamp or a stock certificate)
2: the apparent value or significance[15]

The molecular and digital revolutions envisaged and vitalized species life as a new field of formation.[16] A related transformational shift is the strategic move to modes of reasoning and governance that propose probability as a formative means of political calculation. Fundamental to modern biopolitical imaginaries is the conflation of life not only with species being but its

---

14 Jenny Edkin's study *Face Politics* examines these relations of surveillance, fluidity, and face capture in detail; see Edkins (2015).

15 Merriam-Webster Online Dictionary. https://www.merriam-webster.com/dictionary/face%20value.

16 For a fuller account of this transition, see Dillon (2002).

synthesis with information and code (Kay 2000). The face as living, biological materiality and informationalized code circulates at both the very cusp and crux of this conjunction.

Through the contingency that now distinguishes informationalized life, the figure of Man becomes envisioned as something novelly different. Species life, as unpredictable and contingent, is problematized as emergent life (Dillon and Lobo-Guerrero 2009). This necessitates not simply containing or eliminating certain forms of life imagined as dangerous but the ability to predict potential danger. These cognitions entail and retail both the recognition exercised in technologies of biometric surveillance and identification and practices of precognition beheld in behavioral profiling.

"The creation of novel spaces of governance relates to imaginaries of connectivity in time" (Lobo-Guerrero, Alt, and Meijer 2019, 6). Time counts; it also discounts. Tellingly, the time-telling devices of clocks and watches have faces—faces that count. In the modern biopolitical imaginary, contingency is the ontological condition through which the face is imagined and generated as connectivity. Imagined in terms of connectivities, in circulation and in transit, faces require both screening and securitizing; *real-time profiling* affords this interlocking. Recall the god Janus, looking both forward and backward in time. Through digitalization, time is radically liquefied. Conjoined with the codification of biological life, time is imagined and realized as connectivity. As such it inaugurates novelty: the perpetual fluidity of circulation. Its biopolitical cogwheel, as Dillon and Reid show, is life as being-in-formation (Dillon and Reid 2009). Vitally, real-time transmission augments further temporal and spatial dynamics of biopolitical securitization. Imaginaries corroborating and connecting sequential technologies predicated on the perceived "value" flows of persons, good, capital, and information, specifically through differentiating good from dangerous flows, formulate a biopolitical assemblage that can be, I suggest, encapsulated in the notion of *face value*. Through this accounting of the face, face value in affect becomes the measurement of the real, transmitted in concert with and through the real-time fluidity of digitalized algorithms. The effigy of Janus, god of exchange, was printed on the first coin of the liberal series.[17] The face, in terms of the contingent real, has value: a sight/site of virtual (ex)change, (dis)closures, and (in)securities.[18]

---

[17] Janus' initiating role extended to financial enterprises: Mythology describes Janus as the first to mint coins.

[18] In life insurance policy terms, "face value" has a further meaning: one of the most important factors influencing the cost of a life insurance policy, the face value is the death benefit, the stated dollar amount received by the policy's beneficiaries upon the death of the insured.

Alliances of neoliberal capitalism with security (Ball and Snider 2013), or rather, their very conjunction and (in)formative interdependence in producing and securing the face as a novel space of governance, are reflected in the example of Amazon's Rekognition system. What Jenny Edkins calls "face politics" produces individuals as visual objects of administration (Edkins 2015). It is also, as I turn to explore in greater detail, a novel site of self-governance.

Affect: Confessional Kiosks—Telling Time/Borderline Truths

The affect is what? It is the passage. (Deleuze 1994, 18)

Following Spinoza's definition, "an ability to affect and be affected," this analysis is situated within the theoretical scope of the "politics of affect" (Spinoza 1994). Describing an "axial dimensionality," Peter Adey highlights the interior and exterior surfaces and the pasts and futures that logics of preemption in border surveillance seek to secure (Adey 2009, 275). Not only the body is understood to require securing but the deeper "space" of the unconscious including its "prethoughts" (Adey 2009, 276). The face's mobility represents a further vital domain and dynamic of securitization. The continually changing nature of facial movements are conceived of as indicators of intent. Through sighting/siting affect, behavioral profiling goes beyond the representational imaginaries of biometrics. A kind of "pre-face" might be discerned: a preemptive logic[19] categorizing and profiling facial movements in terms of risk. What this also maps are the dynamics of the face as (bio)markers of time.

Profiling, Adey clarifies, "addresses a future" (Adey 2009, 277). What must be secured is not just the present but the time to come. One is, he notes, "literally touched" through airport processing procedures (Adey 2009, 278). Particularly potent, this illuminates not just the physical touching of security checks but also the deeper, more penetrative touching of the interior inner space. This *interface* is realized as *touchscreen*, a digitalized display of affect. Recognized as a surface that is constantly (ex)changing, the interface, like the body in circulation, is mobile and *interactive*. Connectivities of code within the inner neurological, psychological, and emotional terrain generate facial movements to be deciphered and decoded. Braille-like, this

---

19 For a relevant discussion of preemptive securitizing logics and practices, see Goede (2008). See also Anderson (2010).

profiling articulates a certain kind of topological touching. Affect is the key of its calculus. Through touch and affect, like biometrics, behavioral profiling reads life as encoded. In digitalized profiling, as the "pre-screening" steps of the IBORDERCTRL system show, algorithmic assemblages conjoin precisely the connectivities of encounter (Palladino 2018) and mathematics (Dillon 2015).

Through extended biopolitical governing technologies, Louise Amoore writes, the body "in effect, becomes the carrier of the border . . . inscribed with multiple encoded boundaries of access" (Amoore 2006, 374–78). What I expand upon here, however, is how the face, *in affect*, likewise bears/bares the border, inscribed with but also describing and revealing encoded boundaries of access and intention. The novelty of the preface now is the instantaneous transmission of the facial display, the anticipation of possible futures in real time. This membroid, digitalized boundary, imagined as pluripotent, able to develop into multiple potentialities, is itself emergent. Affect is taken as a novel space of governance—even, as Adey writes, an "object to be known and captured" (Adey 2009, 281).

The nonverbality of these behaviors is essential to the political imaginaries through which they are sighted/sited. The pre-face is deciphered in terms of encoded intent, of *pre-text*, and of risk. Going back to my introductory remarks concerning the biblical siting of Man as "made" in the "image of God," we might likewise retrace Christian theology to the enigmatic opening of the New Testament's heralding in John, Chapter 1, of the beginning: "In the beginning was the Word, and the Word was with God, and the Word was God" (John 1:1). Not only this, the mutually constitutive imaginary of God and Word takes on a further matter, literally. In John 1:14, we read, "And the Word was made flesh, and dwelt among us." This reciprocity of word and flesh, image and matter, illuminates a vital conjunction at the core of Christian mythology. It articulates not only that God became Man but also the entwinement and embedding of power, language, and corporeality. The One in(di)visible God becomes not only visible (sighted) but also touchable and sited, embodied. Christ's "immaculate conception" inaugurated a novel imaginary, a new connectivity between God and Man, Word and Flesh. Fast-forward: What Foucault's studies show is how from the eighteenth century, biopolitics conceived man in quite another register, another imaginary aligned with new forms of governance taking populations and their circulations, species life, as its referent object (Foucault 2007). The face transposed from an imaginary of reflection (God/Man) to one of biopolitical registration (Sovereign/species) whereby not the divine was reflected but the biological nature of species life was made to be known, a novel space of governance.

What Foucault's work also shows is the collaboration of such novel power forms with existing institutions of governance, not least those of the established Church. The confessionary complex Foucault described has been picked up by Mark Salter to explore interrogation techniques in border sites (Salter 2008). Truths, revealed through practices of confessing and only authorizable by a representative of the sovereign, have been formative to the construction of borders. Faces and bodies, as confessional border sites, become physical and affective sights/sites of (dis)closures—spaces where digitalized modes of truth-telling operate as algorithmic elocutions of specific power/knowledge complexes: at face value.

Through the connectivities of digitalization, processes whereby information is converted into a digital, computer-readable format, the materiality of the face as digital image is made fluid, amenable to data processing, storage, and transmission. In digitalization, information is converted into a single binary code.[20] It is deciphered not as Word (as earlier with God/Man imaginaries) but in terms of code, both materially and affectively, in data demarcating "biomarkers of deceit." The digitalization of the confessional kiosk, engendering avatar border guards as authorized representatives of the sovereign, is revelatory of novel transformations.

Amoore suggests the concept of the biometric border to "signal a dual-faced phenomenon" in the contemporary war on terror (Amoore 2006, 336). This biopolitical, Janus-like phenomenon makes migrants and travelers bodies themselves sites of "multiple encoded boundaries" (Amoore 2006, 336). An almost "ubiquitous frontier" (Amoore 2006, 336) in the war on terror, border management has become a biopolitical, mobile site of governance, regulating people's everyday lives. Alongside the biometric border running through bodies, increasingly the face—as biometric and behavioral profile—is seamed and implanted with manifold, encoded boundaries. Biopolitical bordering practices demarcate not just external, territorial borders but also interstitially profiles identity, risk, and threat within the comings and goings (think Janus) of everyday life. And significantly, it is the performing of the *idea* of the biometric border that Amoore highlights as principal to these technologies.

The (inter)face is recognized as a mobile, emergent frontline in the global war on terror and beyond. As inherently manifold topology, its duality resides in its very changeability. While its identity is captured, fixed, and secured

---

20 Lily Kay's seminal work offers a historical account of how through the information revolution DNA-based protein synthesis came to be represented in metaphorical terms of information code and writing technology (Kay 2000).

through its biometric data, its radical potentiality, that is its potential for emergence, is sighted/sited through technologies of behavioral profiling. Sutured interstitially internally within societies as well as national and territorial borders (Stenum 2017), it runs through everyday "real" life, affecting spaces of self-governance. The "multiple borders of daily life" (Amoore 2006, 338) that Amoore observes resurface in the "wild" spaces targeted by the "Janus" program, with its accentuation of daily activities—laughing, smiling, frowning, yawning, the "morphological dynamics" of the face. Amazon's Rekognition likewise heralds the ability to deliver real-time, city-wide surveillance of everyday life. As David Lyon notes, potentially both enabling and constraining, surveillance literally has "two faces" (Lyon 2003, 3). Meaning to "watch over," the French word connotes both protection and control, a control that crucially can extend a moral dimension. Surveillance, and in particular its digitalization, is intricately entwined with modernity's paradigms of freedom. What Lyon has called "surveillance society" vitally impacts the "very order of society" (Lyon 2003, 4), permeating everyday life, its social and racial divisions, directing choices and desires. The connectivities of digitalization create novel spaces of governance and, in the encounters of the everyday, self-governance.

The ubiquity, connectivity, and (liberal) freedom of the interface border site is such that it has become imagined as more than a passport, a fixed identity. It is imagined as a *biomarker* between truth/deceit itself, a contingent, emergent, and ultimately discursive border able to demarcate good from bad, innocence from guilt. This biomarker, a biopolitical bordering of identity, delineates biopolitical imaginaries' force fields of security. Prescribing and inscribing these cartographic and biographic (dis)connectivities are the algorithmic calculations and liberal belief in mathematical probabilities that decipher the (de)coding of life. Foucault's governmentality, whereby the agonisms of power function in an open, unceasing strategic game, resonates within these interactions. The face as living materiality is inter-acted upon and with(in). Its agents are, in some ways, free to act. The annunciatory, algorithmic powers of the biopolitical border avatar, a concept summoning and merging the deific and computational, reflects the duality of Janus the god. Moreover, these self-adapting, generative algorithms inaugurate calculatory powers ad infinitum—calculating forever. Janus signified endings as well as beginnings; digitalized algorithms' ends, meanwhile, are not in sight.

These algorithmic strategies of securitization are no longer simply imaginaries created by the previous conventional entities of the human, state, and sovereign (Amoore and Raley 2016) but imaginaries of radically novel dimensions. The practices, beliefs, and material conditions necessary for these (dis)connections to occur are, through algorithmic assemblages involving artificial intelligence, machine learning, and neural network computations, being reconfigured. Crucially, it is the adaptive capacity of algorithms that both seeks to secure the contingency of species life and simultaneously engenders further generative powers of knowing. As this book's introduction sets out, a political imaginary is connected to the *human* ability to create images. The fields of immanent movement and confrontation of imaginative forces in which algorithms play, however, redefine the very parameters of these dynamics. The face is created as image, profile, and biopolitical identity, in part, through the nonhuman, the border-guard avatar. If politics is made *through* the imaginary, the biopolitical digital politics of identity is now being imagined in truly novel proportions.[21] The politics of "algorithmic world-making" (Amoore and Raley 2016) are not made purely at the level of disembodied automation, however, but generated at the interface of the sovereign, human, and machine. The self-learning, adaptive and generative powers of algorithms may calculate risk ad infinitum. Novelty, as the human ability to "introduce absolute beginnings into reality" (Blumenberg 1985, 169) itself takes on an (in)visible, infinite, and informational dynamic and scale. Janus, god of beginnings and transitions, indeed of novelty, overlooks the very portals of these emerging world orders. That novelty comes into the world precisely as a result of human intellectual creativity, though, must not be forgotten.[22]

Faceless Killing: Forever War

Inside the main Temple of Janus in ancient Rome, a structure with doors on both ends, stood a statue of Janus. The "Gates of Janus," as the doors were called, were closed in times of peace and opened in times of war—transitions between war and peace. Automated forms of warfare being developed by the U.S. military using cloud computing systems, or "algorithmic warfare," signals, in the view of Ben Tarnoff, the "desire to weaponise AI" (Tarnoff 2018). The lack of conventional adversaries in a war without national boundaries or fixed battlefields defines post-9/11 securitization, what Tarnoff calls "forever war" in terms of its continuity, perpetual indeterminacy, and expansion. The porosity of the line between civilian and combatant, its vastness, and vagueness make determining who the enemy is a decisive problem: The U.S.

---

21 See also Goede, Marieke de, Stephanie Simon, and Marijn Hoijtink's exploration of the strategic role of imagination in pre-emptive post-9/11 security (Goude et al. 2014).

22 As Amoore and Raley have noted, human strategy, enterprise, and imaginations have always been involved in this creation (Amoore, Louise, and Raley 2016).

military knows *how* to kill; figuring out *who* to kill remains difficult. The automation of finding who to kill by machine learning speeds this process—the capacity to wage war everywhere forever.

What the face says, Judith Butler proposes, is the commandment "Thou shalt not kill" (Butler 2004). Real-time digitalized imaging enables not just new kinds of recognition and (dis)counting but new kinds of killing.[23] The ultimate question of the sovereign, that of the strategic calculus of necessary killing, Foucault clarifies in "The Right of Death and Power over Life" (Foucault 1978), is how much killing is enough. The interconnected diffusion of the previously distinct actors of human, state, and sovereign with computational powers of machine learning transposes this question informationally—and infinitely.

"The face is a politics," write Deleuze and Guattari in their analysis of the relations of the face and the power assemblages requiring its social production (Deleuze and Guattari 1987, 181). Not exterior to the speaking, thinking, or feeling person, the face is a *white wall/black hole system*, not essentially individual but "zones of frequency or probability" (1987, 167–68). Faces are generated by an "abstract machine of faciality" (1987, 168)—a face that is a surface (facial traits, lines, wrinkles), a map. Fundamentally, facialization operates not through resemblance but through an "order of reasons" (1987, 170). As digitalized, emergent border site, as interactive touchscreen, the face is integrally connected to these very orders, these imaginaries of connectivity. For Deleuze and Guattari the face is not universal but "White Man himself"; indeed, "The face is Christ" (1987, 176). Recall the imaginaries siting God/Man; recall the racial aspect of biometric facial recognition systems. Recognizing its new role as "deviance detector," the abstract machine of faciality operates through the "computation of normalities" (1987, 177–78), uncanny parallels to the algorithmic biomarkers of everyday life. And critically, racism acts not between inside and outside but as *internal* dividing line, propagating "waves of sameness until those who resist identification have been wiped out" (1987, 178)—faceless killing.

Face Value: More Than a Sum of Its Parts (Conclusion)

Something in the world forces us to think. This something is not an object of recognition but of fundamental encounter. . . . It may be grasped in a range of

---

23 The Pentagon's "Project Maven," also known as the "Algorithmic Warfare Cross-Functional Team," is an example of the development of automated recognition systems by military forces (Pellerin 2017).

affective tones . . . its primary characteristic is that it can only be sensed. In this sense it is opposed to recognition. (Deleuze, 1994, 176)

This chapter opened with the two-faced god of beginnings and endings. This deity is invoked now at the *ianua*[24] of its closing. Guardian of the gates of heaven, the initiator of new historical ages and even of human life itself, Janus represented the origin of time, presiding over the concrete and abstract beginnings of the world. The novelty of Janus, we see, scopes the latitudes of this exploration of the face as vital, informationalized biopolitical site of governance, connected in and through (real)time. In his faces, the question of infinity, too, (re)appears.

Through algorithmic calculations that connectivize the digital biopolitics of identity, the connectivity of the face is imagined as more than the sum of its parts: Face value is imagined *as* (in)security. It is thus not merely the connectivities of digitalization through which these imaginaries are animated but the touchscreen display of the interface itself *as* contingent connectivity (inter)acts as force field of imaginations. Biometrics and behavioral profiling are illustrations of real-time connectivities afforded through digitalization and initiated by prevailing biopolitical imaginaries that site/sight life in terms of contingencies, (re)production, and seamless circulation, the attendant (in)securities such pure fluidity demands, and ultimately, face value as the definitive biopolitical watermark of such currency. Amazon's Rekognition, the "Janus" program, and iBorderCtrl and AVATAR systems are revelatory of imaginaries predicated on the confluence and constellations of digitalized life, capital, and global risk markets.[25] That these are predicated on borders and bordering practices, enunciated as security/securities, elicits the very conundrum of liberal modernity as proprietor of freedom as such. Calculating "biomarkers" of risk, algorithmic assemblages entwine the powers of touch and mathematics to profile, predict, and govern. In biometric profiling, the encoded face is rendered as site/sight of exposure; in behavioral profiling, it is one of disclosure—Janus' domain.

As material and as porous, the face offers an extraordinary topological space of governance. Precisely as such, however, as an area of interchange, exchange, and connection, it also offers potent fields of resistances to securitizing formulations. Finally, as the introduction makes clear, claims to

---

24 *Ianua* (noun): any double-doored entrance (e.g., a domestic door or a gate to a temple or city). From the name of the Roman deity *Iānus* (Janus), from *iānus*, "arcade, covered passageway."

25 See the edited volume Ball and Snider (2013).

novelty and connectivity provoke ethical questions. The face as novel space raises the question at the heart of modern security and governance, that of relationalities between connectivity and freedom. Digitalized forms of connectivity constitute the face as a (k)new object of knowledge but more as (k)new subjects of knowledge and self-governance.[26]

Ultimately, the unique connectivity of the face, as encounter, exceeds faciality and the biopolitics of face value. The face, never merely profile but (w)hole, affects and connects. It is, indeed, always already (k)new—a radically different recognition than that of Amazon's propositions or those of IARPA's Janus program, iBorderCtrl, or AVATAR. The unknown of this (k)new is a different novelty, one of the aesthetic (Farago 2016). A politics of aesthetics disrupts, initiating an "aesthetic break" (Bleiker 2012; Rancière 2008; Shapiro 2013). It is the very mobility and freedom of the face, its excess, that initiates its agency, its natality,[27] and mortality—its vulnerability, power, and plurality. Carrying this, baring this novelty, is its everyday terror and its everyday hope.

Post-Face: A Deliberation

It seems curious that Foucault too invoked the image of the face in relation to that of the figure of Man. His description of the possible erasure of "man . . . like a face drawn in the sand at the edge of the sea" traces man and the face as transitory, malleable, permeable, and impermanent (Foucault 1989, 385), an interstitial image that highlights the uncertainties of life itself. Janus, god of transitions, also appeared at the very thresholds of connectivities—and at their cusp.

"Where we perceive a chain of events, the Angel sees one catastrophe," wrote Walter Benjamin in 1940 (Benjamin 1969, 249). Perhaps, like the aporia of Benjamin's "Angel of History," borne in the storm of history, both coming and going, the face is always already a be-leaving. Like Janus, this figure looks both toward the past and future. With Benjamin we encounter a radically different form of connectivities, consisting (paradoxically) of fragmentation and montage. A transparency,[28] this angel displaces notions of

---

26 For a related discussion of the political implications of IT in liberal governance and possibilities of alternative politics of connectivity, see Julian Reid (2009).

27 Hannah Arendt's concept of natality as the capacity to begin something new (Arendt 1958).

28 Artist Paul Klee employed an oil transfer technique involving covering tracing paper with ink, placing a drawing paper underneath, and scratching the top paper to create an impression on the paper below—a different kind of touching, a tracing.

connections and of the singular face we assume to be facing in a certain, linear direction. It displaces notions of progress and borders, spatiality, temporalities, and as angel—corporealities. This chapter's thematics are juxtaposed in its image: displaced and timeless, it sights inside and out.

This chapter hopes to, in a sense, deliberate the face. To (dis)close its meanings, to trace its insights. Perpetually in tension, as simultaneously image and affect, the face can never be fully known or framed; as contrapuntal[29] and radically asymmetrical encounter, it holds power to account.[30] The face is not only a sight/site of identification, accounting, and governance, for the face itself sights. It is a space of movement and of being moved; of touch and being touched. Every thought, Arendt claimed, is already always an "after-thought" (Arendt 1981, 103). The act of thinking, therefore, is inherently one of connectivities. The possibilities of the face, as relational, contrapuntal, and as affect, engenders an immediacy and unpredictability that moves beyond biopolitical imaginaries. Never fully knowable or containable, as expression it exposes and discloses our connectivities—and thus perhaps most profoundly, our humanity.

Bibliography

Adey, Peter. 2009. "Facing Airport Security: Affect, Biopolitics, and the Preemptive Securitization of the Mobile Body." *Environment and Planning, D: Society and Space* 27: 274–95.

Adzima, Chris. 2017. "Using Amazon Rekognition to Identify Persons of Interest for Law Enforcement," AWS Machine Learning Blog, AWS Website, June 15, 2017. https://aws.amazon.com/blogs/machine-learning/using-amazon-rekognition-to-identify-persons-of-interest-for-law-enforcement/. Accessed: October 10, 2018.

Amoore, Louise. 2006. "Biometric Borders: Governing Mobilities in the War on Terror." *Political Geography* 25(3): 336–51. DOI: 10.1016/j.polgeo.2006.02.001.

Amoore, Louise, and Marieke De Goede. 2008. "Transactions after 9/11: The Banal Face of the Preemptive Strike." *Transactions of the Institute of British Geographers*, New Series, 33(2): 173–85. http://www.jstor.org/stable/30133355.

---

29 A musical term originating from the Latin *punctus contra punctum* meaning "point against point," counterpoint is the relationship between voices that are harmonically interdependent (polyphony) yet independent in contour and rhythm.

30 Action by Amazon employees where more than 450 Amazon employees signed a letter to CEO Jeff Bezos strongly protesting the company's push to sell "Rekognition" to local police departments around the country demonstrates this agency. Similarly, Google employees' protests against the Maven Project contract caused Google to announce its decision not to compete for the Pentagon's cloud-computing contract, valued at as much as $10 billion. Microsoft workers have likewise protested the company's bidding for the U.S. Defense Department's Joint Enterprise Defense Infrastructure cloud, or JEDI, which involves transitioning massive amounts of Defense Department data to a commercially operated cloud system.

Amoore, Louise, and Rita Raley. 2016. "Securing with Algorithms: Knowledge, Decision, Sovereignty." *Security Dialogue* 48(1): 3–10. https://doi.org/10.1177/0967010616680753.

Anderson, Ben. 2010. "Preemption, Precaution, Preparedness: Anticipatory Action and Future Geographies." *Progress in Human Geography* 34(6): 777–98. DOI: https://doi.org/10.1177/0309132510362600.

Anderson, Benedict. 1983. *Imagined Communities: Reflections on the Origin and Spread of Nationalism*. London: Verso.

Arendt, Hannah. 1958. *The Human Condition*. Chicago, IL: University of Chicago Press.

———. 1964. "'What Remains? The Language Remains': A Conversation with Günter Grass." In *Essays in Understanding, 1930–1954. Formation, Exile and Totalitarianism*. New York: Penguin, 2005.

———. 1981. *The Life of the Mind*. Boston, MA: Houghton Mifflin Harcourt.

Ball, Kirsty, and Laureen Snider. 2013. *The Surveillance-Industrial Complex: A Political Economy of Surveillance*. London: Routledge.

Bedoya, Alvaro, Clare Garvie, and Jonathan Frankle. 2016. "The Perpetual Line-Up: Unregulated Police Face Recognition in America." October 18, 2016. Center for Privacy and Technology, Georgetown Law. https://www.perpetuallineup.org/. Accessed: October 5, 2018.

Benjamin, Walter. 1969. "Theses on the Philosophy of History." In *Illuminations*. Translated by Harry Zohn. New York: Schocken Books.

Berkowitz, Bruce. 2003. *The New Face of War: How War Will Be Fought in the 21st Century*. New York: Free Press.

Bleiker, Roland. 2012. *Aesthetics and World Politics*. London: Palgrave Macmillan.

Blumenberg, Hans. 1985. *The Legitimacy of the Modern Age*. Translated by Robert Wallace. Cambridge: MIT Press.

Boehnen, Chris, Patricia Wolfhope, Kimberly Foy, and Patrick Grother. 2018. "JANUS: Facial Recognition in the Wild." YouTube video. IARPA JANUS Program, Office of the Director of National Intelligence. Published August 1, 2018. https://www.youtube.com/watch?v=61Ihi3VsTHQ. Accessed October 5, 2018.

Boultadakis, George. 2018. Cited in: "Smart Lie-Detection System to Tighten EU's Busy Borders." European Commission website. Published: October 24, 2018. http://ec.europa.eu/research/infocentre/article_en.cfm?artid=49726

Buolamwini, Joy, and Timnit Gebru. 2018. "Gender Shades: Intersectional Accuracy Disparities in Commercial Gender Classification." *Proceedings of Machine Learning Research*, Conference on Fairness, Accountability, and Transparency, 81: 1–15. Available at: http://proceedings.mlr.press/v81/buolamwini18a/buolamwini18a.pdf.

Burchell, Graham, Colin Gordon, and Peter Miller (eds.). 1991. *The Foucault Effect: Studies in Governmentality*. Chicago, IL: University of Chicago Press.

Butler, Judith. 2004. *Precarious Life: The Powers of Mourning and Violence*. London: Verso.

Cagle, Matt, and Nicole Ozer. 2018. "Amazon Teams Up with Law Enforcement to Deploy Dangerous New Face Recognition Technology," ACLU Northern California Website. Published on May 22, 2018. https://www.aclunc.org/blog/amazon-teams-law-enforcement-deploy-dangerous-new-face-recognition-technology. Accessed: October 15, 2018.

Castoriadis, Cornelius. 1998. *The Imaginary Institution of Society*. Translated by Kathleen Blamey. Cambridge, MA: MIT Press.

Crockett, Keeley. 2018. "Can you fool an AI lie detector? University at Manchester Science Festival." News item, Manchester Metropolitan University website. https://www2.mmu.ac.uk/research/news-and-events/story/?id=8593. Accessed: October 30 2019.

Das, Ranju. 2018. "City of Orlando partners with Amazon to test real-time facial recognition technology". YouTube video. WFTV Channel 9. May 24, 2018. https://www.youtube.com/watch?v=BGq0x2TSHrA. Accessed: October 20, 2018.

Deleuze, Giles. 1994. *Difference and Repetition*. Translated by P. Patton. New York: Columbia University Press.

Deleuze, Giles, and Felix Guattari. 1987. *A Thousand Plateaus: Capitalism and Schizophrenia*. Translated by Brian Massumi. Minneapolis: University of Minnesota Press.

Dillon, Michael. 2015. *Biopolitics of Security: A Political Analytic of Finitude*. London: Routledge.

Dillon, Michael. 2002. "Network Society, Network-Centric Warfare and the State of Emergency." *Theory, Culture & Society* 19(4): 71–79. https://doi.org/10.1177/0263276402019004005.

Dillon, Michael, and Julian Reid. 2009. *The Liberal Way of War: Killing to Make Life Live*. 1st edition. London: Routledge.

Dillon, Michael, and Luis Lobo-Guerrero. 2009. "The Biopolitical Imaginary of Species Being." *Theory Culture Society* 26(1): 1–23. https://doi.org/10.1177%2F0263276408099009.

Edkins, Jenny. 2015. *Face Politics*. London: Routledge.

Farago, Jason. 2016. "How Klee's 'Angel of History' Took Flight." BBC Online, Culture Section. Published on April 6, 2016. http://www.bbc.com/culture/story/20160401-how-klees-angel-of-history-took-flight. Accessed: October 10, 2018.

Foucault, Michel. March 1967. "Of Other Spaces, Heterotopias." *Architecture, Mouvement, Continuité*. Translated by Jay Miskowiec, 5: 46–49.

———. 1978. *The History of Sexuality*. New York: Pantheon Books.

———. 1982. "The Subject and Power." In *Michel Foucault: Beyond Structuralism and Hermeneutics*, edited by Hubert L. Dreyfus and Paul Rabinow. Chicago, IL: University of Chicago Press.

———. 1989. *The Order of Things*. London: Routledge.

———. 2003. *Society Must Be Defended: Lectures at the Collège de France, 1975–76*. New York: Picador.

———. 2007. *Security, Territory, Population: Lectures at the Collège de France, 1977–78*. Edited by Michel Senellart. Translated by Graham Burchell. London: Palgrave Macmillan.

Gates, Kelly. 2013. "The Cultural Labor of Surveillance: Video Forensics, Computational Objectivity, and the Production of Visual Evidence." *Social Semiotics* 23(2): 242–60. DOI: 10.1080/10350330.2013.777593.

Goede, Marieke de. March 2008. "The Politics of Preemption and the War on Terror in Europe." *European Journal of International Relations* 14(1): 161–85. DOI:10.1177/1354066107087764.

Goede, Marieke de, Stephanie Simon, and Marijn Hoijtink. 2014. "Performing Preemption." *Security Dialogue* 45(5): 411–22. DOI:10.1177/0967010614543585.
Kay, Lily. 2000. *Who Wrote the Book of Life? A History of the Genetic Code*. Writing Science. Stanford, CA: Stanford University Press.
Lobo-Guerrero, Luis, Suvi Alt, and Marrten Meijer, eds. 2019. "Introduction." In *Imaginaries of Connectivity and the Creation of Novel Spaces of Governance*. Lanham, MD: Rowman & Littlefield.
Lynch, Jennifer. 2018. "Face Off: Law Enforcement Use of Face Recognition Technology." *Electronic Frontier Foundation*. https://www.eff.org/wp/law-enforcement-use-face-recognition. Accessed: November 14, 2018.
Lyon, David. 2003. *Surveillance after September 11*. Cambridge: Polity.
———. 2007. "Surveillance, Security and Social Sorting: Emerging Research Priorities." *International Criminal Justice Review* 17(3): 161–70. DOI:10.1177/1057567707306643.
———. 2009. "Surveillance, Power, and Everyday Life." In *The Oxford Handbook of Information and Communication Technologies*, edited by Chrisanthi Avgerou, Robin Mansell, Danny Quah, and Roger Silverstone. Oxford: Oxford University Press.
Nunamaker, Jay, Elyse Golob, Douglas Derrick, Aaron Elkins, and Nathan Twyman. n.d. "Field Tests of an AVATAR Interviewing System for Trusted Traveler Applicants." BORDERS Program, University of Arizona. http://www.borders.arizona.edu/cms/sites/default/files/FieldTestsofanAVATARInterviewingSystemforTrustedTravelerApplicants.pdf. Accessed: November 2, 2018.
Palladino, Paolo. 2018. "What's in a Name? On Affect, Value and the Bio-Economy." In *BioSocieties, edited by Nikolas Rose, Catherine Waldby and Hannah Landecker*. New York: Springer.
Pellerin, Cheryl. 2017. "Project Maven to Deploy Computer Algorithms to War Zone by Year's End." *DoD News*. U.S. Department of Defense Website. https://dod.defense.gov/News/Article/Article/1254719/project-maven-to-deploy-computer-algorithms-to-war-zone-by-years-end/. Accessed: October 20, 2018.
Rancière, Jacques. Summer 2008. "Aesthetic Separation, Aesthetic Community: Scenes from the Aesthetic Regime of Art." *Art & Research: A Journal of Ideas, Contexts and Methods*. 2(1). http://www.artandresearch.org.uk/v2n1/ranciere.html.
Reid, Julian. 2009. "Politicizing Connectivity: Beyond the Biopolitics of Information Technology in International Relations." *Cambridge Review of International Affairs* 22(4): 607–23. DOI: 10.1080/09557570903325520.
Reilly, Claire. 2018. "Welcome to the Airport of the Future, Where Your Face Is Your Passport." July 18, 2018. *cnet*. https://www.cnet.com/news/welcome-to-the-airport-of-the-future-where-your-face-is-your-passport/. Accessed: October 15, 2018.
Saar, Martin. 2015. "Spinoza and the Political Imaginary." Translated by William Calison and Anne Gräfe. *Qui Parle: Critical Humanities and Social Sciences* 23(2): 115–33.
Salter, Mark. 2008. "When the Exception Becomes the Rule: Borders, Sovereignty, and Citizenship." *Citizenship Studies* 12(4): 365–80. DOI: 10.1080/13621020802184234.
Shapiro, Michael J. 2013. *Studies in Trans-Disciplinary Method: After the Aesthetic Turn*. New York: Routledge.

Snow, Jacob. 2018. "Amazon's Face Recognition Falsely Matched 28 Members of Congress with Mugshots." July 26, 2018. ACLU website. https://www.aclunc.org/blog/amazon-s-face-recognition-falsely-matched-28-members-congress-mugshots.

Spinoza, Baruch. 1994. *A Spinoza Reader*. Translated by Edwin M. Curley. Princeton, NJ: Princeton University Press.

Stenum, Helen. June 2017. "The Body-Border—Governing Irregular Migration through Biometric Technology." *Spheres, Journal for Digital Cultures*. http://spheres-journal.org/the-body-border-governing-irregular-migration-through-biometric-technology/.

Tarnoff, Ben. 2018. "Weaponised AI Is Coming. Are Algorithmic Forever Wars Our Future?" *The Guardian Online*. Published on October 11, 2018. https://www.theguardian.com/commentisfree/2018/oct/11/war-jedi-algorithmic-warfare-us-military. Accessed: October 11, 2018.

Wong, Julie. 2018. "'Recipe for Authoritarianism': Amazon under Fire for Selling Face-Recognition Software to Police." *The Guardian Online*. May 23, 2018. https://www.theguardian.com/technology/2018/may/22/amazon-rekognition-facial-recognition-police. Accessed: October 20, 2018.

The Holy Bible, King James Version. 1999. New York: American Bible Society.

Websites and Online Articles

"An Open Letter to Microsoft: Don't Bid on the US Military's Project JEDI," Signed by employees of Microsoft, Published on the Medium Corporation Website, 13 October 2018. https://medium.com/s/story/an-open-letter-to-microsoft-dont-bid-on-the-us-military-s-project-jedi-7279338b7132. Accessed: November 12, 2018.

"Amazon Rekognition Announces Real-Time Face Recognition, Text in Image Recognition, and Improved Face Detection." Posted on November 21, 2017. Amazon, AWS Website. https://aws.amazon.com/about-aws/whats-new/2017/11/amazon-rekognition-announces-real-time-face-recognition-text-in-image-recognition-and-improved-face-detection/. Accessed: October 20, 2018.

Amazon Rekognition. 2018. https://aws.amazon.com/rekognition/.

BORDERS, Field Tests of an AVATAR Interviewing System for Trusted Traveler Applicants, University of Arizona, n.d. https://eller.arizona.edu/sites/default/files/FieldTestsofanAVATARInterviewingSystemforTrustedTravelerApplicants.pdf. Accessed: October 3, 2018.

CORDIS, EU Commission website. "Intelligent Portable Border Control System." https://cordis.europa.eu/project/rcn/202703_en.html. Accessed: October 15, 2018.

"Implementing 9/11 Commission Recommendations," U.S. Department of Homeland Security Report, *Progress Report 2011*. https://www.dhs.gov/xlibrary/assets/implementing-9-11-commission-report-progress-2011.pdf. Accessed: February 15, 2019.

EU Commission website. 2018. "Smart Lie-Detection System to Tighten EU's Busy Borders." http://ec.europa.eu/research/infocentre/article_en.cfm?artid=49726. Accessed: October 15, 2018.

Electronic Frontier Foundation. https://www.eff.org/. Accessed: October 20, 2018.

IARPA Broad Agency Announcement. Janus Program, Office of Smart Collection. IARPA BAA-13–07. Release date: November 8, 2013. https://leaksource.files.wordpress.com/2013/11/iarpa-janus.pdf. Accessed: November 18, 2018.

Merriam-Webster Online Dictionary. 2018. Springfield, MA: Merriam-Webster. https://www.merriam-webster.com/.

"Smart Lie-Detection System to Tighten EU's Busy Borders" European Commission website. Published October 24, 2018. http://ec.europa.eu/research/infocentre/article_en.cfm?artid=49726. Accessed November 2, 2018.

"The University of Arizona Licenses Deception Detecting Avatar to Startup." *Tech Launch Arizona*. University of Arizona. Published on August 21, 2018. https://techlaunch.arizona.edu/news/university-arizona-licenses-deception-detecting-avatar-startup. Accessed: October 15, 2018.

CHAPTER THREE

After Ports Were Linked

Paradoxes of Transpacific Connectivity in the Nineteenth Century

Sujin Eom

Introduction

We do know, however, that, like most other grave epidemic diseases, it is one of nature's punishments for filthy habits. That it was the curse of the Middle Ages, was due to the fact that the cities of Europe were, at that time, filthy and insanitary to an extent only comparable with the condition of some of the towns of Asia at the present day. *Filth is the great factor in the development and increase of epidemic disease*; but, having begun in a crowded and dirty environment, and progressed to epidemic extent, the infection often seems to become so intense as to tend to overleap its natural boundaries, and to attack with greater or less violence those living in far better circumstances.[1]

When bubonic plague was found in Hong Kong in May 1894, the *Japan Weekly Mail*, published for a readership of Yokohama's Western residents, featured a number of articles covering the outbreak. Under the title of "The Black Death," those articles associated the epidemic with "uncivilized" pockets of filth and contagion in Asia and with ignorance of "modern scientific discoveries." The news that the plague was rampant in Hong Kong and that Chinese residents were escaping the British colony in large numbers went current even in Japan. Japanese newspapers urged the authorities to "take prompt and full measures for the prevention of the dangerous disease," and

---

1 *The Japan Weekly Mail.* May 26, 1894, my italics.

subsequently strict sanitary precautions were taken to prevent its entry into the archipelago.² The fear of the plague further created anxiety among Yokohama's Western residents. On June 8, 1894, in a letter to the editor for the *Japan Weekly Mail*, a concerned Western resident of Yokohama pointed to the regular import into Yokohama of old cottons from Hong Kong as a suspect and overlooked medium for spreading pestilence and called for a strict investigation of such items.³

The anxious tone of the letter indicated the fear of epidemic disease crossing regional boundaries, especially given the presence of the increasingly networked ports in the Pacific. It also signaled the age in which migrant figures acquired new vectors of metaphorical and moral meaning as control over mobility was now taken "out of hands of the local" and placed "in the hands of the state" (Cresswell 2006, 13). This fear of migrant things is also reflective of the rapidly increasing connectivity during the time, real or imagined, a paradoxical outcome of the imperial enterprise of expansion and mobility: The global spread of the plague was first and foremost facilitated through a multitude of transpacific sea routes linking Asia to Europe and the Americas. This chapter deals with this historical transition, set against a backdrop of drastic changes in global capitalism, which created a hitherto unseen level of transoceanic, transpacific in particular, connectivity.

This chapter looks primarily at the Japanese port of Yokohama and the Korean port of Incheon, two of treaty ports in East Asia opened to foreign trade and commerce in the 1860s and the 1880s, respectively. After these treaty ports were established, Euro-American entrepreneurs who had already engaged in trading in China's treaty ports moved to these new trading outposts with a view to expanding to other markets while bringing with them their own laws and institutions. Chinese migrants, from merchants to laborers, also came to the ports to benefit from the growth of the treaty port economy. I draw attention to the treaty port as the contact zone in which the increased mobility of people and goods both provided economic opportunity and posed constant threats of violence and disease. The Euro-American residents wished to conduct trade and business in new territories, but they had to deal with the problem of co-residence with their Asian neighbors while trying to protect themselves from the fallout of epidemic diseases often attributed to intrinsic traits of Asian races. By situating the two ports within the cross-oceanic network of personnel and knowledge, I argue that

---

2   *The Japan Weekly Mail*, June 2, 1894.
3   *The Japan Weekly Mail*, June 16, 1894.

this dilemma of colonial proximity translated into the built form in the two ports by reflecting circulating ideas of residential separation based on racial distancing.

While this new mobility characterized the increasingly connected economies in the late nineteenth century, it also became subject to surveillance and control by the state, which exerted a "monopoly on the legitimate means of movement" by creating and regulating categories of migrant figures (Torpey 2000: 56). In this regard, I highlight the ways in which the control and management of particular categories of people took "spatial" forms during this period. While acknowledging the benefit of analyzing one specific locality to understand intertwined domains of agency and influence in history of globalization, I am more interested in tracing what was actually moving across different boundaries between seemingly discrete places (Latour 1990, 2007), from migrants and urban forms to policies and ideas. Specifically, I will show how racial and spatial categories traveled across the Pacific Ocean as tools for imagining, managing, and differentiating migration that was the product of increased mobility in the late nineteenth century. The goal of present chapter is therefore to trace how the transpacific connection engendered the circulation of policies and imaginaries through the network of personnel and knowledge, which in turn led to the codification of difference in space and a spread of specific urban models.

Imaginaries of Maritime Connectivity

> The human is a land-being, a land-dweller.
> —Carl Schmitt (1942, 5)

In *Land and Sea*, Carl Schmitt cites the work of the German philosopher of geography Ernst Kapp, who divides the material development of maritime history of the world into three stages: river, inland sea, and ocean. While the Potamic period refers to the river culture cultivated in Mesopotamia or along the Nile, the Thalassic period indicates a culture of inland seas or sea basins of the Mediterranean, which gave birth to trading metropolises such as Venice. The circumnavigation of the earth, European exploration, and conquest of the Americas enabled oceanic culture to emerge (Schmitt 1942, 20–21). With the advent of ocean travel, the nineteenth century witnessed the latest form of what Schmitt termed "spatial revolution" in world history—a revolutionary change that brought about "a transformation of the sense of space" (ibid., 49).

Reflecting Schmitt's own nationalist ideological stance during the turbulent years in the 1940s, *Land and Sea* can be read as a politically driven essay that denigrates sea-bound peoples and cultures—Britain, America, Jews (Berman 2015, xxviii–xxix). While subscribing to "the notion of landed peoplehood as criterion for 'the human'" (Zeitlin 2015, xliii), Schmitt criticizes the foundation of British maritime hegemony while simultaneously dehumanizing "landless wanderers," namely the Jewish people, on the basis that they lack a proper form of dwelling in the land. His contentious ideological commitments aside, it is worthwhile to revisit Schmitt's dichotomous use of land and sea through the employment of two mythical and imaginary figures—Behemoth, "the land animal," and Leviathan, "the powerful whale-fish"—in his analysis of the world historical struggle between land-based and sea-based powers. This use of mythical images not only reveals Schmitt's uneasy relationship with empires and peoples built upon maritime existence but also exhibits the role of the imagery in the creation and deployment of privative categories of people and cultures on the move. As Mitchell Dean points out, "the imagery" as employed in Schmitt's spatial thinking "overtake(s) the argument that is being illustrated by it" (Dean 2006, 18) by electrifying the emotional charges imposed upon sea-bound people.

The nineteenth century witnessed epochal change made possible through the development of steamship technologies, when the increased production and circulation of iron and steam engines gave rise to larger steamers in lieu of sailing ships. As early as the sixteenth century, different parts of the world were already connected by the Portuguese and the Dutch, who founded trading outposts across the Indian Ocean in South, Southeast, and East Asia. Muslim merchants and Jesuit Fathers frequented China's southern ports across the Indian Ocean. The Spanish empire had also initiated the Pacific trade as early as the sixteenth century through the annual voyage of the Manila galleons between the Philippines and New Spain, thereby linking Asia to the Americas and, by extension, Europe. However, the nineteenth century altered spatial concepts more broadly by expanding transpacific maritime connections between Asia and the Americas. Technological advance and competition in the shipping industry was the driving force behind this new flow (Aldcroft 1968). The rise of large-scale enterprise in British shipping contributed to the profusion and diffusion of steamships across the globe in the late nineteenth century (Kubicek 2004, 107–8). In 1867, for instance, the San Francisco–based Pacific Mail Steamship Company (PMSSC) began its first transpacific service by operating a passenger liner between San Francisco and Hong Kong, thereby significantly reducing the trip between the two locations to only a month (Sinn 2011, 229; Yip 1985, 107).

Added to the new infrastructure of mobility was the simultaneous emergence of "narratives about mobility" (Cresswell 2010, 17), or imaginaries therein, which served to amplify what Arjun Appadurai calls "the fear of small numbers" (Appadurai 2006) and galvanize people into violent action. Reflecting on the French notion of *imaginaire* as "a constructed landscape of collective aspirations," Appadurai also maintains that the imaginary (or the imagination) is "an organized field of social practices" (Appadurai 1996, 31). As with contemporary vocabularies of migration ("boat people," "anchor babies," "migrant caravans"), the imaginaries surrounding mobility at the time were often reflective of the fear of global change due to the increased contact between people from different continents.

With the expansion of transpacific sea routes, European migration to the rim of the Pacific Ocean dramatically increased. This was particularly so by the time gold was discovered in the 1850s across the Pacific, from Australia's Victoria Colony to Canada's British Columbia and the U.S. state of California, where Euro-American settlers established large-scale colonies (Nightingale 2012, 136). Equally rising was the transpacific mobility of non-European people, such as Chinese, who found economic opportunity in booming mining towns. About 30,000 Chinese, for instance, migrated to San Francisco in 1852 alone (McKeown 1999, 317). After the gold rush came to an end, the Chinese migrants sought employment in the urban sector, ranging from construction and laundry to domestic labor and restaurant work. The rapid increase in transpacific mobility, as well as "colonial proximities" (Mawani 2009), came to exacerbate a sense of insecurity, especially among Euro-American settlers. This was particularly so when diseases circulated through newly established sea routes among previously isolated regions. At the end of the nineteenth century, for instance, bubonic plague spread rapidly and widely along trade routes consuming tens of millions of people. Newspapers circulating in Asia, while delivering official information, reports, letters, and business advertisements, broadcast anxiety and fear harbored by European and American residents with Asian neighbors.

Transpacific connectivity brought about ample economic opportunity but presented challenges to people from various sectors, from merchants to medical experts sitting on boards of health. At the turn of the twentieth century, for instance, public health officers in the new government of Hawaii faced the dilemma of controlling the spread of plague through rapidly expanding trading routes while relying heavily on economic benefits from the very connection (Mohr 2005). Lack of medical knowledge and misinformation about the link between race and disease turned into an arbitrary policy decision to impose categories of exclusion on Asians, especially Chinese, as if they were carriers of epidemic disease. This led to the disastrous fire that consumed the whole section of Honolulu's Chinatown in the midst of the outbreak of plague, marking itself as "one of the worst disasters ever initiated in the name of public health by American medical officers anywhere" (ibid., 5).

Scholars have observed this paradox—the simultaneous creation of mobility and immobility, of privilege and exclusion, and of integration and segregation—as an inherent function of global connection (Appadurai 1996; Graham and Marvin 2001; Inda and Rosaldo 2008; Ong 2006; Tsing 2005; Urry 2007). Such "frictions" (Tsing 2005) are not necessarily initiated by a *malign* agent but instead integral to "the very complex dynamics of the systems themselves" (Dillon and Lobo-Guerrero 2008, 269). Connectivity is like a double-edged sword—people and places are drawn together by technologies of mobility, from airplane to the Internet, but the same technologies may bring about grave consequences, such as epidemic disease and terrorism, which pose threats to national security. Developed in response to such threats was the monopolization of movement by territorial states, whose fundamental task is "to *striate* the space over which it reigns" (Deleuze and Guattari 1987, 385). It is not the purpose of the state to simply oppose mobility but to channel it into "acceptable conduits" (Cresswell 2010, 24). I would argue that arising out of this paradox is the distinction between different mobilities through differentiation and classification. By the time the explosive rise in mobility came to be associated with the global spread of unruly people and things, real or imagined, what can be termed the "channeling of mobility" (Huber 2013) arose: the increasing bureaucratization of international migration that dictated the terms and conditions of mobility.

This chapter shows how racial and spatial categories traveled across the Pacific Ocean as tools for imagining, managing, and differentiating migration that was the product of increased mobility in the late nineteenth century. To be noted is that urban forms themselves circulate through the cross-imperial network of power and knowledge. The use of urban form as a strategy to govern mobility is not peculiar to the nineteenth century, however, as could be seen, for example, in the containment of mobile Jewish bodies in "ghettos" in Renaissance Europe (Sennett 1994). What made the nineteenth century significant is exponentially increased transpacific connection. The Pacific, a much larger and deeper body of water than any other ocean basins, had long been "a barrier to exchange, a vast watery expanse that took months to cross" (Hoskins and Nguyen 2014, 5). When brought together in contact with each other in an unprecedented way, what was it that connected and disconnected people and places?

Transpacific Mobility and Its Discontents

Intertwined with the new technology of mobility in the late nineteenth century, which increasingly linked coastal cities across the Pacific, was the introduction of the modern mode of trade and commerce known as the "treaty port system" in East Asia. First instituted in China's coastal ports upon the treaty signed between China and Britain after the Opium War, the treaty port system spread further to other coastal cities, including those in Japan and Korea. The treaty port system involved a wide array of legal institutions and practices, from regulations for the conduct of trade to establishment of fixed rates for tariffs, which enabled Asian coastal ports to become hubs of commerce and trade with foreign subjects (Cassel 2012, 4–5). It further granted extraterritorial rights to foreigners, allowing them to trade and live in designated areas called foreign settlements, where European and American settlers could rent or buy houses while subject only to their own country's law. The ideology of free trade helped sustain European economic and political interests in East Asia without all the burdens of empire, without having to control large colonies such as in Africa. Often called "informal empire," this new international order served as one of the key mechanisms whereby informal Western imperialism operated without military occupation (Beasley 1987).

The opening of the ports in East Asia came with the establishment of foreign settlements to accommodate diplomats, traders, merchants, medical doctors, and missionaries. Once the treaty port system had taken strong root toward the end of the nineteenth century, the growth of the treaty port economy in Japan and Korea reverberated along China's coastal ports. Euro-American entrepreneurs who had already engaged in trading in China's coastal cities such as Hong Kong, Guangzhou, and Shanghai moved to Yokohama and Incheon with a view to expanding to other markets. Diplomats frequently moved between different locations, from Shanghai to Yokohama or from Tokyo to Seoul. The Euro-American residents brought with them their own laws and institutions to the new trading outposts, ranging from clubs and bank agencies to boards of health and cemeteries. Modern infrastructure, such as sewage systems and roads, hitherto unfound in Japan and Korea, was introduced, as were parks and gas lamps. Churches, hospitals, hotels, theaters, and racetracks sprang up, adding Euro-American elements to the landscape. Some of these foreigners would later open new businesses in the print industry. Eugene Van Reed, an American born in California, came to Yokohama in 1859, founded a trading company, and published a Japanese-language newspaper there (Munson 2013). Among the most prominent of such periodicals was the *Japan Weekly Mail* that began publication in 1870 in Yokohama. With a range of contributors from British diplomats William George Aston and Ernest Satow to surgeons such as Frederick V. Dickins, the *Japan Weekly Mail* served as a crucial platform on which European settlers in East Asia exchanged information with people in other parts of the world, looking to each other for a better way to conduct businesses in unfamiliar settings.

Added to this migration of Euro-American settlers to East Asia's trading posts was the movement of Chinese migrants. The establishment of the treaty port system in China's coastal cities and the presence of Westerners therein offered "new entrepreneurial freedom" (Murphey 1974, 21) not merely to Western traders but also to the Chinese themselves. In addition to economic opportunities made available in treaty ports, political and economic uncertainty spurred Chinese migration as an escape from mounting internal disorder. In the meantime, the opening of coastal ports elsewhere in Asia lured Chinese migrants who sought better opportunities for fortune and life. Some of them crossed the Pacific Ocean to Cuba or Peru, and some of them went to other Asian cities, where there was increasing demand for construction labor. By the end of the 1880s, the ports of Yokohama and Incheon alike experienced booming economies as well as rapidly increasing populations. As of 1888, the native population of Yokohama was 118,947, whereas foreign residents numbered 4,492, of whom 2,981 were Chinese, 708 British, 255 American, 194 German, 125 French, 43 Swiss, 41 Dutch, and 53 Portuguese and others. In 1886, Incheon had a comparatively small population, yet it was experiencing considerable growth both in population and economy. The native population was approximately 2,000, and the foreign population was 976, including Japanese.[4]

The treaty ports were by no means "El Dorado" as the settlers had previously imagined. After ports were interconnected in ways that produced massive circulation of people, goods, and even animals, the transfer of disease through human and nonhuman passengers made the treaty ports teem with diseases such as smallpox, cholera, and typhoid. The consequences of increased mobility alarmed public health officials in the United States. News of epidemics in Hong Kong, for instance, spread fast across the ocean to Yokohama, Honolulu, San Francisco, and Washington, DC. Medical reports

---

4 The chronicle and directory for China, Corea, Japan, the Philippines, Indo-China, Straits Settlements, Siam, Borneo, Malay States, etc. (Hong Kong: Hong Kong Daily Press Office, 1890).

on the condition of Yokohama were especially important, because the port city was located on the major transpacific sea route. Under these circumstances, such public health journals, from *Public Health Reports* to *Abstract of Sanitary Reports*, functioned as "a system of information exchange to track the spread of epidemic diseases at ports throughout the globe" (Shah 2001, 126). "So long as the disease is kept out of Japan," a medical doctor in Yokohama wrote, after a deadly outbreak of plague in China, "so long will this country be the best bulwark for the United States, against the importation of the disease" (Eldridge 1894, 532). Another important institution brought by American settlers was the board of health staffed by medical experts and civilians. In addition to overseeing health conditions of residents, their responsibility lay with inspecting items and passengers aboard all vessels outbound for the United States. While the primary goal of the medical experts sitting on the board of health was to secure the well-being of Western merchants in the Asian ports, they also played a part in shaping the transpacific network of medical knowledge by submitting medical reports to public health institutions based in the United States. This network of knowledge became one of the mechanisms through which ideas about race, space, and disease were shared across the Pacific.

The presence of foreigners was far from welcome even to locals (Hoare 1994). In the early years of the treaty port, foreigners were attacked and murdered, including the British Legation guards killed in 1862 by antiforeign Japanese samurai. As constant threats of violence against foreigners in the treaty ports increased, the security of Euro-American settlers became a grave issue. The outbreak of cholera and other infectious diseases constituted another security concern, especially when neither sufficient water supply nor sanitary arrangements were provided. The scorching summer heat in the semitropical climate of Japan tormented Euro-American residents even further. Fire was another source of danger that would threaten the safety of settlers as most of structures had been made of wood and thatch.

As such, the treaty port as the "contact zone" witnessed with a dilemma arising out of the increased mobility. The Euro-American settlers wished to conduct trade and business in new territories, but they had to deal with the problem of co-residence with natives while trying to protect themselves from the fallout of biopolitical intercourse, most alarmingly, the worldwide propagation of epidemic disease. How did this dilemma translate into the built form? How did architecture and urban form become an "index" (Schmitt 1942) of this epochal change in mobility by reflecting new (or borrowed) spatial concepts?

Racial Distancing: Circulating Ideas of Race and Space

The treaty port system was a characteristically modern institution unique to East Asia. Not only did it transform the economic order of the region from tributary to treaty (Fairbank 1969), it also gave rise to the modern conception of space in a rapidly interconnected world. More importantly, it was a *mobile* institution that circulated ideas of international law, trade, space, and race. Once a treaty was signed and a port was opened, it became a model for others. After the Japanese ports were opened at the initiative of the United States, Japan soon followed suit by forcing Korea to open its ports. Behind the diffusion of the treaty port system lay the racialized understanding of Asian peoples that homogenized difference among them—if policies were appropriate to one Asian country, they were considered replicable to another, the doctrine of which eventually influenced Japan to enforce the same model to other Asian countries (Beasley 1987, 21). It is in this sense that the drawing of physical layouts in each treaty port was heavily based on the previous models of other treaty ports. Facilitating this urban model among Asian ports was the cross-regional network of personnel, from diplomats and missionaries to treaty-port architects and engineers. Born in Ireland, the British diplomat and Japanologist William George Aston was appointed interpreter to the British Legation in Japan, after which he came to work in British consulates in Tokyo, Kobe, and Nagasaki. In 1884, he was appointed the British consul general in Korea when the port of Incheon was opened for foreign commerce. It was during this time that Aston drew up outlines for the Western settlement in Incheon based on the foreign settlement of the Japanese treaty port of Kobe (Noble 1929).

In Yokohama, a residential settlement for Europeans was established up on the hill with a panoramic view of the harbor. The advantageous location offered a magnificent view, but it was also designed to remove the European district from the water, from the commercial atmosphere of the bund below, and the rest of the city's Asian populations. In particular, Yokohama's Western residents called this mountainous area "the Bluff," which presented visually different facades from the houses of the Japanese quarter. The hill acted as a marker that divided the two spatially distinct areas. The Japanese call the Bluff area *yamate* (up the hill) and the flatland where business facilities were concentrated *yamashita* (down the hill). The creek that flowed between the two separated the residential quarter of Europeans from the commercial streets of the city, native quarters, and the Chinese settlement. This residential division established by the natural dividers, the hill and the creek, was something that the Western residents might have wanted, especially when they often showed contempt toward their Asian neighbors, whom they thought were filthy and lacking in sanitary standards, having little contact with them in everyday life other than in the sphere of commerce (Taylor 2002: 132).

This morphological composition in Yokohama, undoubtedly based on the model of Shanghai as premier treaty port, replicated itself in the port of Incheon. The European settlement was primarily located on the hillside with a commanding view of the harbor. Public gardens and a number of European residences decorated the settlement on the hill, along with consulate buildings, theaters, banks, and bath houses. In order to make room for this new development, Korean residents were removed from the area and forced to live in different sections of the city, which were separated from the European part by racially drawn residential lines.

Residential separation was often based on a medicalized view of racial difference, which also found its expression in the use of building materials. Red bricks were one of those new materials used in a variety of buildings in the European commercial and residential sections, which presented a visual contrast to traditional Japanese houses mainly built of wood and Korean houses with straw roofs and walls of wattle and daub. Especially the straw roofs of Korean houses were denounced as poor sanitation, because the straw would become "rotten after heavy rains in summer," the cause of bad smelling and "unwholesome gasses and germs of disease."[5] The use of building materials in European settlements thereby cast an imperial gaze upon Asia, conveying Western ideas about technological progress and racial superiority in strong association with sanitation and hygiene. The architecture of the European section was supposed to radiate might, just as architecture style aimed to do in colonial settlements elsewhere in the world, such as in Madras in British India (Nightingale 2012, 64).

Racially based residential separation may find its precedent elsewhere, predominantly in British colonies. From the fifteenth century onward, European settlers began to divide cities in Asia and Africa along racial lines, from the Portuguese in Southeast Asia to the British in West Africa, a spatial assertion of colonial force that would later become a circulating model for governing colonial cities based on residential segregation. Among the most influential models in circulation was the practice of building a residential quarter for settlers in hilltops, whose origin may have dated back to the early

---

5 His Corean Majesty's Customs, "The Observation Report on the Climate of Three Treaty Ports in Corea," *Dispatches from Chemulpo*, August 21, 1885.

1800s, when British officials built segregated cities in the highlands of India and coined the term "hill station" (ibid., 48). The practice of racial distancing and the associated term "hill station" traveled across regions afterward to reach Freetown, Sierra Leone, where British authorities developed an all-European residential zone on a small mountaintop a few miles from the city's all-black downtown. By the late nineteenth century, this colonial practice had also traveled to East Asia and become a model for managing difference in its treaty ports.

The residential separation in the treaty ports was meant to provide Euro-American settlers with an opportunity to enjoy metropolitan living standards in far-away places while at the same time asserting and securing political privileges therein. Built on the principle of racial distancing, the built forms were intended to protect "the culturally (and not simply racially) white character of the population" (Elkins and Pederson 2005, 3). Such landscapes provided a provocative reminder of the supreme self-confidence that was characteristic of the nineteenth-century West in relation to the "backward" Asian countries. In many cases, forced removal and segregation in confined quarters was the foundation of bad living conditions that indigenous populations endured, even while the substandard living was often attributed to intrinsic racial traits, not to structural inequality. The economic prosperity of the treaty port system was manifested through new construction of buildings and harbor facilities; these "visible" phenomena assured the Western residents that the treaties with Japan and Korea were a success serving to benefit all. New roads were constructed by the settler communities in order to facilitate trade and commerce—all rationalized and promoted through the rhetoric of "civilization."

Categories of Race and Space on the Move

"Modern states not only naturalize certain distinctions," sociologist Mara Loveman points out, but also "help constitute particular *kinds* of peoples, places, and things" (Loveman 2005, 1655). New economic and technological mobilities in the modern world spurred and facilitated transpacific migration, but at the same time, the increased migration invited new narratives and imaginaries about cross-regional mobility. I would argue that these new narratives created a specific category of migrant figures, rationalizing their subjection to and regulation by modern forms of governance. In the face of a massive influx of migrants in rapidly modernizing cities on the Pacific Rim, my contention is that it was Chinese migrants who emerged as a visual category that evoked moral concerns and aroused emotional responses in an age of uncertainty. Chinese settlements began to emerge along the Pacific coast in the nineteenth century, from San Francisco to Vancouver, along with the technological shift in shipping from sail to steam power as well as the rapidly increasing transoceanic trade and travel. The Chinese settlements in Japan and Korea also developed in step with this global change during the time when mutually constitutive categories of race and space began crossing geographic boundaries.

It was in the American West that one of the first accusations toward the massive influx of Chinese laborers found its expression in political rhetoric advocating for immigration control. A number of white workers took to streets and attacked Chinese migrants as if the Chinese had destroyed the economic and social well-being of the American society. Playing an important role in this antagonism were emerging notions about public health and associations between race, disease, and space. San Francisco, for instance, was among the Pacific port cities where Chinese migration was often singled out in relation to the fear of epidemic disease. In the wake of migration and the perceived by-products of an increasingly connected world, San Francisco's Chinatown was targeted as the object of public health intervention and even described as an incubator of epidemic disease. In one cartoon created and circulated widely in the 1880s, San Francisco's Chinese neighborhood was portrayed as if it were a dead elephant lying on the top of the city. While the carcass was being washed by the San Francisco Board of Health, the imagined relationships among race, space, and disease carried powerful emotional charges with the caption below the image, "Better remove the carcass."[6]

While the transpacific Chinese migration may have originated in Asia, the representation of Chinatowns, and the problematic association between race, space, and disease therein, crossed geographic boundaries across the Pacific back and forth through the expanded network of personnel and communications technologies. When cholera broke out in the early 1880s, D. B. Simmons, an American medical doctor who chaired the Yokohama Foreign Board of Health, organized a committee for the inspection of Yokohama's Chinatown. The inspection was partly initiated by "a great deal of temporary anxiety" among European residents on account of "the presence, in the very heart of the [Foreign] settlement, of a Chinese quarter." According to a medical report written and submitted by Dr. Simmons in 1884, the inspectors

---

6 "Better Remove the Carcass," *The Wasp*, vol. 5, August–December 1880.

found the Chinese settlement to be in a "filthy" condition, but only one clearly authenticated case of cholera was found therein. This unexpected finding disappointed Dr. Simmons, who presumed that Chinatown would be "the very section of the city where the disease was expected to appear in its worst form." He admitted rather unwillingly that the reason behind Chinatown escaping cholera "even better" than it did the European settlement was the supply of good water available to residents in the Chinese quarter. Dr. Simmons wrote, "It was a somewhat remarkable fact that the so-called Chinese town, where some 2,000 of this race are crowded in badly constructed dwellings, and abounding filth, escaped the disease" (Simmons 1884, 163). This instance revealed one of the emerging ideas of race and disease during the time: the unsubstantiated claim that a racialized conception of "filth" is conducive to disease.

The association between race, disease, and space found another expression when bubonic plague swept through ports across the Pacific in the late nineteenth century. Due to the boundary crossing character of the disease, the fear of the plague created grave anxiety among Yokohama's Euro-American residents, as was seen in the quotation at the opening of this chapter. Through the network of information such as treaty-port newspapers, Japanese and Western residents in Yokohama were well aware of the outbreaks of plague in other ports. The anxiety intensified when the British steamship *Gaelic* landed at the port of Yokohama and one of its Chinese crew was immediately hospitalized in a hospital in Chinatown on March 30, 1896, and announced dead the same night. The Japanese authority suspected the possible connection of his death with the plague and thereby dispatched inspectors to investigate the cause of the death. Although the crew member had been already buried, the investigator dug up the grave, dissected the body, and finally diagnosed plague. On the question of how the plague was transmitted to Yokohama, the city government pointed to the year of 1896, when the disease broke on a ship from Hong Kong, as the beginning of an incursion of plague on Japanese shores.

Public sentiments, constructed and amplified through use of images and rhetoric, justify actions and shape policies and laws (Chavez 2008). In the face of massive migration within the Pacific region during the nineteenth century, different cities began to take actions against what they may have considered to be the problem of connected worlds. Cities along the American Pacific coast from San Francisco to Vancouver were collectively pointing to Chinese migration as the root cause of the problem. In San Francisco, the Chinese were depicted as bringing harmful effects to white workers. In Canada, Chinese migration was described as if it would dominate British

Columbia, which had to remain sufficiently white (Anderson 1991, 115). This led to a transpacific chain of immigration policy against Chinese migration in the second half of the nineteenth century, mostly in regions where massive Chinese migration occurred. In 1855, restrictions were imposed on Chinese migration to Australia. In 1882, capping off a series of violent attacks on Chinese property and people, the Chinese Exclusion Act was enacted in California, the first immigration policy against a particular race and class in the United States. Three years later, Canada followed suit in 1885 by enacting the Chinese Immigration Act, which levied an infamous head tax on each Chinese migrant. Since Canada shared borders with the United States, it seemed imperative for the Canadian government to take actions against Chinese migration, especially when Washington complained that "Chinese were smuggling in through Canada" (McKeown 2008, 200).

When Chinese migration was caught up in this web of policies, imaginaries, and racist ideology by the turn of the century, Japan was about to negotiate with Treaty Powers and finally regain its economic sovereignty by abolishing the treaty port system. This in turn left the new empire with several problems arising from the mobility of foreigners. With the end of the treaty port system, Japan intended to regain its sovereignty and diplomatic equality, but doing away with its strictures would also allow foreigners, including Chinese, to reside in the interior, outside of the formerly designated areas at the treaty ports. This inevitably generated heated debate for "the mixed residence in the interior" of foreigners (namely Chinese) with Japanese residents.[7] Japan, as an imperial latecomer, was confronted with the dilemma of how to control flows of people in the wake of new mobilities of foreigners.

The Japanese empire sought to resolve this dilemma in two connected ways. First, different categories were imposed on foreign bodies: Westerners and Chinese. Second, a sense of (im)morality was imputed to the latter group, thereby framing Chinese mobility as a pathological threat to society. Though Westerners were tolerated as neighbors of Japanese people, an argument maintained that the residence of Chinese should be either prohibited

---

7 Among the famous debates was that between the historian and economist Taguchi Ukichi and the philosopher Inoue Tetsujirō. Arguing for mixed residence, Taguchi looked to the United States as "one of the models for a future Japan," in which foreigners were successfully assimilated into law-abiding citizens (Oguma 2002). Inoue, drawing upon the theory of social evolution, viewed the Japanese as an inferior race, which would be overwhelmed by a superior race upon their co-residence. Inoue particularly referred to U.S. prohibition on the immigration of Chinese as one of the examples of "the restriction of the immigration of alien peoples whose migration ran counter to the national interest" (ibid.).

or restricted. (Yasui 2005, 62–67). Beyond the supposed economic threat resulting from near proximity, the Chinese question hinged upon a "moral" geography regarding migrants (Malkki 1992). Influential Japanese intellectual Fukuzawa Yukichi even contended, "Lower-class Chinese were 'a different category of people' who abandoned their country like a shoe and were willing to take any job" (Tsu 2010, 165). What was also often considered to be an inimical and inherent trait of the "base people" was the supposed Chinese propensity for filth and lack of morality and hygiene.

After the debate over mixed residence of Chinese with Japanese, Imperial Ordinance No. 352 was issued in 1899 to restrict Chinese residence and employment to designated areas. In this way, the Japanese empire responded to the problem of connectivity by dictating the terms and conditions of mobility and authorizing legitimate movements. The empire enacted *de jure* residential segregation of Chinese laborers by confining them within the bounds of Chinese settlements while allowing Chinese merchants and industrialists to reside in the interior.[8] Although the restriction based on *occupation* rather than on *race* made it appear as morally superior to Western racism operating in immigration laws, "the categories of exclusion and admission" were in fact "much the same as in the United States" (McKeown 2008: 201). The law targeting migrants, and Chinese migrants in particular, as potential threats was later replicated in Korea under Japanese colonial rule (Eom 2017).

In the first half of the twentieth century, the Japanese government employed a wide range of legal and institutional measures, from deportation to police surveillance, in order to control the flow of Chinese migration into the Japanese empire. This in turn contributed to the making of Chinatowns as an emblematic site of regulated mobility. Even after the abolition of the treaty port system at the turn of the century,[9] the urban color line remained in place. In Yokohama, European settlers continued to live on the hillside and Chinese laborers continued to live within Chinatown but for strikingly different reasons. One was a form of self-segregation, and the other was a form of legalized segregation. The situation was similar in Korea under

---

8 By contrast, Korean migrant workers, most of whom were involved in the mining industry in western Japan at the time, were not mentioned in the discussion of the mixed residence and, subsequently, impacted by the ordinance. Not only did the Chinese remain the largest foreign group until Japan's annexation of Korea in 1910, but the Koreans were not subject to the official treaties Japan had concluded with European countries and China and therefore free to live and work outside the foreign settlements (Yamawaki 1999, 40).

9 The treaty port system in Japan was abolished in 1899. In Korea, the treaty port system finally came to an end in 1914 under Japanese colonial rule.

Japanese colonial rule. Constant surveillance and policing reinforced the association of Chinatown with a sense of illegality. As with the case of the United States, where the representation of Chinese migrants as "fugitives, disease vectors, and communists" (Cresswell 2006, 159) was mobilized to limit their mobility, an equally moralized geography was imposed upon Chinese migrants in East Asia. Chinatowns in this regard served to allay anxieties about Chinese migration, perceived as a threat to public health, social order, and economic interests of the empire—even while Chinese labor was essential to the advancement of the colonial enterprise.

Conclusion

Schmitt was, after all, "a spatial thinker" concerned with the normative assertion of humankind's "earth-bound" origin and orientation (Dean 2006, 7). His use of the two mythical images—Behemoth and Leviathan—not only reveals the latent political intent behind the denigration of sea-bound people and cultures but also informs the constitutive role of narratives and imaginaries in our understanding of "the human" and its ontological foundation. Therefore, the characteristically "telluric" nature of Schmitt's idea paradoxically propels us to a set of questions as to how space, and imaginaries surrounding it, has played a crucial role in dictating the terms and conditions for human existence (ibid., 18). In the late nineteenth century, added to the fear of the global change in the era of massive migration was the explosive increase in the narratives of imagined bodies of "filthy" migrants that would pose a grave threat to the well-being and health of settler communities. This inevitably created the paradoxical situation that gave rise to privative categories of migration in the midst of increased mobility and connectivity across the Pacific.

By looking at the establishment of the treaty port system in East Asia based on circulating ideas of race, space, and disease, this chapter has argued that racial and spatial categories traveled across the Pacific Ocean as tools for imagining, managing, and differentiating migration that was the product of increased mobility in the late nineteenth century. The development of mobility infrastructures drew people and things together across distant urban settings. However, the growing fear of maritime connectivity also engendered the narratives of transregional migration, thereby helping produce and circulate the categories of migrant figures in spatial terms in the two interrelated ways.

First, residential separation based on the principles of racial distancing found its expression in East Asia's treaty ports, which exhibited the paradoxical needs of the Euro-American settlers. The new settler communities wished to conduct businesses in unfamiliar settings; yet they also sought to segregate themselves from the local population through the use of urban planning. Residential division along racial lines became one of the means employed to govern spaces, whereas spatial characteristics of each residential quarter were often used as an explanatory framework to comprehend traits of different racial groups. Second, privative categories of specific groups of migrant people were produced and shared among the Pacific states, which would lay the legal foundation for more restrictive policies toward migration and settlement in each national context. Ironically, the category of Chinese laborers—perceived as a threat to public health, social order, and economic well-being of a given settler community—gained more traction when it was in circulation, contributing to the construction of "Chinatown" as an emblematic site of regulated mobility.

As this chapter suggests, the mutually constitutive categories of race and space have traveled across geographies over time. The transpacific construction of space also exhibits how the creation and regulation of certain groups of people on the move became intertwined with state control over mobility at the height of mass migration. The transpacific circulation of policies, ideas, and imaginaries that legally and spatially codified immobility of a specific form of migrants, while encouraging other forms of migration, reflects the spread of a particular urban model rooted in the colonial geography of exclusion and exemption. This spread further instantiates the paradox of transpacific connectivity in the nineteenth century, when the development of infrastructures of mobility and immobility simultaneously came into being.

Bibliography

Aldcroft, Derek H. 1968. "The Mercantile Marine." In *The Development of British Industry and Foreign Competition, 1875–1914: Studies in Industrial Enterprise*, edited by Derek H. Aldcroft, 326–63. London: Allen & Unwin.

Anderson, Kay. 1991. *Vancouver's Chinatown: Racial Discourse in Canada, 1875–1980*. Montreal: McGill-Queen's University Press.

Appadurai, Arjun. 1996. *Modernity at Large: Cultural Dimensions of Globalization*. Minneapolis: University of Minnesota Press.

———. 2006. *Fear of Small Numbers: An Essay on the Geography of Anger*. Durham, NC: Duke University Press.

Beasley, William G. 1987. *Japanese Imperialism, 1894–1945*. New York: Oxford University Press.

Berman, Russell A. 2015. "Geography, Warfare, and the Critique of Liberalism in Carl Schmitt's Land and Sea." In *Land and Sea: A World-Historical Meditation*, edited by Carl Schmitt, xiii–xxix. Candor, NY: Telos Press.

Cassel, Pär Kristoffer. 2012. *Grounds of Judgment: Extraterritoriality and Imperial Power in Nineteenth-Century China and Japan*. Oxford: Oxford University Press.

Chavez, Leo R. 2008. *The Latino Threat: Constructing Immigrants, Citizens, and the Nation*. Stanford, CA: Stanford University Press.

Cresswell, Tim. 2006. *On the Move: Mobility in the Modern Western World*. New York: Routledge.

———. 2010. "Towards a Politics of Mobility." *Environment and Planning D: Society and Space* 28: 17–31.

Dean, Mitchell. 2006. "A Political Mythology of World Order: Carl Schmitt's *Nomos*." *Theory, Culture & Society* 23(5): 1–22.

Deleuze, Gilles, and Félix Guattari. 1987. *A Thousand Plateaus: Capitalism and Schizophrenia*. Minneapolis: University of Minnesota Press.

Dillon, Michael, and Luis Lobo-Guerrero. 2008. "Biopolitics of Security in the 21st Century: An Introduction." *Review of International Studies* 34(2): 265–92.

Eldridge, Stuart. 1894. *Abstract of Sanitary* Reports 9(29): 527–39. July 20.

Elkins, Caroline, and Susan Pederson. 2005. "Introduction: Settler Colonialism: A Concept and Its Uses." In *Settler Colonialism in the Twentieth Century: Projects, Practices, Legacies*, edited by Caroline Elkins and Susan Pederson, 1–20. New York: Routledge.

Eom, Sujin. 2017. "Chinatown Urbanism: Architecture, Migrancy, and Modernity in East Asia." PhD dissertation, Architecture, University of California, Berkeley.

Fairbank, John King. 1969. *Trade and Diplomacy on the China Coast: The Opening of the Treaty Ports, 1842–1854*. Stanford, CA: Stanford University Press.

Graham, Stephen, and Simon Marvin. 2001. *Splintering Urbanism: Networked Infrastructures, Technological Mobilities and the Urban Condition*. London: Routledge.

Hoare, James. 1994. *Japan's Treaty Ports and Foreign Settlements: The Uninvited Guests, 1858–1899*. Folkestone: Japan Library.

Hoskins, Janet, and Viet Thanh Nguyen, eds. 2014. *Transpacific Studies: Framing an Emerging Field*. Honolulu: University of Hawaii Press.

Huber, Valeska. 2013. *Channelling Mobilities: Migration and Globalisation in the Suez Canal Region and Beyond, 1869–1914*. New York: Cambridge University Press.

Inda, Jonathan Xavier, and Renato Rosaldo. 2008. *The Anthropology of Globalization: A Reader*. Malden, MA: Blackwell.

Kubicek, Robert. 2004. "The Proliferation and Diffusion of Steamship Technology and the Beginnings of 'New Imperialism.'" In *Maritime Empires: British Imperial Maritime Trade in the Nineteenth Century*, edited by David Killingray and Nigel Rigby Margarette Lincoln, 100–10. Woodbridge; Rochester, NY: Boydell Press in association with the National Maritime Museum.

Latour, Bruno. 1990. "Drawing Things Together." In *Representation in Scientific Practice*, edited by Michael Lynch and Steve Woolgar, 19–68. Cambridge, MA: MIT Press.

———. 2007. *Reassembling the Social: An Introduction to Actor-Network-Theory*. Oxford: Oxford University Press.

Loveman, Mara. 2005. "The Modern State and the Primitive Accumulation of Symbolic Power." *American Journal of Sociology* 110(6): 1651–83.

Malkki, Liisa. 1992. "National Geographic: The Rooting of Peoples and the Territorialization of National Identity among Scholars and Refugees." *Cultural Anthropology* 7(1): 24–44.

Mawani, Renisa. 2009. *Colonial Proximities: Crossracial Encounters and Juridical Truths in British Columbia, 1871–1921*. Vancouver: UBC Press.

McKeown, Adam. 1999. "Conceptualizing Chinese Diasporas, 1842 to 1949." *Journal of Asian Studies* 58(2): 306–37.

———. 2008. *Melancholy Order: Asian Migration and the Globalization of Borders*. New York: Columbia University Press.

Mohr, James C. 2005. *Plague and Fire: Battling Black Death and the 1900 Burning of Honolulu's Chinatown*. New York: Oxford University Press.

Munson, Todd S. 2013. *The Periodical Press in Treaty-Port Japan: Conflicting Reports from Yokohama, 1861–1870*. Leiden: Brill.

Murphey, Rhoads. 1974. "The Treaty Ports and China's Modernization." In *The Chinese City between Two Worlds*, edited by Mark Elvin and G. William Skinner, 17–71. Stanford, CA: Stanford University Press.

Nightingale, Carl H. 2012. *Segregation: A Global History of Divided Cities*. Chicago, IL: University of Chicago Press.

Noble, Harold J. 1929. "The Former Foreign Settlements in Korea." *American Journal of International Law* 23(4): 766–82.

Oguma, Eiji. 2002. *A Genealogy of Japanese Self-Images*. Melbourne: Trans Pacific Press.

Ong, Aihwa. 2006. *Neoliberalism as Exception: Mutations in Citizenship and Sovereignty*. Durham, NC: Duke University Press.

Schmitt, Carl. 2015 [1942]. *Land and Sea: A World-Historical Meditation*. Translated by Samuel Garrett Zeitlin. Candor, NY: Telos Press.

Sennett, Richard. 1994. *Flesh and Stone: The Body and the City in Western Civilization*. New York: W. W. Norton.

Shah, Nayan. 2001. *Contagious Divides: Epidemics and Race in San Francisco's Chinatown*. Berkeley: University of California Press.

Simmons, D. B. 1884. "Cholera Epidemic in Japan, with a Monograph on the Influence of the Habits and Customs of Races on the Prevalence of Cholera." *Annual Report of the National Board of Health 1879–1885*, 151–72. Washington, DC: Government Printing Office.

Sinn, Elizabeth. 2011. "Hong Kong as an In-between Place in the Chinese Diaspora 1849–1939." In *Connecting Seas and Connected Ocean Rims: Indian, Atlantic, and Pacific Oceans and China Seas Migrations from the 1830s to the 1930s*, edited by Donna R. Gabaccia and Dirk Hoerder, 225–47. Leiden: Brill.

Taylor, Jeremy E. 2002. "The Bund: Littoral Space of Empire in the Treaty Ports of East Asia." *Social History* 27(2): 125–42.

Torpey, John. 2000. *The Invention of the Passport: Surveillance, Citizenship, and the State*. Cambridge: Cambridge University Press.

Tsing, Anna Lowenhaupt. 2005. *Friction: An Ethnography of Global Connection*. Princeton, NJ: Princeton University Press.

Tsu, Timothy Yun Hui. 2010. "Japan's 'Yellow Peril': The Chinese in Imperial Japan and Colonial Korea." *Japanese Studies* 30(2): 161–83.

Urry, John. 2007. *Mobilities*. Cambridge: Polity Press.

Yamawaki, Keizo. 1999. "Foreign Workers in Japan: A Historical Perspective." In *Japan and Global Migration: Foreign Workers and the Advent of a Multicultural Society*, edited by Mike Douglass and Glenda S. Roberts, 38–51. New York: Routledge.

Yasui, Sankichi. 2005. *Teikoku Nihon to Kakyō: Nihon, Taiwan, Chōsen*. Tokyo: Aoki Shoten.

Yip, Christopher Lee. 1985. "San Francisco's Chinatown: An Architectural and Urban History." Berkeley: University of California Press.

Zeitlin, Samuel Garrett. 2015. "Propaganda and Critique: An Introduction to Land and Sea." In *Land and Sea: A World-Historical Meditation*, edited by Carl Schmitt, xxxi–lxix. Candor, NY: Telos Press.

CHAPTER FOUR

Zones at Sea and the Properties of Connectivity

(A)roundness, (Imm)unity and Liquidity

Barry J. Ryan

On 27 March 2011, in the dead of night, a ten-foot rubber dingy with seventy-two women, men and children pushed off from the port in Tripoli and on a calm sea ventured outwards towards Italy. As they steered out beyond Libya's territorial sea, its contiguous zone and out into the exclusive economic zone, the passengers were simultaneously transversing NATO's maritime surveillance zone. This was a large, highly policed terrain temporarily claimed to secure Libya's air and maritime spaces during NATO's intervention. The engine soon ran out of fuel and the boat began to drift. As the team at Forensic Architecture found, the helpless dingy was known to Italian authorities and its position was verified to be just outside Malta's search and rescue (SAR) zone, the area of sea whereupon responsibility falls to Malta for saving lives (Heller and Pezzani 2014). Not being within their SAR zones, both Italy and Malta made no attempt to save the boat. Fourteen days later, the boat washed ashore on a beach on the Libyan coast with only eleven survivors. While this boat moved through some of the most heavily policed waters of the world, the fates of its passengers were decided by zones of governance that had been inscribed onto the political cartography of the Mediterranean Sea. Those on the boat had no way of knowing which zone they were moving through, and yet their lives depended upon this knowledge. Their existential parameter was the horizon. The gap between the zone of governance and the human zone of experience can seem distant and yet, in this case, the two zones were completely interconnected. Similarly, as they drifted, it was the sea's currents and its winds that guided them back towards the shores of Libya, away from the

SAR zones. The natural world, the sea itself, also decided the fate of the rubber dingy. It is the interconnection of these three spheres of political existence – the human, the state and the non-human domains – that comprises the global politics of the high seas.

The chapter is predicated on the proposition that global space is demarcated by an interconnected and quite complex and organic system of enclosures, which are constituted of human, machinic or non-human life. It seeks these enclosures in the immensity and turbulence of sea, where we can readily discern topographies that derive from an individual's immediate experience – the sea as an object of the human imaginary. We can also discern enclosures that emerge from the state's desire to harness and rationalise oceanic space. These we find in the boundaries drawn to demarcate the sea as a site of political economy, the contiguous zones, exclusive economic zones, conservation areas and so on, that seek to govern the sea, to endow with functionality and rationality. Finally, we can appreciate the non-human maritime sphere, the spawning grounds, habitats and feeding sites, the enclosures naturally created at sea by its flora and fauna.

As on a weather map where isobars surround areas of equal atmospheric pressure, so enclosures coexist formally and informally that demarcate sites of origin, symbolic commonality or a shared fate or outlook. These sites, particularly at sea, might be temporary and highly unstable. In this chapter, I shall refer to these encirclements of differentiated continuous space as zones. Zonation, I argue, is the rudimentary cell-like architecture of all spatial organisation.

Any geographer would immediately recognise the topography I am attempting to map here. Indeed, this vision of global space as an infinitude of various sized, interconnected, interpenetrating zones, in part, derives from the work of an author who saw himself as a 'macrohistorian' of spatial anthropology. Peter Sloterdijk's (2011, 2014, 2016) *Spheres* trilogy demonstrates the historical omnipresence of enclosures from the micro to the macro levels of existence. Sloterdijk's spheres can be readily translatable as zones, whose function is to break-up space in order to reconstitute it as something manageable, understandable or protectable. The defining quality of these zones, according to Sloterdijk, is a sense of shared or solidaristic immunity. And while the zones I analyse through these three perspectives are very different, they exhibit a number of interesting qualities. I propose that these qualities are global and common across the three perspectives. The global constitutive properties I identify with zonation at sea are: (a)roundness, (imm)unity and fluidity. And it is these properties that give rise to the particularly interconnective nature of maritime zonation.

What Is a Zone?

If for instance we look at state practices of zonation, or zones of governance, we can quickly see that they present with identifiable characteristics. A zone of governance is a multifunctional, often multidimensional, demarcated place through which the movement of things or people is regulated, modulated or affected. By its very presence, any zone signifies a difference between what happens within and what happens beyond. It is an encirclement of space that perpetuates a particular mode of behavioural or physical control. In the field of governance each zone operates upon that which is passing through, or inhabiting it, in a specific manner that ranges from subtle alterations within the most inclusive zones to the stringent demands of its more exclusionary manifestations. Foucault's account of quarantine in Middle Ages France is an indicative zone of state governance. In his account of the measures taken in Paris to manage the movement of the sick and the healthy during the plague, Foucault catalogued how urban space was segmented and redistributed. He observed how spatial quarantine formed the blueprints of a more general mode of policing that 'called for multiple separations, individualizing distributions' (Foucault 1991, 197).

The problem arises when we admit that zones of governance are not fully capable of capturing human (or communal) experience of space – when societal place-making persists despite the state's best efforts. It is to these that Sloterdijk's topography speaks. Unlike Foucault's panopticon schematic, where power is centrifugal and redistributed around a desire to repurpose the human through the surrounding architecture, Sloterdijk's topography is chaotic; a radically decentred, unmappable and hence ungovernable mass of spheres. When one goes beyond the symbolic topography of state zonation and incorporates human experiential and non-human place-making, the sovereign claims of the state over global space fall away. There is no centre. At least, none that can hold. The state is not capable of governing the organic anarchy of the world.

I would suggest that from around the period of the Treaty of Westphalia up to the era of state-building in the late twentieth century, the planet's landmass has been subdivided into large macrozones we refer to as states. The state system is an arrangement of interconnected macrozones, an order based upon a universal logic of uniform organisation. The purpose of the state is, in Sloterdijk's terms, to immunize its occupants through the performance of nationhood mediated by a coherent and specific set of sociocultural, legal and economic mores. As well as existing within larger zones at a regional level, the state in is turn subdivided into a number of sub-administrative zones under the control of local or provincial government. These zones are subdivided again into boroughs, post-code zones, planning zones, residential zones, business zones, industrial zones, security zones (established for military, commercial or conservation purposes), quiet zones, speeding zones and so on down to the very micro level of human spatial organization. Yet, Sloterdijk's vision suggests that the state itself is no longer the sum of these zones. Within it and around the state are zones experientially derived, encirclements that are more dynamic, more immune and more temporal. Such zones can persist invisible to the state, beyond its reach; often being more informal, local and more globally connected. Organic segmentation and the differentiation of space has multiplied the number and type of zones to the point that they have outgrown the mother zone; if you like, the state has become a somewhat congealed macrozone. In fact, one gets the impression from Sloterdijk that he considers the state to be obsolete, a macrozonal container that has outlived its usefulness. The fences, firewalls and exclusionary visa regimes being erected around the late modern state are thus markers of its own morbidity.

Having said this, the chapter observes important differences between the way states striate sea space and land space. Zones of governance at sea are remarkably less rooted, less rigidly defined around the concept of sovereignty than zones of governance on land. They certainly mirror the practices of zonal governance we find on the planet's landmass, but the reflection is less steady, it ripples and flows. In short, it becomes liquid. When state power extends into the maritime sphere, it adapts to the materiality it is operating upon. In order to do this, it incorporates novel attributes which are akin to the sorts of adaptations made by humans and non-humans at sea.

The purpose of this chapter is to deduce these attributes in order to gain a better understanding of the global politics emerging from zonation. De Landa (2011), while exploring the contingent identity of objects, has usefully distinguished between the differing ontological status between the *properties* of a thing and its *capacities*. He uses the example of a knife. The primary property of a knife is its sharpness, measured by examining the triangular cross-section of its serrated blade. Ascertaining whether the knife is blunt or sharp, observes De Landa, is entirely different from surmising its capacity to cut things. In order to cut things the knife must be manipulated by someone onto something cuttable, and the correct amount of force needs to be applied. Thus, De Landa (2011, 5) explains, 'A capacity may remain only potential if it is never used'. It is a potential *event* within a space of possibilities. Together the state of an object, its properties and its capacities make up the 'structure of the space of possibilities'. Indicatively, when examining a zone we need to outline what its properties might be, and then explore what its potential capacities are, and we need to comprehend with what it interacts in order to operationalise these properties. Together, these qualities that comprise zonation, as a thing and as a possible event, when understood, afford us insight into the political affect of zoning.

In order to tease out the qualities of zonation, this essay is organised around three sections. The first examines the phenomenology of zonation and seeks to describe the qualities of human or communal understanding of sea space throughout history. The second section examines the evolution of state-based zonation at sea, detailing the forms it has taken over the past few centuries. The final section looks at ecological zones in order to propose a tentative claim that they share similar qualities with human and state place-making efforts.

I am indebted to Levi R. Bryant (2011) for this organisational structure. Bryant has developed an interesting framework based on Lancanian theory to investigate the qualities of objects. As with De Landa, for Bryant, knowing an object requires knowing its powers or capacities. These are deduced from the functionality of the object, which in turn is deduced from its specific geographical situation or material context (Bryant 2011, 90). The properties of an object always relate to topography, the social relations in which the object participates. In a lecture on 'Onto-cartography',[1] Bryant introduces three registers through which we might gain some foothold over the particular qualities of any object.[2] These three orders are interconnected in such a way that to separate one would mean disentangling the entire set. Loosely put, Bryant explains that one register to explore global politics is through human ontology, a study of experience, human perception and imagination. Another is to explore our social institutions, the artefacts of social organisation produced by human intersubjectivity. The third order introduced by Bryant is the ontology of non-human experience or *onticology*. This is the register of object-oriented philosophy, where the material vitality, the being-in-itself of a zone, is presumed to subsist independently from human awareness or knowledge.

Through these orders, the chapter shall explore three general properties of zones. It will demonstrate that as sharpness is a property of a knife, so liquidity or plasticity, (a)roundness and immunity are three *properties* found in all three

---

[1] https://www.youtube.com/watch?v=bUxVKTg0RtI, accessed 28 January 2019.
[2] He bases his framework on Jacques Lacan's three orders of fetishism – the imaginary, the symbolic and the real.

orders of spatial organisation. What this means is that any zone at sea, from the exclusive economic zone to the habitats of salmon in the wilderness, is identifiable as a zone by virtue of it possessing these topographical characteristics.

The *capacities* of a zone are doubtlessly manifold. These are the attributes that operationalise and fuel its potential as an event in a field of possibilities. They make possible the functionality of the zone and reveal both the sociospatial relations of the zone and the specific context in which it operates. The chapter will identify three *capacities* of zonation that are found to some degree in the three registers: inclusivity; global connectivity and vitality; and routinization.

Zones in Human Spatial Imaginaries

When it comes to the zones produced by human experience of the world, the property of (a)roundness is ascendant. The property of (a)roundess is key to all zonation practices. It constitutes the primary property of zonation. In this section, I will outline how it is deeply embedded in the human primordial tendency to organise the chaos of the surrounding world into a manageable sort of holistic order. Gestalt theory informs us that this is a perceptual instinct derived from our immediate reaction to the environment around us, and that it is primarily visual. The external world in this sense is experienced as unitary and personal. I look around. I am always surrounded. The world around me is indistinguishable from who I am. As Heidegger (1982, 64) observes, 'A specific functionality whole is pre-understood. . . . Existing in an environment, we dwell in such an intelligible functionality whole. We make our way throughout it. As we exist factically, we are always already in an environing world'. One's reaction to the world around is an experience that, according to Heidegger, is pre-understood. (A)roundness is therefore a pre-ontological understanding of being – it precedes our beliefs or interpretations about the world. It is instead a practical instinct, a form of knowledge that precedes cognition (Smith 2016, 29). As Malpas (2017, 45) explains, 'What first appears is just the appearing of a place that is a certain definite region, *bounded* and yet also thereby *gathered*, in which we and the things around us are given *together*'. Place, place making, clearing and dwelling are topographical experiences that play a profound role for Heidegger in the history of being. The outer boundaries, the circumferential limits or the horizons of our *umwelt*, or environment, are not the end of place, however, but only the beginning.

Morin's (2012, 82) insightful critique of Sloterdijk's variations on Heidegger outlines how the latter defines humans by their capacity to break through this local primordial horizon(e) into the world beyond. Existence is in this sense an enlarging of the enclosure of being; 'there is always more to come, more to be expected'. 'The world as the horizon of horizons', she writes, 'is the unreachable enclosure around the whole that gives to everything that exists, appears or happens a final aggregation, i.e., its connection and coherence [*Zusammenhang*]'. Morin's essay contextualises Sloterdijk's philosophy of spheres in terms of Heideggerean (a)roundness. Sloterdijk's argument is that this breakthrough is made possible by the human's insulation and distantation from its *umwelt*. As Morin insinuates, Sloterdijk shows how the human gains requisite security from its environment to stand in the clearing and observe the limits. And it develops techniques, or technologies, to project itself onto that limit and out into the world. The innovation in Sloterdijk's thought is that the sphere becomes a sort of spaceship, a projected capsule in which the individual travels from his or her *umwelt* out into the world. The sphere is therefore a limbo, a protected space, a 'between-world'.

> The sphere are these intermediary worlds or intermediary openness: they are membranes that protect against the outside but are not airtight and impervious like environmental enclosures. They separate the human from the pressure of the environment, allow him to develop in a non-adaptive way and prepare the world-opening of the human, that is, prepare his sensibility for what is either spatially or temporally remote. (Morin 2012, 84)

In other words, the *property* of (a)roundness, which we ascribe to our horizon(e) is closely linked to the *capacity* to connect, of connectivity. It is the metaphysical geometry of being round that simultaneously insulates and provides the individual a perceptual grip on the world.

Moreover, in this vision of differentiated global space, individuals, in our personal spheres, exist together in separate forms, like bubbles in a mass of foam. The *property* of technological (imm)unity is manifest. These zones possess a security function; they are places quarantined from the natural environment, but they are also exposed to the 'winds of freedom' generated by globalisation so that within them we mass together, huddling as it were. Individual exclusivity, it would appear, invokes an identitarian inclusivity.

Long before Sloterdijk, Gaston Bachelard (1994, 234) came to the conclusion that roundness is ontological; *das Dasein ist rund*, he writes. So, for Bachelard (1994, 240) roundness is not a metaphor (a metaphor is a crude intellectualism); roundness is being itself; 'the world is round around the round being'. It constitutes concentrated being, the perfect unity, an instinctual and perceptual harmony of interpenetration between mind and the world. Citing Arnaud, Bachelard (1994, 137) observes, 'I am the space where I am'. Experiencing this roundness requires 'the purest phenomenological meditation' (1994, 233). Bachelard draws on poetry by Michelet, who described the profound force of a passing bird as completely spherical. Round being, Bachelard (1994, 237–38) writes, is 'a centralization of life, guarded on every side, enclosed in a live ball and consequently at the maximum of its unity'. The clue to what he means by this is found in an earlier passage in *The Poetics of Space*, where he describes the anxiety he feels when he is in Paris, away from his rural home, his clearing in the woods. Bachelard writes how he imagines the chaos of the city to be the sea and his room to be a boat, an enclosure of calmness and certainty surrounded by pummelling waves. There is thus much in common between Bachelard's imaginative roundness and Sloterdijk's technological spheres. Both seek to describe projections of phenomenological (imm)unity when thrown into an unknown surrounding liquid world. Both experience themselves to be always enclosed in space, always inside.

The earliest known poetry of Scandinavian and Anglo-Saxon coastal populations reverberates strongly with the ontology of (a)roundness. In fact, looking at these poems it is evident that the sea and the land were experienced as a unity of space. In eleventh-century Scandinavian poetry, the sea was that which encircled the land. The etymology of the modern word 'zone' originates in the language used at this time to describe the sea; it was a belt, a girdle, a ring, a band, the harness strap, the sheath and so on.[3] Drawing upon a literary device known as 'kenning', the sea was the 'storm twisted enclosure of man' (cited by Gade 2017, 166). Elsewhere Skaldic poets called the sea, 'the encircling band of all land' (cited by Townend 2017, 232). Boats in these poems were described as horses, bears, oxen or stags, beasts that carried man as swift and as safe over the sea as over land. In other words, these fishing communities perceived that the domain of the land flowed into the domain of the surrounding sea. Poems, myths and songs of coastal communities throughout the world describe men and women looking out at the horizon, perceiving it as the limit of their *umwelt*, the beginning point of the unseen, the world, the adventure beyond.

A concrete example of this encircling instinct is available from the herring communities of north Scotland who in early modernity practised what was known as 'land kenning'. The connection between the Scandinavian

---

3 For a selection of common metaphors in which the sea is derivative of zonation, see Skaldic Poetry of the Modern Middle Ages, https://skaldic.abdn.ac.uk/m.php?p=kenning&i=53.

and the Scot here is remarkably clear. Kenning, as I pointed out, is the literary device that was used instead of metaphors and similes in Norse, Anglo-Saxon and Celtic poetry. The word comes from the Old Norse verb *aðkenna*, which means 'to describe' or 'to understand'.[4] Traceable to the fourteenth century, and most probably practised earlier, the fishing communities of Scotland understood that the waters (and fish) in firths, bays and coasts within a 'land kenning' were an indivisible part of their existential habitat (Johnston 1988, 79). A 'land kenning' refers to a measurement unit of human vision, at sea approximately fourteen nautical miles, 'not nearer than where they [the foreign ship] could discern the land from the top of their masts' (Fulton 1911, 84). A similar tradition has been found to be operating throughout northern Europe at the time. In a period when navigation was primarily reliant on reading the landscape of the coastline, the 'land kenning' effectively demonstrates the existence of a tensile phenomenological horizon(e). Moreover, it exhibits direct etymological lineage between premodern spatial understanding and zonation.

The practice of 'land kenning' also serves to introduce the tension between human zonal topography and the territorial, functionalist, spatial imagination of the early state. As James C. Scott (1999) implied, seeing like a human differs significantly than seeing like a state. First, we see the tension in the attempt to introduce 'double land kenning' or to extend the limit to twenty-eight nautical miles in certain places. This plainly makes little sense without the technology to extend human vision, but it marks the commencement at the turn of the seventeenth century of the instrumentalisation of human experience by the centralising and expanding macrozone state. The draft Treaty of Union between England and Scotland incorporated this custom in 1604 and legislation in Denmark was passed in 1618 to restrict fishing around the Faraoe Islands to its inhabitants (Johnsonton 1988, 342). Morieux (2017, 116) in his study of the development of the French and English sea border institutions and coast guards documents both the rationale of the state and the tensions it created between it and those whose *umwelt* it altered. In France, in particular, the coastline was perceived by the centralising authorities as a defensive barrier, a limit that closed off the outside world rather than opened it: a symbolic, rigid, anchored barrier that would be established beyond the coastal horizon. Commenting on the manner by which the

---

4 https://www.asnc.cam.ac.uk/resources/mpvp/wp-content/uploads/2013/03/What-are-kennings.pdf. Accessed 6 February 2019.

state has historically imposed itself on local experiential-perceptual space Henri Lefebvre observed,

> The state is consolidating on a world scale. It weighs down on society in full force; it plans and organises society 'rationally', with the help of knowledge and technology, imposing analogous, if not homologous, measures irrespective of political ideology, historical background or by the class origins of those in power . . . it neutralizes whatever resists by castration or crushing. (1991, 23)

And yet, as Lefebvre later observes, what he calls social space, or what Sloterdijk (2016) refers to as spheres, persist, resist even. These are the informal, dynamic, existential zones we inhabit and move through. Despite its best efforts to adopt and extend the (ar)oundness of our existence and to provide it with a machinic regularity and state rationality, the macrozone has been unable to contain or fully capture ontological zonation. Despite its efforts to mimic and reproduce (imm)unity properties, state zonation has not succeeded in replicating the capacity of connectivity that is inherent to perceptual horizon(e)s, where limits are perpetually shifting openings to the world, rather than forming defensive territorial traps.

Zones in Symbolic Spatial Governance

The distinction between the experiential-imaginary register and the governance zone is analogous to the way the sketch of a knife by a famous artist becomes a hundred times more valuable than the knife itself. The state order recreates human topography; it territorialises, rationalises and endows it with virtual capacities. Therefore, we can commence with the assumption that the state zone is made of nothing but language and practices. It is experienced through signs and signifiers, protocols, directives, laws and police power. It is symbolic and has no physical presence in the world, other than the effects it produces on human behaviour and whatever accompanying physical enforcement is deployed to ensure compliance with its parameters. It is for this reason the governance zone is best approached as an artefact of knowledge. Whereas the order of the imaginary compels us to examine ontological zonation, the order of the symbolic impels us towards epistemological zonation. Consequently, at issue is the capacities of governance zones to bring a rational structure to the chaos of the world.

While the chapter argues that all zones share similar global properties, zones differ when it comes to capacities. To begin, it needs to be pointed out that all zones of governance possess some degree of inclusiveness. Zones control chaos by managing movement. Inclusiveness is what permits perpetual motion through the zone – understood at sea as freedom of movement. Moreover, all governance zones possess the capacity for routinization. The level of inclusiveness determines the amount of freedom they generate. The degree of inclusiveness is indistinguishable from the level of routine operating in a zone, which ultimately determines the degree of security it possesses. Traffic enters one secured zone, having left a previous one, and exits into another. Each zone contains its own functional context, which is established by policies that determine what is permitted to enter, what needs to take place at entry and what activity and rules take effect within the zone. Thus, all governance zones operate according to a homogenising machinic logic that we refer to as the routinisation. The properties of (a)roundness and (imm)unity are manifest in the modern zone. The property of liquidity is evincible from the ease with which the policies can alter, the context change and the function manipulated.

These properties have certainly been evolving in global space from modernity, from the time William Harvey published *De Motu Cordis* in 1628. This book demonstrated the circulatory system around the heart and reverberated with Copernicus' *On the Revolutions of Heavenly Spheres*, published in 1528. Very quickly the circular perpetual model was adopted by natural philosophers who saw it as analogous to the necessity of a strong and healthy economy of a free unhindered movement. Modernity heralded a new *nomos*, according to Carl Schmitt (2006, 79), 'founded on new spatial divisions, new enclosures, and new spatial orders of the earth'.

A founding father of this new *nomos*, Hugo Grotius (2004), wrote his *Mare Liberum* on the basis that commercial circulation needed to mobilise the natural environment for the good of the state. He accomplished this by declaring a natural distinction between land and sea. This is fundamental to the rationality he codes into sea space, which is constructed as a commons for the 'naturalness' of free trade. His aim was to radically reconceptualise the geopolitical conditions under which free trade with the global south could be guaranteed, to overturn local custom and practice. As Thumfart (2009, 80) has observed, Grotius was upholding the 'primacy of universal principles over local sovereignties'. Grotius' argument against private property in the ocean commons tended to hold back the process of enclosure in the colonised waters of the global south. It had, however, little effect on European sea space. As Rossi (2015, 16) documents, 'there was hardly any part of the European seas free from proprietary claim' at the time Grotius was writing. It is worthwhile to note that Grotius supported 'land kenning' in Europe, arguing that the range of human vision constituted a more practical and authentic delimitation than did the more arbitrary state limits that were proposed around European waters in this period.

These limits had been around since the fourteenth century. They commence with Baldus de Ulbadis who leaned on the tolls extracted from passing ships by the Venetian thalassocracy to argue that a 100 nm mile limit would help maintain order and suppress piracy (Johnston 1988). Economic and rational management of the sea as well as security and safety were new themes included in William Wellwood's *Abridgement of Sea Laws* (2011) [1613], which sought an enclosure within two days voyage. He believed that sovereign stewardship of this space would lead to a more rational and sustainable use of sea resources. The tragedy of the commons argument was also drawn upon by John Selden (1972) [1652] in his rebuttal of Grotius. Selden is not opposed to freedom on the high seas. He barely mentions it (Steinburg 2001, 97). Instead he is interested in exploring the possibility of dominion at sea and in revealing the distinction drawn by Grotius between sea space and land as a contrivance, one contrary to theological tradition. It should be noted that *Mare Clausum* envisaged anything but a closed sea. In it, Selden defines the British seas as stretching from the western coast of Ireland to the northern coast of Spain, northwards to the limits of habitable space and eastwards only a short distance until it meets the German sea (ibid.).

Less imperialistic, more reasonable and more in tune with the properties of zonation, Van Bynkershoek's (2013) [1703] book *De Dominio Maris* introduced the famous cannon-shot rule – a sort of technological type of land kenning – which is incorrectly associated with the three-mile limit that develops as a European maritime norm in the eighteenth century (Kent 1954; Wyndham 1945). The cannon-ball limit was of very little economic utility; it concerned land defence, seeking 'protected zones, fortified by coastal defences which demonstrate territorial authority over the sea' (cited by Fulton 1911, 556–57).

In accounts of these somewhat commercial but primarily militaristic claims to a state prerogative to create enclosures, the contribution of John Locke is rarely acknowledged. In his Two Treatises on Government (2003) [1689], Locke's arguments in favour of the economic efficiency of private property bring a very modern foundation to the emerging new spatial order at sea by intertwining circulation and enclosure as prerequisites to freedom and rationality. Synthesising Grotius and Selden, Locke is able to uphold freedom of navigation and demonstrate a potential right to private property at sea in sites where human labour has improved the 'production or extraction of extractable resources' (Pemberton 2017, 20). Locke's 'systematic political theory of the seas' (ibid.) prefigures contemporary zonation practices that are based on the establishment of multifunctional blue economies which add value to ocean space.

In any event, it is not until 1736 that maritime zonation, of a sort that properly gives form to our zonal properties, occurs. In that year Britain introduced the first of a series of Hovering Acts, which mark the birth of maritime zonal architecture as we recognise it today. This legislation created a maritime customs and excise jurisdiction within two leagues of Britain's coast. These legal enclosures provided for self-limiting jurisdiction, granting authorities powers for the seizure of commodities and the forfeiture of vessels used for smuggling. Representing 'zonal thinking at its most explicit' (Johnston 1988, 53), plasticity was embedded in these zones by tying their legal power to a functional logic – the zones tended to enlarge further into the high seas, but their jurisdiction expanded and contracted according to the needs of national security (Masterson 1970, 58). In 1753 a sanitary zone was created which overlapped the hovering zones, in order to manage the quarantine of ships emanating from countries struck by the bubonic plague (Johnston 1988, 53). This provided the state the capacity to ensure spatial inclusivity and at the same time to routinize freedom of movement to and from its ports. The Acts evolved to divide the seas around the island into seven regional categories (The Kings Chambers). Similar zones established by Norway and Denmark in 1812 had the effect of institutionalising this novel, functional, self-limiting mode of zonation in territorial seas. Bilateral treaties, including the one agreed by the mixed French-British Commission in 1834, served to refine the capacities of these zones, introducing police regulations on fishing behaviour and standardising the numbering and lettering of vessels travelling through them (Morieux 2017). The three-mile limit from the low-tide water mark was codified among European states as standard during the 1881 Hague Conference, which agreed on exclusive fishing limits.

Indeed, we need to consider the Hovering Acts as a new spatial political technology – the invention of an object that would, over the next 130 or so years, disseminate universally and radically redesign the architecture of the maritime sphere. Prior to the invention of a functionally (imm)une, inclusive, liquid enclosure that generated freedom of movement and established what was deemed to be the rational use of sea space, Schmitt's (2006) new *nomos* was a mere theoretical possibility. The year 1881 thus marks the moment in time when zonation becomes a practice in its own right, unmooring enclosure from the rigid spatial absolutism of the sovereign state. Henceforth, zones that seek to replicate the sovereign state; zones in the image of land rather than liquid, with stagnant boundaries; and zones based on military rather than policing modes of control will be deemed illegitimate.

An early indicator that these zones possessed the capacity to connect was seen in the 1920s when the Committee of Experts for the League of Nations decided that 'beyond the zone of sovereignty, States may exercise administrative rights on the ground of custom or vital necessity' (Leiner 1983, 976). The logic behind the contiguous zone was to create a site of limited state-administered jurisdiction, wherein crimes or risks of global import, affecting the coastal state and the political economy of the entire state system, would be policed. This in effect would create a network of coastal zones girdling the world's land mass, each connected to the other by a jurisdictional inter-capacity to manage a burgeoning portfolio of maritime crimes.

At the first United Nations Convention for the Law of the Sea (UNCLOS) in 1958, a contiguous zone allowing for customs, fiscal and sanitary regulation within a belt of twelve nautical miles offshore was agreed. Overlapping this belt, and extending fifty miles seaward, the Convention for Prevention of Pollution of the Sea by Oil was an early extension of jurisdictional authority in the high seas which afforded states the right to act in emergency situations at sea (Johansson and Donner 2015, 23). The convention also added a third dimension to coastal and high seas zoning by awarding sovereign rights to seabed resources.

Over the following two decades, the formerly blank blue map of the world's oceanic space was transformed into a complex cartography of various sized, overlapping regulatory encirclements. SAR zones were established by the World Maritime Organisation in 1979 to divide the global seas into thirteen large zones within which lie subzones (SAR regions) for which states have been tasked with responsibility. National zones proliferated in the meantime: Chile and Peru, for instance, declared zones stretching 200 nms and Iceland a 50 nm zone; Canada in 1970 declared a 100 nm environmental protection zone into the Arctic circle; the Organisation for American Unity (OAU) and the African Union (AU) lobbied hard for extensive zones around their continents.

UNCLOS III was convened to homogenise these claims, to routinise, if you like, the zonal epistemology that was rapidly and chaotically restructuring oceanic space. It led to the creation of a spatial regime for the world's oceans, adding to the contiguous zone an exclusive economic zone (EEZ) with powers to regulate fishing stocks and to protect the sea from pollution. Already, states are seeking to expand this jurisdiction (Scovazzi 2001, 162). Exemplary zonation systems, EEZs on safety grounds, permit the coastal state to regulate the ships and cargoes that are permitted to pass through (Scovazzi 2001). Beyond the EEZ, the continental shelf – an area up to 350 nms from the coast – the law also affords some police powers (reasonable measures) to protect investments and critical infrastructure on the seabed.

In the twenty-five years since the Law of the Sea was ratified, zonation has spread rapidly across the maritime sphere. A post-UNCLOS generation of zones with economic, scientific, military, conservationist and commercial functions are developing within and outside the global EEZ. The EEZ itself has become a novel site of global maritime political economy entirely fuelled by integrated zonation systems that are multidimensional – zoning the seabed, the sea column, the surface and the skies above. These are enclosures for private and public investment in marine energy, aquaculture, biotechnology, tourism and marine mineral resources (Ryan 2015). In order to manage these maritime economic parks, new security technologies are evolving, novel networks of intelligence gathering and distribution are spreading and states are investing heavily in coastal police vessels, drone surveillance technology and the establishment of land-sea governance agencies. Novel Selden-sized zones in the high seas are, in addition, proliferating. The United Kingdom, for instance, has created a large exclusion zone on the premise of environmental conservation around the Chagos Islands, where it leases to the United States a strategically important military base. The Australian government recently announced a maritime identification zone that stretches 1,000 nm from its coastline, designed to gain surveillance and interdict incoming asylum seekers. An entirely new sort of politics has arisen at sea around the capacities for zones to routinize movement, interconnect and to bring managerial rationality and order to the most chaotic of spaces.

And yet, we need to remind ourselves that these zones are sociotechnical constructions, cartographic expressions, legal discourse, symbols on the GPS system, a blueprint of rationality that has been overlaid upon imaginary space. They cannot be seen with the naked eye. They cannot be experienced other than through the practices of policing that maintain them. Strong winds do not shift them, and high waves will not destroy them. They are the symbolic order of the topography of human power. And although we live within them, and they shape our destiny, and bring to our experience of the world (a)roundness, (imm)unity and plasticity, we must be always aware that they are not *real*.

Zones in Non-Human Spatial Forms

What I mean when I say that governance zones are not real is that they are not ontologically real. Zones in the order of the symbolic foreclose the non-human. Human culture exists within its own magnificent zone, with its species specific 'kenning', while non-human culture is kept outside, in a state of nature, so to speak. And yet, maritime flora and fauna are entangled in the net of human culture and its machinic logic, despite being entirely unaware of human horizon(e)s and the epistemological architecture of freedom and rationality. Conversely, humans have only a rudimentary understanding of the ontological topographies shaping other modes of being, particularly in the maritime world.

The hypothesis I wish to introduce proposes that liquidity, (a)roundness and (imm)unity are properties that are found in non-human spatial ontology. Were this to be even accepted as a question, it opens the space of possibility that the capacities of connectivity and vitality structure a primal experience of enclosure common to both the human and the organic non-human. Thus, it is to the topography of the human and non-human zones we now briefly turn in order to animate the third and most planetary order – the order of the real.

The question naturally arises as an implication from the phenomenological perspective. According to the arguments posed above, human nature has a perceptual drive to expand its consciousness spatially. Human evolution then is the process by which we continually expand our horizon(e)s outwards. The claim that this is pre-ontological, primal, makes it valid to hypothesise that all animals experience the world (a)round them in a similar unified manner. A recent GPS tracking study of wolf habitats in Voyageurs National Park clearly shows how six separate wolf packs respect each other's territory (Helmberger 2018). But what is immediately apparent from the movement patterns is that they are spherical. The wolves live and move in surprisingly well-defined circular zones. There are relatively few studies of the shape of animal topography but research into the territoriality of sandpipers (and other non-colonial birds) in the Arctic suggests their habitat is polyhedral in shape (Grant 1968), while other species exhibit a more hexagonal topography. It's also interesting to note research which illustrated that the shape of a juvenile salmon's territory is influenced by the visual limits of its habitat. This non-human type of kenning has been observed in other studies of birds, fish and crabs (Eason and Stamps 1991). Moreover, animal territories demonstrate varying degrees of inclusivity and overlap (Leyhausen 1965). One can surmise with some certainty that all animal zones are places of (imm)unity; that their zones tend to be (a)round; interconnected; and that their strength derives from boundaries which are tensile.

Animal (including insect) zones therefore correspond somewhat to Sloterdijk's (2014) topography of foam relations. We could say that humans and non-humans share a common experience of the *umwelt* at the pre-ontological level – that this *umwelt* is a complex assemblage, a multiplicity of interacting, overlapping, organic zones. Assemblages, so Bennett (2010,

23–24) reminds us, are 'living, throbbing confederations . . . with uneven topographies . . . not governed by any central head'. Sloterdijk's thesis argues that humans have departed from this assemblage, having left it outside to enter technological spheres that isolate the human from the dangers and uncertainty that emerges from it. I'm not quite sure it is possible to entirely detach ourselves from the originary *umwelt*. In any event, the order of the real reveals a persistent will-to-zone which thrives across all forms of life and covers the entire planet from the molecular to the planetary level. The tension between the complex zonal order of the real and the artificial zonal order of the symbolic constitutes the most profound biopolitical issue of the Anthropocene.

Conclusion

Utterly symbiotic, and yet leagues apart, the three spatial registers of global political existence are constituted of zones that possess the capacity to connect. The experience of the ill-fated passengers aboard a rubber dingy floating for a fortnight around the Mediterranean was occluded by the zones of governance that were ultimately responsible for their death. Their horizon(e) was a limit through which they needed to transgress, and it was formed within a complex series of boundaries which functioned to prevent this from occurring. These zones of governance are not founded upon state sovereignty; they are encircled representations of state power within constant flowing space: They function to secure a certain segment of global space, to make it immune to certain risks.

Zones of governance constitute the world picture of a symbolic order that projects certainty and permanence onto a planet that is turbulent, heaving at the seams and incomprehensible. Were we even to attempt drafting a world picture that represents this immanent chaos, we would first have to de-emphasise the potency of sovereignty as the foundation of universal spatial demarcation. Second, we would have to connect the state's symbolic order with those modes of being it has throughout history tried to assimilate, colonise or commodify. A truer world picture of global politics would map out the zonal planet. The zone, I have argued, is a timeless unit of spatial existence. All life is connected by a will-to-zone. It is the origin of human comprehension about the world around us. We cannot escape zonal existence – there is no outside. Any representation of the world we attempt must begin from the inside, the cartographer looking around at his or her own limits.

When it enters the sea, the state changes. It substitutes the rigid concept of sovereignty for the properties of plasticity, (imm)unity and (a)roundness. I have argued that these properties are also found in the ontology of coastal dwellers and maritime flora and fauna. These properties are fecund for a range of political capacities such as inclusivity; global connectivity and vitality; and routinization. When it comes to the sea, zones in the three orders I identified eventualise these capacities to a varying degree. The order of the governance, with its emphasis on permanence, constructs inclusive zones of freedom that operate to rationalise, or routinise, all human and non-human movement. Connectivity is manifest in the uniform epistemology of risk that integrates the various formations of maritime zonation. Coastal communities historically perceived land and sea as unified. The horizon(e) formed a gateway to their surroundings that, once opened, connected them to the wider world. This same horizon(e) is interpreted by the state as a defensive barrier, a technology of disconnection. Within the order of the real, the ontological *terra nullus* of the state order, we find assemblages of zones overlapping, interconnected and throbbing with vitality. This is a vitality we have only begun to appreciate politically. One can only conclude that the limiting epistemology of the state territorial world picture presents us with horizon(e)s that we are compelled to project ourselves towards. The study of international relations, if it is to remain relevant, must stop simply critiquing the symbolic order of the map and begin connecting it with local spaces of human imagination and non-human experience.

Bibliography

Bachelard, Gaston. 1994. *The Poetics of Space*. Boston, MA: Beacon.
Bennett, Jane. 2010. *Vibrant Matter: A Political Ecology of Things*. London: Duke University Press.
Bryant, Levi R. 2011. *The Democracy of Objects*. Ann Arbor, MI: Open Humanities Press.
De Landa, Manuel. 2011. *Philosophy and Simulation*. London: Bloomsbury Academic.
Eason, Perri K., and Stamps, J. A. 1991. 'The Effect of Visibility on Territory Size and Shape'. *Behavioural Ecology* 3(2): 166–72.
Foucault, Michel. 1991. *Discipline and Punish: The Birth of the Prison*. Translated by A. Sheridan. London: Penguin.
Fulton, T. W. 1911. *The Sovereignty of the Seas*. London: Blackwood.
Gade, Kari Ellen. 2017. 'Einarr Skúlason, Fragments 16'. In *Poetry from Treatises on Poetics. Skaldic Poetry of the Scandinavian Middle Ages 3*, edited by Kari Ellen Gade and Edith Marold. Turnhout: Brepols.
Grant, P. R. 1968. 'Polyhedral Territories of Animal'. *The American Naturalist* 102(923): 75–80.
Grotius, Hugo. 2004. *The Free Sea*. Translated by Richard Hakluyt. New York: The Free Press.

Heidegger, Martin. 1982. *The Basic Problems of Phenomenology*. Revised Edition. Translated by Albert Hoftstader. Bloomington: Indiana University Press.

Heller, Charles, and Pezzani, Lorenzo. 2014. *The Left-to-Die Boat Case*. Forensic Architecture. Available on https://www.forensic-architecture.org/case/left-die-boat/. Accessed 18 March 2019.

Helmberger, Marshall. 2018. 'A Picture Tells the Tale'. *The Timberjay*, 13 December. http://timberjay.com/stories/a-picture-tells-the-tale,14665. Accessed 18 February 2019.

Johnston, D. M. 1988. *The Theory and History of Ocean Boundary-Marking*. Montreal: McGill-Queen's University Press.

Johansson, T., and P. Donner 2015. *The Shipping Industry, Ocean Governance and Environmental Law in the Paradigmatic Shift*. London: Springer.

Kent, H. S. K. 1954. 'The Historical Origins of the Three-Mile Limit', *American Journal of International Law* 48: 538–39.

Lefebvre, Henri. 1991. *The Production of Space*. London: Wiley-Blackwell.

Leiner, F. C. 1983. 'Maritime Security Zones; Prohibited Yet Perpetuated'. *Virginia Journal of International Law* 24: 964–91.

Leyhausen, P. 1965. 'The Communal Organization of Solitary Mammals'. *Symposium of Zoological Society of London* 14: 249–64.

Locke, John. 2003. *Two Treatises of Government*. New Haven, CT: Yale University Press.

Malpas, Jeff. 2017. *Heidegger and the Thinking of Place*. Cambridge, MA: MIT Press.

Masterson, W. E. 1970. *Jurisdiction in Marginal Seas*. Reprint of 1926 edition. London: Bailey Bros. and Swinfen.

Morieux, R. 2017. *The Channel. England, France and the Construction of a Maritime Border in the Eighteenth Century*. Cambridge: Cambridge University Press.

Morin, Marie-Eve. 2012. 'The Coming-to-the-World of the Human Animal'. In *Sloterdijk Now*, edited by Stuart Elden, 77–95. Cambridge: Polity Press.

Pemberton, Sarah. 2017. *Locke's Political Thought and the Oceans*. London: Lexington.

Rossi, Christopher, R. 2015. 'A Particular Kind of Dominium: The Grotian Tendency and the Global Commons in a Time of High Arctic Change'. *Journal of International Law and International Relations* 11(1): 1–60.

Ryan, B. J. 2015. 'Security Spheres: A Phenomenology of Maritime Spatial Practices'. *Security Dialogue* 46(6): 568–84.

Schmitt, Carl. 2006. *The Nomos of the Earth*. New York: Telos.

Scott, James C. 1999. *Seeing Like a State*. New Haven, CT: Yale University Press.

Scovazzi, T. 2001. *The Evolution of the International Law of the Sea: New Issues New Challenges*. Leiden: Nijhof.

Selden, John. 1972. *Of the Dominion or Ownership of the Seas*. Translated by Marchamont Needham (1652). London: Arno Press.

Sloterdijk, Peter. 2011. *Bubbles: Spheres I*. Los Angeles, CA: Semio(text)e.

———. 2014. *Globes: Spheres II*. Los Angeles, CA: Semio(text)e.

———. 2016. *Foam: Spheres III*. Los Angeles, CA: Semio(text)e.

Smith, Joel. 2016. *Experiencing Phenomenology*. London: Routledge.

Steinburg, Philip E. 2001. *The Social Construction of the Ocean*. Cambridge: Cambridge University Press.

Thumfart, Johannes. 2009. On Grotius's *Mare Liberum* and Vitoria's *De Indis*, following Agamben and Schmitt, in *Grotiana*, vol. 30.

Townend, Matthew. 2017. 'Hallvarðrháreksblesi, *Knútsdrápa* 2'. In *Poetry from Treatises on Poetics. Skaldic Poetry of the Scandinavian Middle Ages 3*, edited by Kari Ellen Gade and Edith Marold. Turnhout: Brepols.

Van Bynkershoek, Cornelli. [1703] 2013. *De Dominio Maris Dissertatio*. Gale: The Making of Modern Law.

Wellwood, William. [1613] 2011. An *Abridgement of Sea Lawes*. Maritime Law Digital. http://maritimelawdigital.com/uploads/PDFs/Welwod-Sea_Laws.pdf. Accessed 18 February 2019.

Walker, Wyndham L. 1945. 'Territorial Waters: The Cannon Shot Rule'. *British Yearbook of International Law* 22: 2223–24.

CHAPTER FIVE

From *Tian Xia* to Sovereignty

The Shift of the Chinese Imaginary of Connectivity in the Nineteenth Century

Ariel Shangguan

Introduction

There is an old tale about the genesis of the Chinese political system: Approximately 3,000 years ago, when the Mycenean age was coming to an end and the Western part of the world was witnessing the rise of the classic Greek civilization, in the Middle Kingdom of the Eastern hemisphere, a small tribe known as the Zhou rebelled against the ruling elites of the Shang, overthrew the polity, and eventually established a dynasty that lasted longer than any other Chinese dynasties that have ever existed.[1] Upon the success of their revolution, the rulers of Zhou were faced with one major question, that is, how to establish a lasting form of governance? At that time, there were more than 1,000 culturally and ethnically different tribes in China. In order to ensure the absolute harmony among those tribes, King Cheng of Zhou then argued that the only way to govern the new polity was to make it "an open network" where any tribe could participate as long as it could be at peace with the existing ones (Zhao 2009, 8). There would be one "world government" that overlooks the well-being of each tribe and is responsible for the allocations of wealth and resources. All tribes were independent of each other in terms of their economic output and cultural and social values; and yet, they all share the universal political obligations to the central government. The rulers of Zhou also sincerely believed that it was "天 (tian),"

---

1 The Zhou reigned for about 800 years.

meaning "Heaven," that had given the Zhou a mandate to rule (Keightley; cited in Loewe and Shaughnessy 1999). Accordingly, they called their system of governance: "天下 (tian xia)," namely, "all under heaven."

This chapter is about a changing Chinese imaginary of connectivity in the nineteenth century; but it is also about how a foreign idea became transplanted into the minds of Chinese people amid the country's evolving relationship with the rest of the world. It is often argued that China had never encountered anything resembling the "international" prior to its interaction with the European powers in the nineteenth century (Chen 1987, 57). By this I do not mean that Chinese people had never met any Europeans prior to the first Opium War—such a claim would be factually incorrect as the initial encounter between Europe and China can be traced as far back to the sixteenth century when the Jesuit missionaries went to China in an attempt to spread Christianity. What China had indeed never experienced, however, was the idea of "international" as a novel form of political order that is based on the independence of and equality among states. The European-dominated modern state system presented China with considerable challenges, as it was antithetical to the traditional Chinese conception of world order that implies hierarchy and inequality among individual nations. Historians—whether Chinese or Western, radical or conservative—hence regard the Opium War as the starting point of modern China, as it highlights not only the first successful attempt made by foreign powers to penetrate China's self-sufficient economy but also the collapse of the Confucian worldview that had prevailed in Chinese political thinking for millennia (Chan 1999). As such, in the first half of the nineteenth century, China began a series of social, political, and intellectual transformations that ended up changing the country forever.

The main aim of this chapter is to tell a story of one of those transformations. Specifically, it will illustrate how in a span of less than half a century, the traditional Confucian view of hierarchical world order was replaced in Chinese imagination by the Western conception of international society that presupposes mutual recognitions of state *sovereignty*. Few concepts are as central to the disciplinary debates of international relations (IR) as the notion of "sovereignty."[2] However, it was not until the late nineteenth

---

[2] There is a considerable amount of research on the concept of "sovereignty." Katzenstein (1996, 515), for instance, argues that although the logic of sovereignty seems to be taken for granted in realism, "it is not a natural fact of international life. Instead it is politically contested and has variable political effects." Bartelson (1995) also wrote a genealogy of the concept and showed how sovereignty is bound up in knowledge practices. For more on debates on sovereignty, see Bartelson (1995) and Katzenstein (1996).

century when Western knowledge and technology were introduced into the country that the concept began to be known by the Chinese people for the first time. The present chapter hence attempts to explain the process of introducing the concept of sovereignty into Chinese discourse as well as some of the consequences of this conceptual transplanting. The first section will briefly outline the concept of "天下 (tian xia)," that is, "all under heaven," and explain how this Chinese understanding of connectivity was subverted and eventually replaced by the Western idea of sovereignty after China's heavy defeat in the Opium Wars. The second section will then discuss the consequences of this change in the Chinese political imaginary. It will argue that, while the introduction of the notion of sovereignty enabled China to effectively defend itself against Western imperialism, the internalization of the modern conception of statehood has also led to the rise of essentialism in Chinese intellectual discourse.

The Collapse of *Tian Xia* and the Emergence of Modern Sovereignty in Chinese Political Imaginary

Scholars of international relations (IR) are not foreign to the Chinese concept of "天下 (tian xia)." In 2005, Chinese philosopher Zhao Tingyang famously proposed the term as a new analytical concept for the discipline of IR, and since then, the concept has been a topical theme for discussion among both Chinese and Western scholars. Although the concept of "天下 (tian xia)" did not appear in IR discourse until 2005, it is in fact one of the most frequently adopted concepts in ancient Chinese texts. In *Mencius* (2010), for example, one passage reads,

> Thus, it can be said that people cannot be controlled simply by closing the borders; a state cannot be protected simply by being surrounded by steep mountains and a raging torrent; all under heaven ("天下 (tian xia)") cannot be conquered simply by using forces [my translation].

A common translation of the Chinese concept of "天下 (tian xia)" is "all under heaven." The most significant contribution of the concept to the disciplinary debates of IR lies in that it connotes a radically different view of connectivity from that of the Westphalian state system. Unlike the Westphalian system that stresses the equality of each individual state, Chinese "天下 (tian xia)" emphasizes a family-state system that favors hierarchy (Zhao 2005). In his book, Zhao outlines four theoretical underpinnings of the Chinese "天下 (tian xia)" that distinguish the concept from the Westphalian system:

1. The world must be seen as a political entity under a commonly agreed institution;
2. The world should be the highest level of political measurement; from the perspective of international relations, this means that *world affairs and issues should be analyzed by a world standard, not a nation-state standard*;
3. Political institutions at each level must be of the same essence. The political principle must be able to be universalized and transitively run through all political levels;
4. The legitimacy of a political institution should be rooted in the ethical [my translation and emphasis].

According to Zhao (2005, 2006), the world governed by the state system is a "non-world," for interstate institutions cannot solve trans-state problems. The "天下 (tian xia)" system, on the other hand, sees "the whole world as one family" and therefore is capable of creating a global system, thus solving global problems (Zhao 2006, 31). In other words, in contrast to the Westphalian system where nation-states are deemed as the primary actors in the international system, the Chinese "天下 (tian xia)" defines a political order that sees and analyzes the world as one totality—namely, borderless.

One important implication of such a Chinese imaginary of borderless world is that, unlike the Westphalian system where the boundary between "self" and "other" is clearly delineated through the idea of territory, the Chinese "天下 (tian xia)" implies a much more ambiguous relation between self and other. This is most clearly manifested in China's relations with foreign countries: Looking back in history, it can be noticed that up till its encounter with the Europeans, China had had a long history of absorbing and assimilating foreigners; "barbarians" who came to reign over the Chinese heartland, such as Mongols and Manchus, had all been sinicized and assimilated into the mainstream Chinese society one way or another (Chan, 1999). What can be concluded from this Chinese approach to its relations with foreign nations is that, since the concept of "天下 (tian xia)" implies hierarchical relations between individual states, it essentially allows for the more powerful states to absorb the weaker ones and consequently assimilate them into their own cultural, political, and intellectual orbits. In the case of China, especially, the strength and persistence of its cultural identity resulted in the country's sense of civilizational superiority that in turn serves as what Emilie Durkheim (2014) once called "collective conscience," bonding the Chinese population throughout the history.

This sense of civilizational superiority was finally tested, if not displaced, in the face of the dynamic and expansionist Europe. The Chinese absorption did not work with the Europeans, as they were simply too rich and technologically too advanced. What is more, both the Chinese and the Europeans claimed their own superiority based on different worldviews and consequently, they collided head on. A letter by Griffith John (cited in Thompson 1906, 254) to the London Missionary Society vividly described the irreconcilable identifications between the two cultural groups:

> Are we not much superior to them? Are we not more manly, more intelligent, more skillful, more human, more civilised, nay, are we not more estimable in every way? Yes, according to our way of thinking. No, *emphatically* no, according to theirs. And it would be nearly as difficult to alter out opinion on the subject as it is for them to alter theirs.

European merchants and diplomats repeatedly protested that they were not being treated as "equal" by Chinese traders. Accommodations thus had to be made by the government in order to "tame" the complaining Europeans—on *their* terms and in accordance with *their* understanding of international rules [my emphasis] (Gong 1984). "Self-knowledge develops through knowledge of the Other" (Todorov 1999, 254); for the very first time in their history, China realized that they were speaking from the position of weakness, not of strength.

Europe's scientific advancement as well as overwhelmingly superior military force eventually led Chinese intellectuals to conclude that the only way for them to defend their country against foreign encroachment is to learn from them. As such, from the late 1830s, a growing number of intellectuals and ruling elites began to advocate for the study of Western knowledge. This is also commonly known as the beginning of China's "Western learning." In 1839, an official named Lin Zexu instructed a number of scholars to translate English texts on international law; his intention was to use international law to ban the British merchants from importing opium into the country (Chan 1998). In 1862, an academy named *Tongwenguan* (College of Foreign Languages) was set up by the Qing government, whose main purpose was to train translators to handle foreign affairs. Two years later, Henry Wheaton's *Elements of International Law* was translated by then American missionary W. A. P. Martin and distributed to public officials. The book soon became a primary reference for them to conduct diplomacy (Chan 1998).

The adoption of international law and the country's official involvement in international diplomacy then brought some Western political concepts into China, with the most important one being "sovereignty." What is particularly interesting about the transmission of the concept of sovereignty was that, before the introduction of Wheaton's *Elements of International Law*, the Chinese term for sovereignty, that is, "主权 (zhu quan)," did not possess any meaning that could connote the power of the state. The Chinese expression of sovereignty consists of two characters: "主 (zhu)," meaning ruler, master; and "权 (quan)," which means rights but also power (not in the positive sense of the power of a legitimate authority but in the negative sense of one's privileged position to manipulate rules). Hence, in the premodern Chinese language, or at least before the nineteenth century, "主权 (zhu quan)" means the rights, or power, of the master. In *Guanzi* (2010), a seventh-century BCE political and philosophical text, for example, one paragraph reads,

> If we reward the subjects too much we will risk exhausting the national treasury; if we are too lenient towards the subjects we will risk undermining the authority of the national law. The exhaustion of the national treasury will undermine the power of the monarch ("主权 (zhu quan)"); and the leniency towards the subjects will undermine our national security. Thus, everything has to be balanced and nothing can be overdone. [my translation]

Similarly, in *Qianfulun* (2011), philosopher Wang Fu from the Han Dynasty says,

> Those in power have greed; so they hate those with integrity. Those in power will do anything to hide those with integrity; because they pose threats to the power of the monarch ("主权 (zhu quan)"). [my translation]

In both of these cases, it can be seen that "主权 (zhu quan)" was used to refer to the power of the monarch rather than the authority of the state.

This conception of sovereignty, however, began to change after the publication of the Chinese version of Wheaton's *Elements of International Law*. This is mostly because, when Martin was translating Wheaton's text, he equated the meaning of the Chinese "主权 (zhu quan)" with that of the English "sovereignty." Unlike in the above two texts where "主权 (zhu quan)" was used to describe the power of the monarch, in his translation of Wheaton's text Martin deployed the Chinese term "主权 (zhu quan)" explicitly to translate the English "sovereignty." For example, one passage from Martin's translation reads,

Thus what is the absolute power of a state, is what we call sovereignty ("主权 (zhu quan)"). Such a sovereignty ("主权 (zhu quan)") can be exercised within the state, or outside of the state. When exercised within the state, it is the highest of all legal orders. When exercised outside of the state, it symbolises the absolute autonomy of the state and also protects the state from any foreign interferences [my translation]. (Wheaton, translated by Martin, 2003, 27)

This was the beginning of the Chinese obsession with the concept of sovereignty. According to political scientist Gerald Chan (1998), when the definition of "主权 (zhu quan)" as the power of the state was first introduced into the Chinese intellectual discourse, it quickly took hold among intellectuals and political elites; Li Hongzhang, one of the most distinguished diplomats in Chinese history and also one of the earliest advocates of the Western learning, for example, allegedly used the concept on many occasions to resist European influence in the Chinese territory. Also, in his study of the Chinese foreign policy in the late Qing period, John Schrecker (1971, 253) discovered a steady increase in the frequency of Chinese officials' employment of the term "sovereignty" in their political rhetoric; from 1875 to 1894, the Chinese term "主权 (zhu quan)," that is, sovereignty, appeared on an average of only once per 100 pages in the Qing government's foreign policy documents. Then between 1895 and 1899 it grew to 2.5 times per 100 pages, and by the period between 1902 and 1910, the frequency soared to about 22 appearances per 100 pages. It was obvious that from the late nineteenth century, sovereignty of the Chinese state had become the prime topic of concern for the Qing government. This also explains why Martin's translation of "sovereignty" is now the default definition for "主权 (zhu quan)" when most of the neologisms he crafted in his translation of Wheaton's book could no longer be found in Chinese discourse today (Callahan 2001): because the introduction of the English concept of sovereignty had led to the shift in the Chinese imaginary of connectivity from the previous borderless "天下 (tian xia)" to the modern international system that consists of bounded territories.

Sheldon Wolin (2004, 218) argues, "The need to establish a field of intelligible meanings among political phenomena become acute when traditional social and political arrangements appear to be breaking down into a kind of primal condition." Indeed, from the rise of continental philosophy in the nineteenth century to the recent revival of Marxism within Western academia, it is almost a truism that every theoretical innovation has to be spurred by moments of crisis – as if human mind became particularly lucid when threatened by its own extinction. This chapter has so far illustrated how the concept of sovereignty became transplanted into Chinese thinking in the aftermath of the Opium Wars, thus subverting the traditional Chinese imaginary of connectivity. It is probably worth mentioning here that, before the arrival of the Europeans, it was almost unimaginable for Chinese intellectuals to accept any foreign knowledge, since they firmly believed that China had everything and therefore there was no need to borrow anything from the outside world. The shift of Chinese imaginary from "天下 (tian xia)" to modern sovereignty in this sense was highly significant, as it marked China's proactive transition of its knowledge production from Chinese to Western precedents or what Leigh Jenco (2015, 4) calls "the painful process of de-parochialisation": that is, the realization that one's norms and values that were formerly presumed as universal and incontroversiable turned out to be particular, thus insufficient.

What, however, needs to be pointed out is that this process of transplanting a foreign concept into a different cultural and political context came with certain consequences. With reference to Japan's importation of Western liberal theory during the nineteenth century, Douglas Howland (2002, 2) argues that "westernization [in Japan] was not a linear process—unlike the tree that arrives with its roots secured in soil and burlap, there was no transplanting of the West in a neat package." The same can also be said about introducing the notion of sovereignty. As mentioned before, the traditional Chinese imaginary of connectivity before the nineteenth century was an antithesis to the Westphalian state system, as it presupposed a borderless world. What this implies is that when the notion of sovereignty was incorporated into Chinese political and intellectual discourse, it did not translate very well as the concept did not have a natural fit within the existing Chinese knowledge system. Hence, when the concept was first brought in, its arrival was bound to generate certain side effects. The following section of this chapter will therefore examine some of these side effects.

After Sovereignty: The Rise of Essentialism in Chinese Political Thinking

The first side effect resulted from the transplanting of the notion of sovereignty in Chinese political thinking was that it gave rise to a new Chinese understanding of the concept of "国 (guo)," meaning country as well as China's obsession with the idea of territorial integrity. In contemporary Chinese language, the character "国 (guo)" is used to refer to all three English concepts: country, state, and nation. Yet, just like "主权 (zhu quan)," that is, sovereignty, before the late nineteenth century, the character was not exclusively associated with the idea of a sovereign state. This means that within Qing China, for instance, there could be a number of states with different governors in charge. Those states did not have clearly defined boundaries, nor could they make their own laws. In *Mencius: Li Lou II*, for instance, we can even notice that there is one paragraph where the character was used to describe a city:

> Accordingly, she got up early in the morning, and privately followed wherever her husband went. Throughout the whole city, there was no one who stood or talked with him. (China Text Project 2019)

However, since the introduction of the concept of sovereignty, the character "国 (guo)," it can be noticed, gradually began to be used to exclusively describe the idea of a "sovereign state," namely, a bordered state with a centralized government. For instance, in 1866, two years after the publication of Wheaton's book in Chinese, Li Hongzhang accused European powers of aggressive conducts in Chinese territory with reference to his reading of international law:

> Every country ("国 (guo)") knows its purpose is to serve people, but only to Chinese people they want to put up more restraints. They want to control people by threatening officials, and control officials by threatening the imperial court. . . . This is against the clause listed in the public law of foreign country ("国 (guo)"). This conduct is devoid of emotion and reason, and it is not fair and just [my translation]. (Li 1866; cited in Shen 1966, 9)

It can be observed that, in the above passage, Li used the word "country"— or, in the Chinese original, the character "国 (guo)"—to refer to sovereign states ("foreign country"). This is quite unusual since, as mentioned earlier, the character could also mean "home," "feud," "city," etc. After reviewing other scholarly writings on foreign countries during this period, it became clear that this exclusive usage of "国 (guo)" as a sovereign state might have resulted from China's attempt to use a concept of European origin to defend itself against the European aggression in Chinese territory. Because if China accepted the European claim on the inherent sovereign right of the state, it could use the same logic of sovereign statehood to prevent any European activities in its territory.

Two examples can be found to illustrate such a Chinese strategy to "use the foreign against the foreign": The first one is the trajectory of Guo Songtao, China's first permanent diplomatic representative in the West. In 1842, following the first Opium War, Britain and China signed the treaty of Nanjing, opening the Chinese market for foreign trade. Although the Chinese officials were not happy with the high tariffs and extraterritorial jurisdiction listed on the treaty, it wasn't until thirty years later, in the 1870s, that the treaty was described as unequal and humiliating (Lorca 2014). This was to a great extent due to the influence cast by Guo who repeatedly protested that "the West should treat China as *equal*" and that "Westerners in China should fall under the *jurisdiction* of the Chinese local authority [my emphasis]" (Wang 2005, 24). By accepting the European conception of sovereign statehood and reapplying it to the context of Western imperialism, Guo Songtao managed to transform himself from non-European actors being subjected to European legal discourse to using international law as a means of resistance against foreign domination.

Another example was from Xue Fucheng, also a key advocate of Western learning in the late nineteenth century, who made the following remark soon after Japan made its entrance into the European-dominated international society:

> The West has a book called *Public Law for Ten Thousand Countries* (the Chinese translated title for Wheaton's *Elements of International Law*). It is used to equalize the power imbalance between nations and has a set of rules to be followed. . . . Only that Asian countries have different traditions, different political conducts, different languages; we simply do not fit with their scale of the public law. The book also never mentions the Eastern countries. In the past thirty years, Japan and Thailand have been endeavoring to conduct themselves to suit the West's public law. Ever since Japan has changed their time, they became obedient, luring the people from the West; and in return, the Western people incorporated them into the governance of the public law [my translation]. (Xue 1892, 414)

Xue's basic argument here is that the Western international law only concerns people of the West—not only because the book itself was designed *in* the West but also *for* the West (thus no mentioning of the Eastern societies). Everywhere else, especially Asia, is not—and probably should not—be part of the Western "public." Although Japan eventually managed to be incorporated into such "public," this is mainly because they had to perform in a certain way to be accepted *by* the West. However, in order for this argument to be valid, Xue first of all had to acknowledge and *essentialize* the political and cultural differences between the Western countries and those of the East; as he argued in the above passage, "*Asian countries have different traditions, different political conducts, different languages*; we simply do not fit with their scale of the public law" [my emphasis].

What is particularly interesting about Xue's account is that it demonstrates not only the changing Chinese political imaginary but also the changing Chinese conceptualization of the self/other binary. As mentioned earlier on, in contrast to the Westphalian state system, the Chinese connectivity of "all under heaven" allows for a much more ambiguous relation between the "self" and the "other." It presupposes the idea that one's cultural identity can be simply transformed and assimilated into the more powerful state with civilizational superiority. In his *Liberal Barbarism*, with reference to the British and French destruction of the Chinese garden in the late nineteenth century, Erik Ringmar describes such a Chinese thinking as follows:

> The Europeans were indeed barbarians, yet a barbarian, in the Chinese tradition, was not a destroyer of civilization as much as uncouth outsiders who had not yet benefited from the privileges of a Chinese-style education, and as such they were more to be pitied than feared. Barbarians were ignorant children—without knowledge of morality, philosophy, and proper ritual—and this was indeed why they had showed up at China's borders. The foreigners had, in the Chinese expression, "come to be transformed." (2013, 5)

However, if this logic is to be taken seriously, it also means that, given China's heavy defeat in the Opium War, China could be considered to have occupied the position of an inferior state and therefore should be absorbed into the Western civilization. But this obviously is not what Xue argued. Instead of willingly subduing China under the European domination, Xue used the logic of equality among states—a key assumption in the Westphalian system—and essentialized the cultural, political, and social differences between the European and the Asian countries. At this point, it can be argued, Chinese elites were already thinking of the world order from the perspective of the Westphalian system instead of their own "天下 (tian xia)."

Such an essentialist conception of cultural differences reached its zenith in the late nineteenth century and the early twentieth century under the influence of the second wave of Western learning. The end of the Sino-Japanese War brought about a new wave of Chinese intellectuals advocating for Western knowledge. The main difference between this time and the previous movement was that intellectuals who were advocating for the adoption of Western technology in the previous movement did not genuinely believe in the superiority of Western knowledge, while scholars pioneering the second wave were actively calling for thorough national reforms at all political, intellectual, cultural, and education levels.

One of the key proponents of the second wave of Western learning was Kang Youwei, a senior official of Guangxu Emperor and arguably China's most influential thinker of the nineteenth century. As a prominent advocate of Western learning and constitutional reforms, Kang's writings were heavily influenced by his readings of Western classics. His most well-known theoretical contribution to the history of Chinese political thought was the concept of "大同 (da tong)," meaning the "great unity." The concept "大同 (da tong)" first appeared in the Confucian classic of *The Book of Rites*, and it was principally used to describe a society where the Confucian ethics of benevolence was practiced by all members of the society. Drawing on the original Confucian understanding of the concept as well as insights from other philosophical doctrines, between the late nineteenth century and the early twentieth century, Kang then took a more radical approach to the understanding of the concept of "大同 (da tong)" and eventually came up with a depiction of what he called the most ideal society of "great unity." Kang basically argued that most of the world's sufferings arise from human-imposed boundaries, such as boundaries of nation, class, gender, and even family. Therefore, by eliminating those boundaries, in Kang's view, humankind can eliminate most of the unnecessary sufferings and miseries. As he wrote,

> There is a saying that "all under heaven is one nation." But whenever there are small boundaries, they all become the obstacles to tackle the big boundaries. The more we set up small boundaries, the more they cause problems to eliminate the big ones. Because the boundary of family is preventing individuals, and the boundary of a state preventing the citizens, it is very difficult for us to reach the great unity and peace. If in China, we set up the boundaries of province, government, state, county, local, village, last name, and household in order to differentiate ourselves from a different province, government, state, county, local, village, last name, and household—how can we ever reach the harmony among people? Therefore I say that the happiest order is of a great unity [my translation]. (Kang 1935, 137)

What is interesting about Kang's work is that, it shows that by the late nineteenth century, not only that Chinese intellectuals had completely accepted the European-dominated Westphalian state system as the default world order but also that they were trying to overcome such an order by (re)introducing the Chinese concept of "天下 (tian xia)"—without realizing that before the arrival of the Europeans, it had always been China's traditional conceptualization of the world order. In Kang's book, *The Great Unity*, we can see clearly how, at the beginning of the early twentieth century, Chinese intellectuals had already presupposed the existence of sovereign, bounded nation-states; as he wrote in the section titled "the harm of having nation-states,"

Today if we want to save people from potential disasters, want to give everyone in the world happiness, want to seek the benefit of the great unity, we must first destroy the boundaries of nation-states and deconstruct the meanings of nation-states. . . . However, with that being said, nation-states are the highest form of human collectivity. Apart from the Divine above, there is no universal law above nation-states. Each nation-state acts in accordance with its own interests. This is not something that can be restrained using the public law [i.e., international law]; this is not something that can be changed using abstract ideas [my translation]. (Kang 1935, 86)

The above passage shows that, at this point, even with the introduction of international law in China, Kang already acknowledged that nation-state was the highest form of political entity at the international level and that "there is no universal law above nation-states." This is a clear indication of the complete shift of the Chinese political imaginary of connectivity from the previous borderless world of all under heaven to the modern sovereign statehood.

Following this thread, Kang then proposed a few suggestions that he believed that if we could follow them, we could enter the utopian age of "great unity": first, no bounded territories, no borders. There should be one central government for the entire world that is elected democratically. Second, no families. Coinhabitation between a man and a woman should be no longer than one year maximum. Third, free nurseries, health care, and schooling. Jobs will be assigned by the state when a child passes his or her schooling age. Fourth, all men and women should serve in the military for a few years. Free public accommodations, canteens, and properly trained police officers. And finally, encourage and reward intellectual achievements in any areas of study (Kang 1935).

Upon its publication, Kang's propositions were greatly embraced. His argument regarding the human-imposed boundaries being the source of sufferings was especially echoed by then Chinese intellectuals. However, what is rarely mentioned in the debates regarding Kang Youwei's work is that his notion of "great unity" illustrated not only the internationalization of the Westphalian modern statehood in the Chinese thinking but also the internalization of the racial and biological essentialism that were prevailing in the Western intellectual discourse in the late nineteenth century. As mentioned earlier, Chinese intellectuals began to engage with Western knowledge as part of the "Western learning" movement in the 1860s. During that period, scholars such as Kang Youwei began to engage with Western scientific theory. The ideas of Darwin, Lamark, and Spencer, for example, are said to have begun to circulate among Chinese intellectuals as early as 1870 (Tsu 2005). In other words, they were introduced into the Chinese discourse around the same time as the concept of sovereignty.

According to Historian Emma Teng (2013), of all the ideas Chinese intellectuals were exposed to, none was more powerful than those of social Darwinism that assert the superiority of the white race over the yellow due to the superior progress of Western civilization. Facing the mounting pressure of European imperialism, Teng (2013) argues that Chinese scholars of the late nineteenth century became obsessed with the theories concerning the idea of an international struggle for the survival of the fittest. Hence, essentialist theories such as social Darwinism that portrays a global conflict between the white and yellow resonated strongly with them both on intellectual and emotional levels at that time.

If we read Kang's *The Book of Great Unity* carefully, we can also discover that Kang's understanding of the world was deeply influenced by, if not rooted in, the ideology of social Darwinism and Western racial theory. As mentioned before, the basic premise of Kang's *The Book of Great Unity* is to eliminate human-imposed boundaries. With a view of racism as a global issue, Kang accordingly dedicated the fourth chapter of his book to discuss "Eliminating Racial Boundaries and Amalgamating the Races." Kang (1935) first categorized the world into four races—white, yellow, black, and brown—and argued that it was the physical differences among these groups that gave rise to the problem of racial inequality. As he wrote,

> In a peaceful world of great unity, everyone is equal and everyone exists in great unity—this is of course a fair thing to say. However, things do differ and that is an inevitable truth. If we were to have everything as equal, then those things much be equal in its intelligence, level of knowledge, shape, and physique. Only then we can have true equality. . . . Lincoln freed the black slaves, but look now what is happening in America: (white) Americans are reluctant to brush their teeth with the blacks; they do not allow to dine or even sit with the blacks; blacks are not allowed to use the first class of their cars, or enter a restaurant. If a black is elected to be an official, white Americans bully him; if a black is intellectual, they mock him that. (Kang 1935, 138–39, my translation)

Kang hence proposed that the way to solve such a problem is simply to "unify" all human races—or, in his own words, "racial improvement" (Kang 1935, 142). He explicitly denigrated the black and brown as inferior races and proposed a detailed plan for them to "improve" on their "racial quality" through interracial marriages:

> If the blacks and browns were to move elsewhere to settle, then they should live with the yellow and the white. Then we will set up a rewarding system for men who are willing to marry the brown and the black ladies as well as for women who are willing to marry the black and brown men. The reward will be called the "racial improvement award." Some might ask: if we keep mixing the superior races with the inferior ones, would that not lead to the deterioration of the human race in general? I say: no, not necessarily. In a hundred thousand years' time, there will be much less blacks and browns. The world will be full of white and yellow, and only a few blacks and browns. This is the way to improve to racial quality [my translation].

At this point, it is probably not too difficult to speculate that in Kang's ideal society of "great unity," there are probably two races living, namely, the yellow and the white.

In his study of the expansion of the international society in East Asia during the nineteenth century, Shogo Suzuki (2009, 14) argues that Japan's invasion of China soon after becoming a member of the international society indicates that Japan did not only accept the Western standards regarding what means to be a "civilized" state but also accepted the idea about how they should *act* as a "civilized" state. That is to say, during their socialization process in the international society, Japan emulated the "civilizing" mode of action conducted by the Europeans by invading China. A similar argument can also be applied to the case of Kang Youwei and possibly other Chinese intellectuals of the nineteenth century who shared his views: The rise of such a racial essentialism in Chinese intellectual discourse after the shift of the Chinese political imaginary shows that China did not only accept and internalize the European notion of modern statehood but also emulated *what they thought a modern state should be doing* by essentializing the racial and cultural differences. Ringmar describes the sentiment of the Chinese intellectuals in the late nineteenth century as follows:

> Before 1860, the Chinese could just be themselves, but after 1860 they were forced to become either pro- or anti-European, pro- or anti-modern, and pro- or anti-railroads, electricity, democracy, Darwinism, Spencerism, Freud, canned vegetables, the Charleston, and cigarettes. (2013, 11)

By imitating the theories of social Darwinism and committing themselves to the ideology of Western racial discourse, the Chinese intellectuals were trying to prove that China was now a modern, pro-European state. Scholars such as Emma Teng (2013) accordingly argue that modern Chinese racial theory was formulated within such a context of intellectual transformation in late Qing China, drawing on both the nation's long history of thought on ethnic difference as well as new ideas derived from the West. The transplanting of the concept of modern statehood, it can be argued, to a great extent facilitated and legitimized this intellectual invention. In this regard, Kang's work is both a demonstration and a reminder of the consequences of the conceptual transplanting of the idea of sovereignty and modern statehood in Chinese political imaginary in the nineteenth century.

Conclusion

This chapter has examined how the modern conception of sovereignty became transplanted in the Chinese political imaginary in the nineteenth century. It has demonstrated how, in a span of less than half a century, the Chinese imaginary of connectivity has shifted from the traditional Chinese idea of "天下 (tian xia)" that presupposes a borderless world to the modern Westphalian system that is based on the mutual recognition of state sovereignty. However, it has been argued that such an act of transplanting a foreign concept that did not naturally fit within the existing Chinese knowledge system was not a linear process and therefore it had also generated certain consequences in the process of this conceptual transplanting: By the late nineteenth century, the Chinese intellectuals had not only accepted the Westphalian state system as the default world order but also tried to (re)introduce the Chinese "all under heaven" as a way to overcome the shortcomings of the state system. Yet, such a complete acceptance of the modern world order also led to the rise of racial essentialism in Chinese intellectual discourse. This was mostly due to the Chinese intellectuals trying to prove that China was now a modern, pro-European state by imitating the essentialist depiction of racial differences. The present chapter is a very preliminary study on the subject matter and more research is definitely in need to further substantiate what has been argued. What is called for here, however, is that there is always a dualistic nature to the translation of a European political concept into the intellectual discourse of the non-European countries and more attention should be paid to this area of study and its link to the study of IR.

Bibliography

Bartelson, Jens. 1995. *A Genealogy of Sovereignty*. Cambridge: Cambridge University Press.

Callahan, W. A. 2001. "China and the Globalisation of IR Theory: Discussion of 'Building International Relations Theory with Chinese Characteristics.'" *Journal of Contemporary China* 10(26): 75–88.

Chan, G. 1998. *International Studies in China: An Annotated Bibliography*. New York: Nova Science.

———. 1999. *Chinese Perspectives on International Relations: A Framework for Analysis*. London: Macmillan.

Chen, L. 1987. "Mantan Xifang Guoji Guanxi Xue (On International Relations Studies in the West)." *Guowai Zhengzhixue* 1: 57.

Durkheim, E. 2014. *The Division of Labour in Society*. New York: Free Press.

Gong, G. W. 1984. The Expansion of International Society. In *The Expansion of International Society*, edited by H. Bull and A. Watson. Oxford: Claredon Press.

Guanzi, Qi Chen Qi Zhu (Seven Officials and Seven Rulers). June 2010. *Gushiwen Wang* [online]. https://www.gushiwen.org/GuShiWen_37b591a524.aspx. Accessed September 18, 2017.

Howland, R. D. 2002. *Translating the West: Language and Political Reason in Nineteenth-Century Japan*. Honolulu: University of Hawaii Press.

Huidun (Wheaton, H.). 2003. *Wanguo Gongfa (Elements of International Law)*. Translated by Ding Weiliang (W. Martin) Beijing: University of Political Science and Law Press.

Jenco, L. 2015. *Changing Referents: Learning across Space and Time in China and the West*. New York: Oxford University Press.

Kang, Y. 1994 [1935]. *Datong Shu (The Book of Great Unity)*. Shenyang: Shenyang Renmin Chubanshe.

Kazenstein, J. Peter, ed. 1996. *The Culture of National Security: Norms and Identity in World Politics*. New York: Columbia University Press.

Liang, Q. 1988 [1897]. *Du Chunqiujie Shuo (On the Readings of the World of Chunqiu)*. Beijing: Zhonghua Shuju.

Loewe, M., and L. E. Shaughnessy, eds. 1999. *The Cambridge History of Ancient China: From the Origins of Civilization to 221 B.C.* Cambridge: Cambridge University Press.

Lorca, A. B. 2014. *Mestizo International Law: A Global Intellectual History 1842–1933*. Cambridge: Cambridge University Press.

Ringmar, E. 2013. *Liberal Barbarism: The European Destruction of the Palace of the Emperor of China*. New York: Palgrave Macmillan.

Schrecker, E. J. 1971. *Imperialism and Chinese Nationalism*. Cambridge, MA: Harvard University Press.

Shen, Y., ed. 1966. *Chouban Yiwu Shimo (Foreign Affairs in their Entirety)*. Beijing: Wenhai Chubanshe.

Suzuki, S. 2009. *Civilization and Empire: China and Japan's Encounter with European International Society*. London: Routledge.

Teng, E. J. 2013. *Eurasian: Mixed Identities in the United States, China, and Hong Kong, 1842–1943*. Berkeley: University of California Press.

Thompson, R. W. 1906. *Griffith John: The Story of Fifty Years in China*. New York: A. C. Armstrong.

Todorov, T. 1999. *The Conquest of American: The Question of the Other*. New York: University of Oklahoma Press.

Tsu, J. 2005. *Failure, Nationalism, and Literature: The Making of Modern Chinese Identity, 1895–1937*. Stanford, CA: Stanford University Press.

Wang, D. 2005. *China's Unequal Treaties: Narrating National History*. Lanham, MD: Lexington.
Wang F. June 2011. *Qianfulun (Comments of a Recluse)* [online]. http://www.zwbk.org/MyLemmaShow.aspx?lid=180778. Accessed September 18, 2017.
Wolin, S. 2004. *Politics and Vision*. Princeton, NJ: Princeton University Press.
Xue F. 1892. *Xue Fucheng Xuanji (Selected Works)*. Shanghai: Shanghai Renmin Chubanshe.
Zhao, T. 2005. *Tianxia Tizi: Shijie Zhidu Zhexue Daolun (The Tianxia System: A Philosophy for the World Institution)*. Nanjing: Jiangsu Jiaoyu Chubanshe.
———. 2006. "Rethinking Empire from a Chinese Concept 'All under Heaven.'" *Social Identities* 12(1): 29–41.
———. 2009. "A Political World Philosophy in Terms of All-under-Heaven (Tian-xia)." *Diogenes* 221(56): 5–18.

CHAPTER SIX

'Making up Germans'

Colonialism, Cartography and Imaginaries of 'Germandom'

Zeynep Gülsah Çapan and Filipe dos Reis

Introduction

On 30 July 1896, Martin Gosselin, chargé d'affaires at the British Embassy in Berlin, sent a diplomatic cable to Prime Minister Lord Salisbury in London reporting on a recently published map in Germany.[1] The map was issued in June 1896 by the cartographer Paul Langhans and it delineated the position of various European populations in southern Africa. It was part of Langhans' larger project of a *Deutscher Kolonial-Atlas* ('German Colonial Atlas'), which he published in fifteen installments between 1893 and 1897 with *Justus Perthes*, one of the leading private cartographic publishing houses on the continent located in the small German town of Gotha (Langhans 1897).

Gosselin reported to Lord Salisbury that the map 'is entitled "the extension of German influence (Deutschtums) in South Africa," the towns underlined in red being places where High German colonies are said to be in existence, in the British colonies, and in the South African Republic' and, as the British diplomat continues, 'the spelling adopted in these maps is uniformly that of the Boers, who are styled "low Germans"' (as cited in Seligmann 1998, 179). The map was published in the midst of Anglo-German imperial rivalry in the Cape region. Germany had established its colony of South West Africa in 1884 and during the 1890s discussions came up in the German public, but

---

[1] For a longer reconstruction of this anecdote, see Seligmann (1998).

also within official circles, of whether Germany should extend its colony from South West Africa to the Cape and, thereby, gain hegemony over the southern part of Africa as a whole, to the disadvantage of the British. In this climate, sympathies arose with the Boers in their conflict with the British government as the Boers were seen by many as part of a larger Germanic community. The conflict between the British and the German governments would culminate in the Kruger telegram in January 1896, where the German Kaiser Wilhelm II congratulated President Paul Kruger of the Transvaal for defeating an unofficial British insurrection. Langhans published his map on the region only six months after the telegram. Gosselin's report on Langhans' map should spark three matters of concern within the British administration. First, as the map was not an official document of the German government but published by *Justus Perthes*, a private cartographic press, and as it addressed the general public, it was unclear whether the British government should react to it. After three months of careful considerations and the exchange of several memoranda, the Foreign Office concluded that 'the Kolonial Atlas appears to be a private publication by the firm of Justus Perthes of Gotha, for which the German government is not responsible' and, consequently, 'Lord Salisbury is therefore inclined to the opinion that it will be preferable to take no official action in this matter' (as cited in Seligmann 1998, 180). Thereby the British government developed a policy concerning the unofficial cartographic publications, namely not to react to these kinds of publications even if they were against British interests. Second, the Intelligence Division in the African department of the Foreign Office complained about the lack of accuracy of the map. According to the Intelligence Division, these errors were to the disadvantage of the British empire and, in turn, to the advantage of German territorial claims in the region. However, these inaccuracies were mainly about border disputes between German and British colonial territories and did not touch on the question of hegemony over the region as a whole.[2] Third, Gosselin was afraid of how the map portrayed the whole region of southern Africa in a specific way, namely as part of a larger project of *Deutschtum* (Germandom).[3] As

---

[2] Yet, in January 1897, an anonymous correspondent should come to an opposite conclusion in a review article in *The Geographical Journal*, a journal which was published by *The Royal Geographical Society* (with the *Institute of British Geographers*), namely that 'there is no doubt that the map of P. Langhans is at present by far the best map of South Africa produced on the continent' (Anonymous 1987, 64).

[3] A note on translation: Some of the concepts used in this essay are difficult to translate from German into English. This is, in particular, the case of the core notion of this chapter: *Deutschtum*. While some authors have translated it as 'German influence' or 'Germanness', we use the term 'Germandom', as it resembles the particular tonality of the German original in the best way.

such, the Boers were portrayed as 'low German' and thereby part of a greater German empire.

In this chapter, we take up this last thread and explore how the notion of Germandom, as part of the idea of a greater German empire, created new imaginaries of connectivity at the turn of the twentieth century. By investigating this, the chapter discusses the relationship between population, territory and state and how this relationship has been imagined through different connectivities. We focus in particular on articulations of Germandom in the context of the *völkische Bewegung*, of which Langhans was a part. This ethno-nationalistic movement was represented through organisations such as the *Alldeutscher Verband* ('Pan-German League') and also active in German colonial circles. Imaginaries of Germandom reveal how connectivities worked in establishing specific 'modes of reasoning' and ways of imagining time and space. This chapter reconstructs how the complex relationship between defining population, territory and the nation-state was tied to connectivities and to different 'colonial fantasies' (Zantop 1997). As the editors of this volume put it in the Introduction (page 5), 'The terms under which what is being connected, the processes through which connections are made possible, and the ideas, practices, and beliefs and material conditions that need to be in place for a particular form of connection to take place, produce a specific order'. The aim then is to underline the 'politics of connectivity' that led to different imaginations of the relationship between population, territory and state and 'different modes of reasoning about order, power and governance'.

In order to do so, the chapter unfolds as follows. It starts by providing a short overview of how nineteenth-century Germany discussed the relationship between population, territory and the state. It argues that there existed competing imaginaries with respect to how to understand where Germany was and who constituted that space. These different imaginaries had different 'modes of reasoning' with regard to population and territory. In order to substantiate our claims, the article reconstructs empirically the specific imaginary of *völkisch* authors and, in this regard, particularly the work of the cartographer Paul Langhans at the *Justus Perthes* publishing house in Germany. Therefore, the chapter proceeds by outlining the importance of the *Perthes* publishing house and discusses Langhans' role in it. Finally, the chapter focuses on connectivities that were imagined with respect to spatiality and reconstructs Langhans' project of 'translating' ethno-nationalistic ideas into maps and statistics. In order to illustrate this, the chapter introduces examples from Central and Eastern Europe, as well as from the southern part of Africa.

Germandom and the Politics of Connectivity

The process of 'making up people', as Ian Hacking (1986) has characterised it, necessitates to imagine the ways in which 'the people' created are connected to a specific space and time. One of the main issues thus far in tracing the process of 'making up people' has been the spatio-temporal hierarchies through which the relationship between population, territory and state has been analysed. In this context, two points are noteworthy. First, the space of 'Europe' is taken to be separate from the 'non-European' space and as such processes occurring within the space of 'Europe' are analysed on their own without considering their connectivities with the colonies. Second, the spaces designated as outside of 'Europe' are temporally assigned as being behind the space of 'Europe' (Çapan 2017).

This, in turn, has usually two repercussions for historical analysis in international relations (IR). First, it means that developments within the spaces of 'nation-states' and developments in the colonies are taken as two different processes. As such, the question of the making of the 'German people' is separated from the colonial fantasies through which that imagination was formulated (Fabian 2002). Second, it means that the 'beginnings' and 'endings' assigned to processes become spatially and temporally limited whereby discussions concerning the making of the 'German people' commence with the 'unification' of the German *Reich* under Prussian leadership in 1871. These two dynamics produce a couple of blind spots as a variety of connectivities are overlooked when analysing the relationship between the making of a people, the imagination of a territory and establishment of a state. As Timothy Mitchell (2000, 3) has noted, 'The methods of managing persons, self-identities, space and movement that Foucault presents as essential to the formation of European modernity in many cases came to Europe from its encounter with what lay beyond'.[4] This is important also in understanding how 'colonial alterity centrally participated (and participates) in the production of the European self' (Fernández and Esteves 2017, 150).

Recent literature on German colonialism has done significant work in demonstrating the different connectivities involved (Ames, Klotz and Wildenthal 2005; Eckert 2009; Naranch and Eley 2015). For example, James Sheenan (1981, 4) argued that 'we have too often allowed the

---

4 For more about how a Foucauldian analysis can be extended through attention to colonial modernity, see Stoler (2002) and Vaughan (1991).

political sovereignty of the nation-state to become the basis for the conceptual sovereignty of the nation as a way of thinking about the past' whereas there was 'a much wider pattern of connections, made possible by shared language and literature, and sustained by a complex web'. These 'connectivities' go beyond the bounded entities of 'nation-states' or 'empires' and have to be understood as operating at multiple levels. As Zantop (1997, 2) has argued, 'a colonialist subjectivity emerged in Germany as early as the 1770s, during the so-called coloniopolitical half of the eighteenth century, and . . . it grew into a collective obsession by the late 1800s'. German 'fantasies' or imaginaries about colonies cannot be limited in time to the 'official' beginning of the German state nor to the 'official' beginning of colonisation. Moreover, as we discuss below, even after the establishment of the German *Reich* the spatial imaginaries of colonial fantasies might extend its official borders. This is why rather than underlying the temporal and spatial bounded categories, the chapter focuses on connectivities in the manner in which 'Germans' were imagined as a population.

'Germany' was imagined and reimagined throughout its history with rival imaginings articulating different conceptions of space. These reimaginings demonstrate the unfixity of the notion of 'Germany' but also how the concept of the nation was articulated in connection with the colonial fantasies. The instability and transformation at the beginning of the nineteenth century along with the economic and social systems that were already under transition led to an agricultural crisis which increased emigration in the 1840s. The debates around the meaning of 'Germany' were exacerbated during this time (Fitzpatrick 2008). Political discourse in Germany from the middle of the nineteenth century onwards focused on different ways of characterising 'Germans abroad' whether it be *Auswanderer, Auslandsdeutsche, Auslandsdeutschtum* and *Deutschtum*. The debates around these concepts reveal varied imaginings of what it means to be 'German' (O'Donnell, Bridenthal and Reagin 2005; Penny 2017; Penny and Rinke 2015; Perraudin and Zimmerer 2011; Walther 2002). The discursive shift from *Auswanderer* to *Auslandsdeutsche* reveals different imaginations of what it means to be German but also different politics of connectivity. As Naranch (2005) explains, 'unlike the term *Auswanderer* (one who "wanders out"), which implied movement, mobility, and national dispersal, the connotations attached to the newer image of the *Auslandsdeutsche* imparted a sense of timelessness and enduring self'. *Auslandsdeutsche* remain German, sometimes even after generations abroad, while *Auswanderer* might lose their connection to Germany within a generation.

Even before the unification, there had been controversies with respect to what emigration meant in terms of Germanness. As Fitzpatrick (2008, 28) notes, 'many liberals of this period' including figures such as Hans Christoph von Gagern, Friedrich List and Hermann Blumenau, 'when discussing the necessity of the nation-state couched their arguments in terms of the need to expand overseas as a means of alleviating internal population pressures'. As such, 'the history of Germany is inextricably tied to Germans outside the homeland', since there was no centralised state until 1871 they emigrated 'from Central Europe as colonists to Czarist Russia and the East' and later 'to the New World' (O'Donnell et al. 2005, 1). In that sense, not only were the 'colonial fantasies' important in the imagination of identities in the metropole, imperialism was inextricably linked with liberal notions of nationhood.[5] As these discussions demonstrate, 'Germany' as such cannot be thought of as being a separate entity with no relation to the colonial endeavour at that period. There were, of course, different imaginaries of 'nationhood' that connected state, population and territory differently. These different imaginaries of 'nationhood' were not 'spatially fixed', nor were they based on a 'racially enclosed nation-state' but rested rather on 'a complex "imperial formation": an uneven and "mobile macropolity" centred on a nation-state core but radiating outward in a complex "architecture" of multiple, ambiguous, and gradated zones of territorial and nonterritorial sovereignty and anchored in discourses about diverse human populations and shifting "categories of subject and citizen" within Europe and overseas' (Sweeney 2014, 267). For example, as Woodrow D. Smith (1986, chapters 4 and 5) points out, at the end of the nineteenth century *Weltpolitik* ('world politics') and *Lebensraum* ('living space') were two concepts that imagined the relationship between population, territory and the state differently with different ways of defining the relationship to the colonies as well as the definitions of subject and citizen. *Weltpolitik* imagined the state as central where the colonies were an outward expansion of its economic interests, whereas *Lebensraum* – a concept that goes back to the German geographer Friedrich Ratzel – imagined people and culture as central where the colonies became the extensions of Germandom.

In the remainder of this chapter, we reconstruct imaginaries of connectivities of Germandom in terms of *Lebensraum* imperialism in the context of the *völkisch* movement. Dennis Sweeney (2014, 266) has characterised 'radical

---

5 For further discussions on this point especially with respect to British and French empires, see Hall (2002) and Pitts (2005).

or *völkisch* nationalism' as 'a new ideological formation on the German right, emphasizing the ethnoracial unity of "Germandom," the centrality of the "people" to all policymaking, and aggressive imperial expansion'. To do so, we focus on the cartographic work of Paul Langhans at *Justus Perthes* press at the turn of the twentieth century. The next section will provide some background information on the *Perthes* publishing house and Langhans in order to contextualise their importance for debates around defining 'Germandom'.

On *völkisch* Cartography

Based in the small German town of Gotha, *Justus Perthes* was one of the leading European and German-language publishers between the second part of the nineteenth century and the first half of the twentieth century with respect to the collection, evaluation and distribution of geographical knowledge. It became recognised for its production of various maps and atlases depicting the European and non-European world; its flagship journal *Petermanns Geographische Mitteilungen* was 'a benchmark for maps on global exploration' (Demhardt 2015, 1095). In general terms, the cartographic press of *Justus Perthes* published extensively on non-European territories and can be understood as part of the German colonial movement – sometimes as a reflection of it, sometimes as a driving force by creating novel imaginaries of space. In order to grasp the discourse on Germandom, we focus in this chapter on the work of (and the circles around) one of its most influential cartographers and demographers at the turn of the twentieth century, Paul Langhans (1867–1952). Langhans was one of the protagonists in the *völkisch* and *pan-German* movement and, in this context, Langhans' project at *Justus Perthes* was to produce maps and writings for the *völkische Bewegung* – and to translate their ideological programmes into maps, statistics and other forms of publications. Before joining *Justus Perthes* officially in 1889,[6] Langhans had studied at the University of Leipzig, where he had been influenced by Friedrich Ratzel. Langhans would become later a member of several extreme nationalistic and anti-Semitic organisations and parties such as the *Deutschbund* ('German Federation'), the *Alldeutscher Verband* ('Pan-German League'), the *Deutschsoziale Reformpartei*

---

6 Langshans was in contact with *Justus Perthes* before officially joining the press. For example, in 1885, at the age of seventeen, he had submitted a map of the 'German slave coast' (today Togo) and two years later a map on German settlements in Rio Grande in Southern Brazil (see correspondence between the journal editors of *Petermanns Geographische Mittheilungen* and Paul Langhans, Forschungsbibliothek Gotha, Sammlung Perthes, SPA ARCH PGM 558).

('German-Social Reform Party') or later, in 1931, the NSDAP (for more biographical details, see Meyer 2017). More recently, Langhans has been described as the 'doyen of German-nationalistic cartography' (Demhardt 2009, 17), the 'most important representative of ethnocentric geopolitics' (Kienemann 2018, 69) in Germany and as a supporter of a German 'settler empire' (Lerp 2013, 568).

We will focus in this chapter mainly on Langhans' work in the most productive and creative period of his career, namely during the last decade of the nineteenth and the first years of the twentieth century. In this time span, Langhans was part of different attempts to redescribe the German colonial enterprise by reprojecting it from the non-European south to Central and Eastern Europe. We explore this shift by primarily reconstructing the imaginaries of connectivity presented in two atlases, the *Deutscher Kolonial-Atlas* (1893–1897) and the *Alldeutscher Atlas* (1900), as well as the journal *Deutsche Erde*, which was established and edited by Langhans between 1902 and 1914. The focus on the role of private institutions such as *Justus Perthes* publishing house and individuals such as the *völkisch* cartographer and Pan-German League activist Langhans goes hand in hand with Jason D. Hansen's (2015, 3) observation that most initiatives of '"ordering" the central European landscape was less an imperial process of state-backed experts imposing national knowledge "from above"'. The private nature of these projects does, however, not signify that the government of the German empire did not pursue a politics of expansion, but that this politics of expansion sometimes diverged (as in the case of the 'acquisition' of non-European 'protectorates'), sometimes overlapped (as in the case of the Prussian Settlement Commission) with the imaginary of radical nationalistic circles in Germany (Liulevicius 2009, chapter 5).

Statistics and the Cartographic Space of Germandom

This section aims to elaborate on how different technologies of power were put into use in order to imagine these novel connectivities and the space of Germandom. It was in the nineteenth century that both cartography and statistics gained importance in terms of imposing *certainty* and constructing categories (cf. Desrosières 1993; Hacking 1990, 1986, 1982). Both cartography and statistics were essential instruments in how the relationship between population, territory and nation was imagined, and both often worked in tandem. Cartography and maps also work to delineate the 'territory' that the state and nation become associated with and as such it is an 'explicit tool for the transformation of social, economic and political spaces of the state' (Pickles 2004, 111). This production of spaces also works when it comes to 'making up people', subjects and actors. As Hacking (2002, 100) states, 'new slots' are created 'in which to fit and enumerate people' and 'counting', for example, through censuses 'creates new ways for people to be'. It is in this process that different connectivities are made between population, territory and nation. As such, a colonial space is imagined where 'Germandom' might reside and which then has to be 'populated'. The following subsections will focus on these processes of producing spaces and subjects. First, we discuss the imagination of novel spaces through maps by underlining the different connectivities that were articulated between territory and people and construction of a 'colonial' space for Germandom. The second subsection focuses on the role of statistics in the construction of the 'people' linked to the imagination of a 'colonial' space. As such, it expands upon the first subsection by underlining how the spaces that were imagined were 'populated'. The third and fourth subsections introduce specific examples of these processes: the way a German sphere of influence, as *Mitteleuropa*, is constructed in Central and Eastern Europe, and, by coming back to the anecdote at the outset of this chapter, how the Boers are 'made' German.

Colonial Space

In 1893, Paul Langhans started at the *Perthes* press to, as we can read on the cover, 'design, execute and edit' the *Deutscher Kolonial-Atlas* ('German Colonial Atlas'). The *Deutscher Kolonial-Atlas* was published in unregular instalments of two main maps each, and it was concluded in 1897 after fifteen instalments with thirty main maps in total. As a feature, over 300 smaller supplementary maps accompanied the main maps at the margins. The unregular completion of the instalments over five years produced the impression of cartographic and colonial novelty and progress.[7] In retrospective, the atlas would become 'one of the last highlights of overseas cartography at the Perthes press' (Demhardt 2009, 17), and it would help Langhans to launch a 'career as one of the major political cartographers in Germany' (Lerp 2013, 567).

---

7 Langhans' atlas was one of only two major German colonial atlases at that time: While Richard Kiepert's (1893) *Deutscher Kolonial-Atlas* was produced for official use, Langhans' atlas was the product of a commercial cartographic publishing house and addressed a broader public – in particular, a public on the nationalistic spectrum of society being enthusiastic for German expansionism.

In the Preface (*Vorwort*), which was published with the first instalment in 1893, Langhans contextualises the atlas by weaving the history of German state-building and German colonisation together. As it was typical for *völkisch* circles, Langhans develops a progressive narrative of colonialism:

> Since the economic unification of Germany, both the German industry and the German trade are in a steady upturn. This upturn gained even more momentum when the economic unification was followed by the political one. Since then, the German people [*Volk*] is able to provide effective protection to all its members and relatives even in the most distant countries and oceans. The economic growth, as well as the growing national spirit of the German people [*Volk*], required finally the expansion of the German economic sphere through colonies that are politically connected to the mother country. Hand in hand with these efforts of making accessible to the German trade new spheres of action are the attempts to preserve and strengthen the Germandom [*Deutschtum*] abroad. (Langhans 1897, Preface)

In this quote, Langhans does not only provide us with a progressive narrative of colonialism, but he also connects the imperial imaginaries of *Weltpolitik* and *Lebensraum*: While the economic unification can be attributed to the idea of *Weltpolitik*, the emphasis of Germandom is part of the discourse on *Lebensraum*. Depicting the spread of Germandom would become the main theme not only of the *Deutscher Kolonial-Atlas* but also of Langhans' various publishing projects at the turn of the century. As we have argued above, the analytical bifurcation of the 'European' and 'non-European' space in how the past is narrated has obscured the different connectivities through which space was imagined. As Hacking (1986) has underlined, 'making up people' and the creation of categories are inextricably linked. As such the imagination of 'Germandom' reinscribed the category of 'Germans' – hence 'making up people' – but it also reinscribed the category of 'colony' in order to delineate the relationship between territory and people. We see this in Langhans' line of argumentation: In order to be able to link the official policy of oversea 'protectorates' with the *völkisch* discourse on Germandom, Langhans introduces a broad and rather uncommon definition of colonialism – a definition that extends the economic vocabulary of *Weltpolitik* – when he describes the scope of the atlas as the 'account of the German protectorates [*Schutzgebiete*], the German settlements abroad, the dissemination of the Germans, their intellectual and material culture on the whole globe, this is the purpose and aim of the *Deutschen Kolonial-Atlas*' (Langhans 1897, Preface). By rearticulating the concept of 'colonialism', Langhans is able to link the official colonialism of non-European 'protectorates' (*Schutzgebiete*) in Africa, Asia and the Pacific with *völkisch* ideas of settlement and migration.

Colonialism is thereby detached from a mere focus on official state-run projects as it could, in addition, include other initiatives such as by the church (in the form of missionary work) or by individuals (e.g., settlers). This signifies that not the German *Reich* but the notion of Germandom becomes the connecting feature between different, often loosely interacting, populations: In the end, every German migrant and every German abroad could become a participant in the German colonial enterprise; all phenomena, which are associated to the spread of Germans over the world, are subsumed under the label of colonialism (see Kienemann 2018, 71); and everywhere where there is a German share of population abroad there is a legitimate claim for German colonisation. Thus, being a member of – what Langhans identifies as – the German people (*Volk*) and even tribe (*Stamm*) creates new connectivity effects:

> The thousand ties of affiliation and friendship, the shared language and conventions preserve and foster the economic exchange with the home country automatically, but only as long as the German national spirit is kept alive. A number of significant associations, which are full of men full of enthusiasm, have aimed at not only not losing the intellectual tie to German language and culture that brings together all Germans, but to further tighten it, so that the German tribe brothers [*Stammesbrüder*] who migrated abroad preserve their nationdom [*Volkstum*] and, by keeping together all German forces in this way, to provide a counterbalance to the aspirations of other nations with regard to the political and economic domination of the world. (Langhans 1897, Preface)

This new form of connectivity is illustrated in the first map of the *Deutscher Kolonial-Atlas*, which is headlined as *Verbreitung der Deutschen über die Erde* ('Dissemination of Germans over the Earth') (Figure 6.1). This map features hardly any topographical detail and, with the exception of the German 'protectorates', the map does not contain any political borders. Even Europe – and here the territory of the German *Reich* itself – is depicted without borders. Yet, what is illustrated in shades of various colours, ranging from brown and yellow to pink, are regions with an allegedly larger number of German population: Parts of Australia, South America, Southern Africa, North America and Europe are coloured. In particular, as Christoph Kienemann (2018, 71) has elaborated recently, the map indicates a closed German settlement space in Eastern Europe, covering even Western parts of Czarist Russia. However, according to the map legend, only 1–5 per cent of the population in this region is German. The impression of a homogeneous space of German population is also enforced by the stark contrast with regions with less than 1 per cent of Germans. These are left white and could be interpreted as 'blank' spaces for further German colonisation.

138 ~ Zeynep Gülsah Çapan and Filipe dos Reis

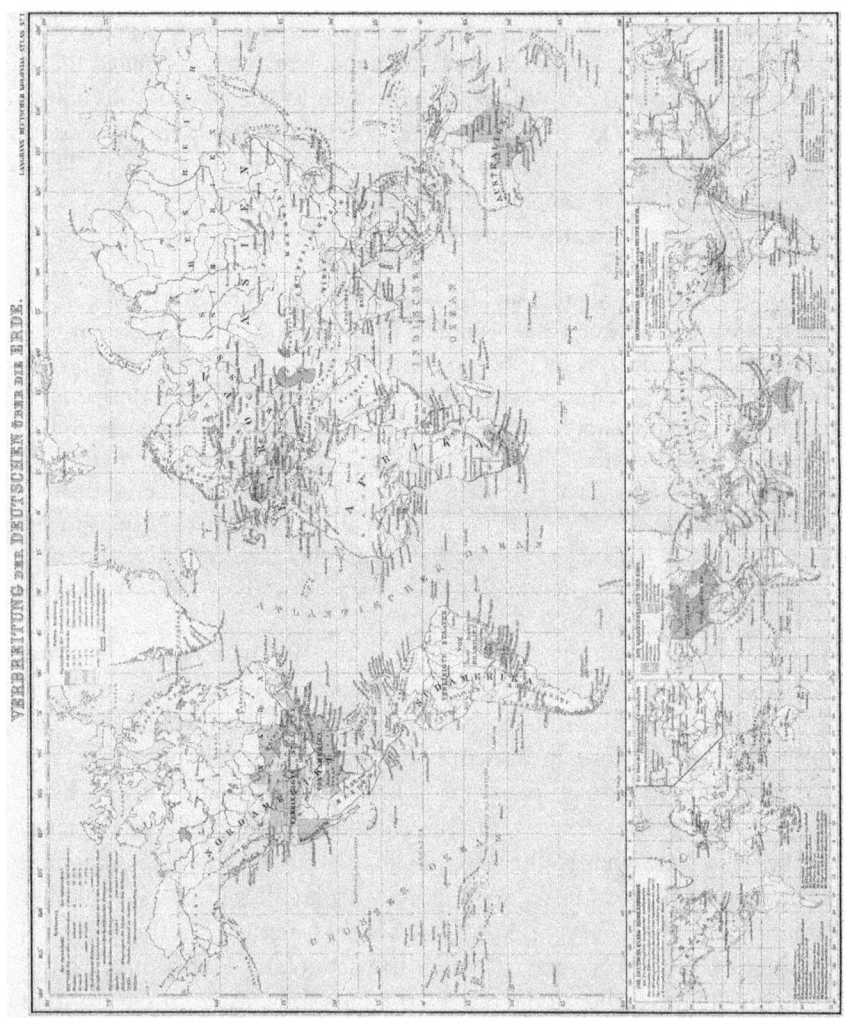

Figure 6.1 Map of 'The Dissemination of Germans All over the World' in *Deutscher Kolonial-Atlas, Justus Perthes Gotha*, 1897

Thereby, Germandom, as an imaginary of connectivity, creates novel spaces of imperialism, colonialism and government. The map helps to create the 'geobody' of this entity (Winichakul 1994): Cartographic representations of Germandom do not simply reveal the geography of Germany but rather articulate the boundaries of Germandom and 'Germany', even before a possible realisation. This claim is brought forward more frankly in a new Introduction (*Einleitung*), which was added as a supplement to the last instalment of the *Deutscher Kolonial-Atlas* in 1897. Where the Preface of 1893 was still an attempt at articulating German expansionism in a rather moderate way – and where the maps had to 'speak for themselves' – the tone of the new Introduction is openly aggressive, imperial and *völkisch*. Again, the main rhetorical move consists of a redefinition of 'colonialism'. As Langhans laments in the new Introduction,

> The recent movement in favour of the acquisitions of State-sponsored oversee protectorates has one-sided the use of the concept of the colony so much, namely to the one of the State-colony, that it might be bold, to give the name colonial atlas to all settlement activities of Germandom. (Langhans 1897, Introduction)

By situating German colonialism within a 'century-long' history, Langhans is also able to shift and relocate the potential space of German colonial activities. For Langhans, this space is not that much situated outside of Europe but rather in Germany's neighbouring countries: the German colonies in the East. As he writes,

> Alongside with the *Reich*-German protectorates, those countries are most intensively examined [in the Atlas], which were for the settlement activities of German migrants the most beneficial and in which Germandom could preserve more or less its independence against alien-national influences; these are the German agricultural colonies. Here, the tough conquest and settlement policy of the Guelphs, the Ascanians, the Hohenzollerns and also the Habsburgs, as well as of the Teutonic Order towards the East, did Germanize the lands between Elbe and Vistula and large areas of the Hungarian lands and mountain districts. (Langhans 1897, Introduction)

Statistics and the Construction of Population

In 1900, three years after the completion of the *Deutscher Kolonial-Atlas*, Langhans published with *Justus Perthes* another atlas, the *Alldeutscher Atlas* ('Pan-German Atlas') (Langhans 1900). As the title suggests, this atlas was directly supported by the Pan-German League and, as such, opens with a declaration of the organisation's aims and structure. In contrast to the

Deutscher Kolonial-Atlas, the *Alldeutscher Atlas* lacks any introduction or preface. Instead, it opens with several statistics on the 'Germans and other inhabitants of the *Reich*'.

In doing so, the *Alldeutscher Atlas* explicitly links maps and statistics. Institutionally, *Justus Perthes* press had a vast collection of statistical data, which were published through the *Diplomatisch-Genealogische Jahrbuch* ('Diplomatic Genealogical Yearbook'). The yearbook was a collection of statistical knowledge covering all countries of the world. If available it published official statistics, if not its editorial team directly requested information from German embassies, consulates and other sources abroad. Langhans was included in the editorial team of the yearbook at the turn of the century. But also, on a more general level, both statistics and cartography had become pivotal technologies of power in the second part of the nineteenth century, often working in tandem. This was, in particular, the case with regard to the counting, categorising, ordering and governing of populations. States started to perform censuses on a regular basis and ethnographic maps had become a popular genre of thematic maps. One of the main issues discussed in the late nineteenth century was how to 'measure' national belonging. In the context of Germany, the most popular category created for measurement was 'language spoken at home' (*Familiensprache*) which was thought to reflect true national consciousness. But also, for example, mother tongue, nationality langue or place of birth were possible categories in discussions on how to determine German nationality.[8]

Langhans' *Alldeutscher Atlas* uses statistics for two purposes: on the one hand, to chart the number of 'foreigners' not only in the German *Reich* but what is considered as German sphere of influence; on the other hand, the atlas also attempts to count the number of Germans, understood in terms of the 'spread of Germandom', throughout the world. With regard to the former, Langhans includes statistics on the German *Reich*, Belgium, the Netherlands, France, Italy, Russia and – as two distinct entities – Austria and Hungary. With regard to the latter, we find numbers on the United States, Canada, Chile, Brazil, southern Africa and Australia. These statistics are based on various census results. Due to the lack of a standardisation between different censuses, but also due to Langhans' interest in depicting Germandom as big as possible and counting as many Germans as possible, different statistics use different criteria in order to determine the nationality of individuals. While, for instance, in the German *Reich* or Hungary mother tongue is used in order to determine the number of Germans, it is in Austria the *langue parlée* and in

---

8 For a detailed reconstruction of the use of these different categories in the case of Germany, see Hansen (2015).

Belgium the 'nationality language'. In the United States, in turn, Langhans considers those as German who were born in the *deustche Sprachgebiet Mitteleuropa* ('German language area of Central Europe'). In the end, Langhans is able to count nearly 85 million Germans, which he contrasts with the official numbers of approximately 55 million *Reich*-German citizens. Langhans seeks to further document and illustrate that the 'spread of Germandom' exceeds official statistics significantly by providing a table on *Die deutschen Großstädte der Erde* ('The German Metropoles of the World') (Figure 6.2). As in the *Deutscher Kolonial-Atlas* before, Langhans is in this list not interested in existing political borders, as he does not care in which country a metropole is located but in how many of its inhabitants are German (or better what Langhans counts as such). While Berlin, the capital of the *Reich*, is on top of the list, Vienna, the capital of Austria-Hungry, is second. The list is, however, not restricted to cities of a 'greater Germany' (consisting of the Second Empire and Austria-Hungary) but also includes, among others, New York, Chicago, Milwaukee, Amsterdam, Brussels, Antwerp, Zurich or Riga.

Yet, in contrast to the *Deutsche Kolonial-Atlas*, the *Alldeutscher Atlas* refrains from including the official German colonies – the 'protectorates' of Togo, Cameroon, German East Africa and Tsingtao are not even mentioned – and is restricted to the *völkisch* project of mapping German emigrations in terms of the 'spread of Germandom'. These 'silences', as Harley (1988) called them, are also significant in the construction of the imagination: It is what is included as much as excluded that signals the specific imagination and connections that the map aims to project. In that regard, the exclusion of official German colonies is related to how the space of Germandom and its connections were being imagined not just in terms of state-led expansion but primarily through emigration. In this regard, it presents an alternative German colonial empire through maps of 'the five main centres of Germandom', namely Central and Eastern Europe, North America, South America, the southern part of Africa and south-eastern Australia. This is further illustrated, for example, in a supplementary map on *Das Deutsche Reich einst und jetzt und seine Bewohner* ('The German Empire back and now and its inhabitants)' (Figure 6.3), which is located at the margin of a map depicting the spread of Germandom in Europe. The small auxiliary map is interesting for four reasons. First, it distinguishes between regions with Germans – where Germans are in the majority in a lighter colour, where they are in the minority in a darker colour – and those without Germans, the latter described as *undeutsch* ('non-German'). This term has, as Kienemann (2018, 77) noted, a 'culturalist connotation' and is to some degree value-laden. This impression is enforced by the fact that those *undeutsche* regions are depicted in white, whereby its population seems not

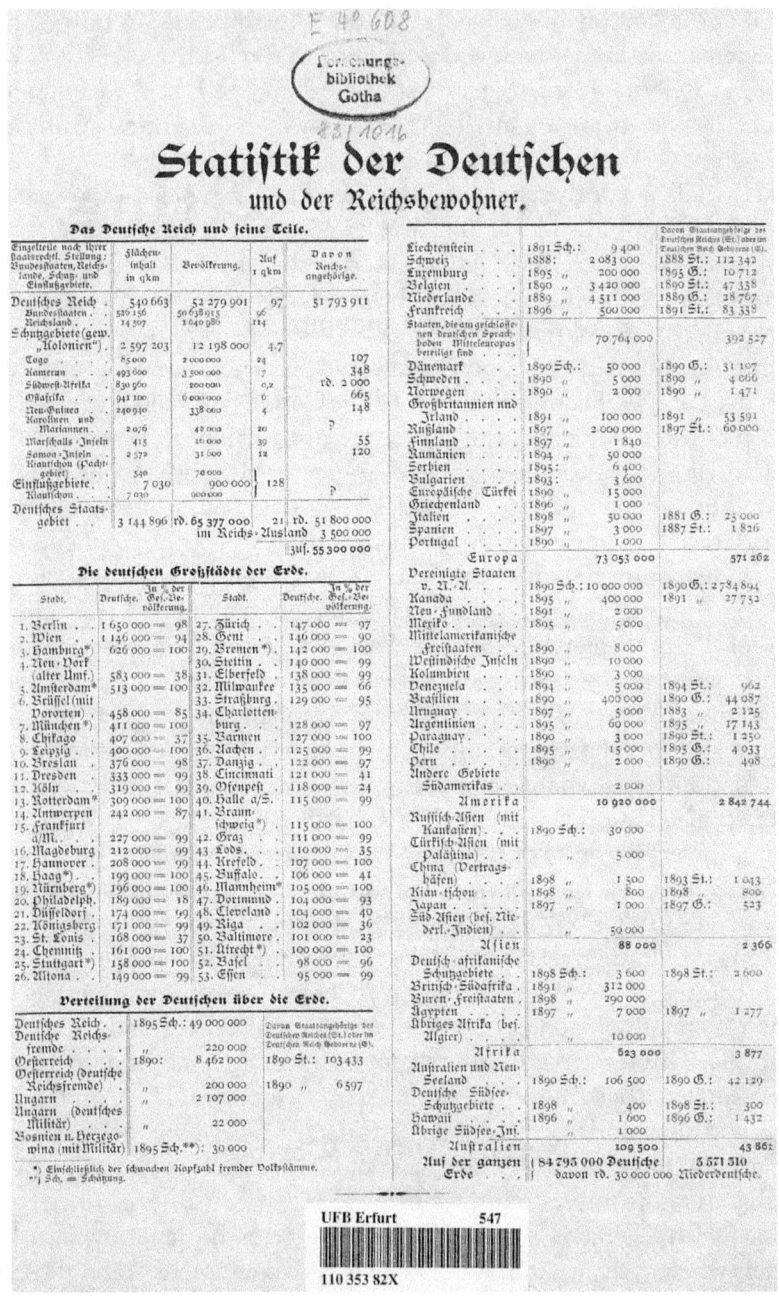

Figure 6.2 Statistics of 'The German Metropoles of the World' in *Alldeutscher Atlas, Justus Perthes Gotha*, 1900

only to be non-German but non-existent at all. Second, the map contains, in broad and strong strokes, different political borders of the German *Reich*. The political border of 1899 is contrasted with the ones of the sixteenth century during the reign of Emperor Karl V and the Linzer programme of 1882, a position paper of the far-right *deutschnational* ('German-nationalist') movement in Austria. By presenting these different borders, Langhans seeks to show that the contemporary border of 1899 does not overlap with territories populated by Germans. This, in turn, is something which is rather the case with the border as proposed in the Linzer programme. Third, while in the west with regard to France and in the north with regard to Denmark the political border of the *Reich* and the extent of the German population more or less overlap – something which could be read as the result of the two wars of 1864 and 1870/1871 – this is not the case with Central and Eastern Europe. The impression is created that these regions are in permanent turmoil as questions of nationality are not set (yet). Only active politics of population, it seems, could bring stability. Towards the east, the map plots a story of 'colonial islands of Germandom' in regions mainly dominated by Polish and Russian population. The eastern border region of Germany is, in terms of nationality, not presented as a linear line of demarcation but as a multi-ethnical frontier zone of struggles between the German and Polish population. It was in Langhans' maps that Central and Eastern Europe was first presented as a 'patchwork rug' (*Flickenteppich*) – a cartographical topos that would become popular during the first part of the twentieth century (Weger 2010, 245). Finally, if we move to the west, the Netherlands and Flemish parts of Belgium are presented as German.

In the remainder of this chapter, we discuss briefly two imaginaries of Germandom, which are tied to the discussion above. This helps us to underline how previously seperated spaces and populations are connected through the notion of Germandom, as well as the centrality of maps and statistics in these processes. First, we introduce the idea of *Mitteleuropa* as a new sphere of influence of a 'greater Germany' towards the east and, second, we reconstruct how the Boer population was categorised as German. As we will see, Langhans played an central role in both examples: not as the main author but in the background through his role as editor and cartographer at *Justus Perthes*.

The Space of *Mitteleuropa*

In the two popular conceptions of German expansionism at the turn of the twentieth century, *Weltpolitik* and *Lebensraum*, depictions of a 'greater German' sphere of influence extending towards Central and Eastern Europe found their way into the German public. One mode to frame this potential sphere

Figure 6.3 Auxiliary Map of 'The German Empire and Its Inhabitants Then and Now' in *Alldeutscher Atlas, Justus Perthes Gotha*, 1900

of influence was through the concept of *Mitteleuropa* ('Central Europe'). As with so many geopolitical imaginaries at that time, a plethora of articulations existed and the idea of *Mitteleuropa* could be mobilized for different projects – ranging from liberal to conservative and far-right circles – with different borders and novel ways of connecting territory, population and nation (for an overview see Schultz and Natter 2003). Within *völkisch* and other far-right circles *Mitteleuropa* was promoted in particular through the work of the German geographer Joseph Partsch (1904) and his monograph *Mitteleuropa: Die Länder und Völker von den Westalpen und dem Balkan bis an den Kanal und das Kurische Haff*. Already the subtitle demarcates this newly imagined political space clearly: ranging in the south from the Western Alps (Swiss territory) to the Balkan and in the north from the German-Danish border to the region around Klaipeda (in today's Lithuania) (Figure 6.4).

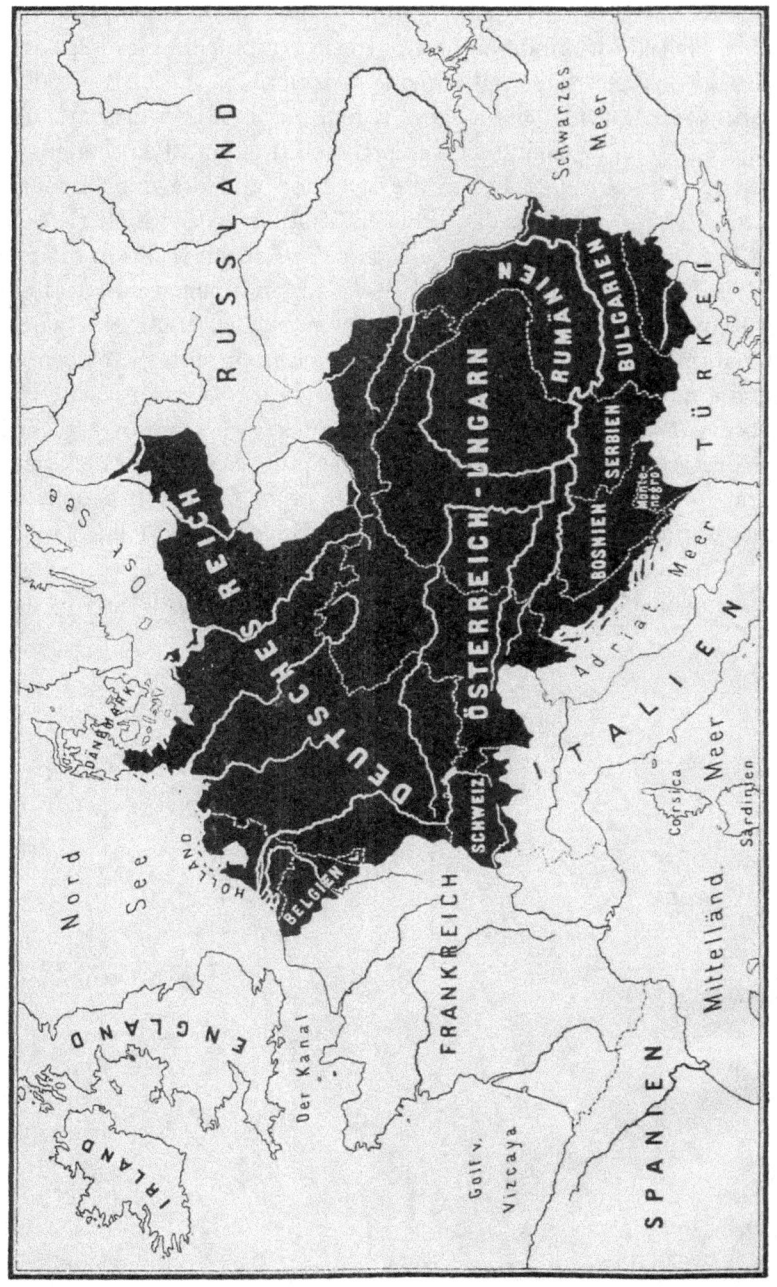

Figure 6.4 Map of 'Central Europe' from Joseph Partsch's *Mitteleuropa, Justus Perthes Gotha*, 1904

The idea of *Mitteleuropa* would become influential in geopolitical thinking. The book was first published in 1903 in English, commissioned and edited by Harold Mackinder as part of the geographical series *Regions of the World*, and one year later in German. The German version was published by *Justus Perthes*, with whom Partsch had published various monographs and journal articles earlier, as an enlarged edition, and Paul Langhans was the responsible cartographer for the selection and drawing of maps and diagrams. It were, in particular, these illustrations with which Partsch had hoped to augment the potential readership. As Partsch writes in the preface, these 'fine additions', that is, Langhans' maps and diagrams, would help to promote the book in the German 'patriotic public' (Partsch 1904, viii). The combination of the spatial imaginary of *Mitteleuropa* with the categorisation of its nationalities through statistics should link it to a larger *völkisch* notion of *Lebensraum*. As earlier in Langhans' *Alldeutscher Atlas*, categories of nationality are assembled in such a way that they exceed the official number of Germans: This time the historical notion of the Germanic peoples is used in order to include Dutch and Flemish populations as members of a 'greater German' nation. Thereby, new hegemonic claims are fostered as the Germanic people considerably outnumber all other nationalities of *Mitteleuropa*

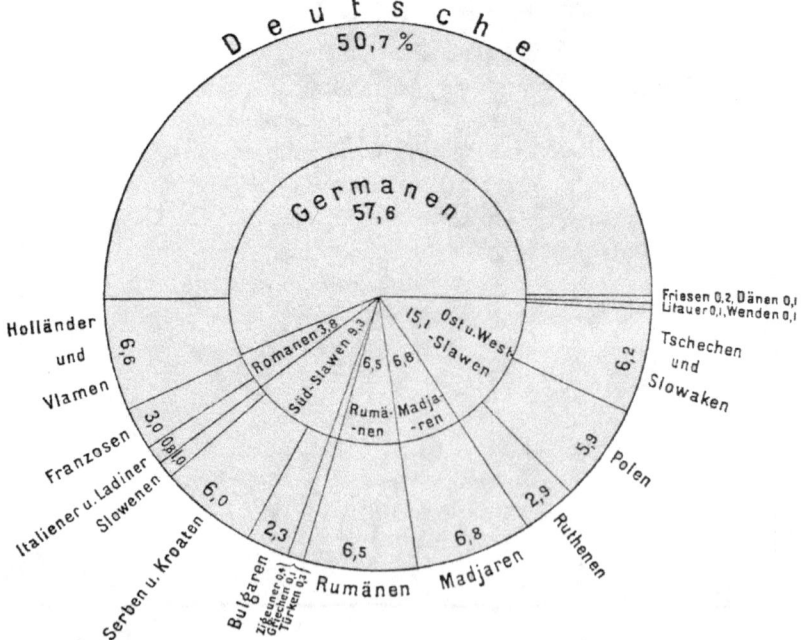

Figure 6.5 Statistical Graph on 'Nationalities of Central Europe' from Joseph Partsch's *Mitteleuropa, Justus Perthes Gotha*, 1904

(Figure 6.5). To include the Dutch and Flemish had, however, an additional connectivity effect, as it helped to 'make' the Boers German.

Making the Boers German

Langhans' project of Germandom culminated in the creation of the journal *Deutsche Erde* ('German Soil'). Langhans was able to establish this journal at *Justus Perthes* in 1902 and would operate as its editor-in-chief until its end in 1914. The journal quickly became one of the major organs for *völkisch* positions, raising its copies sold from 800 in 1902 to more than 75,000 in 1908. In particular, its maps, which were usually drawn by Langhans, enjoyed great popularity as over 100,000 of its maps were additionally sold to other organisations and publishing outlets (Hansen 2015, 116). Moreover, the journal was able to publish numerous articles written by main representatives of the *völkische Bewegung*. For example, Ernst Hasse, the long-time leader of the Pan-German League, contributed articles regularly; but also figures such as Joseph Partsch would publish here. The journal combined articles on the history of 'Germanic' peoples and travelogues of far-distant 'colonies' of Germandom with large sections on statistics and reviews of recent publications on Germandom. In addition, it included on a regular basis large, coloured maps mostly drawn by Langhans himself.

In order to further illustrate how novel spaces of governance were created through the notion of Germandom, we focus in the remainder of this section on how the Boers in South Africa were portrayed as German within several articles published by the *Deutsche Erde* during the Second Boers War (1899–1902). As we have seen, in both the *Alldeutscher Atlas* and in Partsch's *Mitteleuropa* the Netherlands as well as the Flemish parts of Belgium were depicted as German. Moreover, as the short episode at the outset of the chapter has indicated, large parts of the German public became sympathetic with the Boers population in southern Africa during the 1890s. While the German government (with the Kruger telegram as its high point) supported the Boers initially, it abandoned, after signing a secret agreement with Britain in 1898, any aspiration for South Africa and, consequently, refrained from any interference in favour of the Boers. Yet, the radical-right continued its support, in particular during the Second Boers War, as it considered the Boers of being of Germanic origin. It were these discussions, which were taken up in the *Deutsche Erde*. In two articles, published in 1902 and 1903, respectively, Max Robert Gerstenhauer, a member of both the Pan-German League and the German Colonial Association, attempted to present the Boers as members of Germandom. Gerstenhauer's line of argumentation is interesting as it presents, at least for Pan-German circles, an early attempt to move in the definition of nationality from language (or sometimes culture) to race. As Gerstenhauer (1903, 4) makes it explicit, one should recognise 'how infinitely important race, racial diversity, racial purity, racial mixture for the history of the world and for the fate of the individual people' is. To 'prove' this point, Gerstenhauer inquiries into the southern part of Africa, that is, the region encompassing German South-West Africa and the British Cape Colony. In line with *völkisch* ideology, Gerstenhauer distinguishes in a first step between citizenship and nationality, the latter understood as peopledom (*Volkstum*) (Gerstenhauer 1902; see also Hasse 1902). To rely on citizenship in counting people would be 'misleading and worthless' (Gerstenhauer 1902, 104). Instead, Gerstenhauer suggests that one should consider Germandom as consisting of two 'tribes' (*Stämme*), the 'high Germans' (*hochdeutsch*) in the central and southern part of Germany and the 'low Germans' (*niederdeutsch*) in the northern parts. By reconstructing the pedigree (*Stammbaum*) of the Boers, Gerstenhauer (1903, 7) argues that the Boers are 'by descent low Germans, as their race is of 50% Low German Dutch, of 27% Reichs-German, French of only 17%, and Coloured of less than 1%. Since the Dutch with regard to their race, meaning in their blood, do not differ from their low German neighbours in the Reich, one can say that the Boers are to 77%, i.e., to more than three quarters, of German descent.'

By arguing this, Gerstenhauer makes clear, on the one hand, that the German government should support the Boers in their war with the British government and, on the other hand, that the Boers should serve as an example for newly arrived settlers from the German *Reich*, as they did not 'mix up with coloured women' as this would 'degrade the reputation of the German race in the eyes of the black population' and endanger the fact that Germans become the 'Herrenvolk' due to their 'racial superiority' (Gerstenhauer 1902, 105). In this regard, Gerstenhauer (1903, 7) claims that the German government should produce accurate statistics and count the 'numerous half-breeds from marriages with coloured women'. This kind of knowledge, of course, would then facilitate politics of segregation in order to keep Germandom 'pure'.

Conclusion

By introducing the imagined community of Germandom, new forms of connectivity and novel spaces of governance were created. Such an understanding follows Sweeney's (2014, 268) observation of how the Pan-German ideology connects nation, empire and colony, namely by 'creating a greater

German empire via two interrelated means: an aggressive colonial policy overseas and the formation of a German-dominated sphere of influence in central and eastern Europe'. Maps and statistics are important technologies in this regard: They do not only depict political communities of the past or present, but they help to create new imaginaries about the future. As we have argued, maps and statistics are not neutral depictions of the world out there but should better be understood as sides for the creation of novel spaces of governance and the contestation between different political projects. In this regard, although the *völkisch* circles around Langhans make us believe that they 'know' what Germans are, where Germany is or what German history is, they were, in reality, aware about the uncertainty of what they categorise as German and where they situate Germany in time and space. They had to 'make up Germans'. These spaces, temporalities and subjectivities do not simply exist but were produced through maps and statistics. Although Langhans' imagined community of Germandom might have only existed in maps and statistics, these technologies are essential devices in the creation of future projects of German expansion.

The imaginations of the relationship between territory, state and population have been discussed through the imposition of spatial and temporal boundaries and the chapter problematised these boundaries by focusing on the way in which far-right circles imagined Germany at the turn of the twentieth century. It explored, through the example of Paul Langhans and the *Justus Perthes* publishing house, and different connectivities that were imagined in order to 'make up people'. Being German – or being a member of 'Germandom', as it was called in the *völkisch* movement – was not a fixed entity but rather something that was imagined through different ways of connecting the relationship between population and territory. The chapter has examined a specific way in which these connectivities worked in the case of Paul Langhans and how he imagined 'Germany'. These connectivities were discussed through spatial imaginations. The spatial connectivities that were imagined demonstrated a series of tensions/dynamics through which the different re-articulations of the relationship between population, territory and state occurred. For example, the familiar dichotomy between 'empire' and 'nation-state' as two different forms of political organisation collapsed. As we have shown, the *völkisch* circles imagined Germany as an 'imperial nation-state' operating on a logic of expansion, which is usually ascribed to empires, while demanding at the same time the idea of 'ethnic' homogeneity of its population as we know it from the nation-state. Yet, as we have seen introducing the imaginary of Germandom makes it possible to think both, empire and nation-state, as connected.

Bibliography

Ames, Eric, Marcia Klotz and Lora Wildenthal, eds. 2005. *Germany's Colonial Pasts*. Lincoln: University of Nebraska Press.

Anonymous. 1987. 'South-West Africa in Langhans' Colonial Atlas. (From a Correspondent)'. *The Geographical Journal* 9(1): 62–64.

Çapan, Zeynep Gülşah. 2017. 'Writing International Relations from the Invisible Side of the Abyssal Line'. *Review of International Studies* 43(4): 602–11.

Demhardt, Imre Josef. 2009. 'Paul Langhans und der Deutsche Kolonial-Atlas 1893–1897'. *Cartographica Helvetica* 40: 17–30.

———. 2015. 'Petermanns Geographische Mitteilungen'. In *The History of Cartography*, edited by Mark Monmonier, 6: 1095–99. Chicago, IL: University of Chicago Press.

Desrosières, Alain. 1993. *The Politics of Large Numbers: A History of Statistical Reasoning*. Cambridge, MA: Harvard University Press.

Eckert, Andreas. 2009. 'Germany and Africa in the Late Nineteenth and Twentieth Centuries: An Entangled History?' In *Comparative and Transnational History: Central European Approaches and New Perspectives*, edited by Heinz-Gerhard Haupt and Jürgen Kocka, 226–46. New York: Berghahn Books.

Fabian, Johannes. 2002. *Time and the Other: How Anthropology Makes Its Object*. New York: Columbia University Press.

Fernández, Marta, and Paulo Esteves. 2017. 'Silencing Colonialism: Foucault and the International'. In *Foucault and the Modern International: Silencing and Legacies for the Study of World Politics*, edited by Philippe Bonditti, Didier Bigo and Frédéric Gros, 137–53. New York: Palgrave Macmillan.

Fitzpatrick, Matthew P. 2008. *Liberal Imperialism in Germany: Expansionism and Nationalism, 1848–1884*. New York: Berghahn Books.

Gerstenhauer, Max Robert. 1902. 'Die drei südafrikanischen Nationalitäten in Deutsch-Südafrika'. *Deutsche Erde* 1(3): 102–5.

———. 1903. 'Entstehung des Niederdeutschen Volksstammes in Südafrika'. *Deutsche Erde* 2(1): 4–7.

Hacking, Ian. 1982. 'Biopower and the Avalanche of Printed Numbers'. *Humanities in Society* 5: 279–95.

———. 1986. 'Making Up People'. In *Reconstructing Individualism: Autonomy, Individuality, and the Self in Western Thought*, edited by Thomas C. Heller, Morton Sosna and David E. Wellbery, 222–36. Stanford, CA: Stanford University Press.

———. 1990. *The Taming of Chance*. Cambridge: Cambridge University Press.

———. 2002. *Historical Ontology*. Cambridge, MA: Harvard University Press.

Hall, Catherine. 2002. *Civilising Subjects: Colony and Metropole in the English Imagination, 1830–1867*. Chicago, IL: University of Chicago Press.

Hansen, Jason D. 2015. *Mapping the Germans: Statistical Science, Cartography, and the Visualization of the German Nation, 1848–1914*. Oxford: Oxford University Press.

Harley, J. B. 1988. 'Silences and Secrecy: The Hidden Agenda of Cartography in Early Modern Europe'. *Imago Mundi* 40(1): 57–76.

Hasse, Ernst. 1902. 'Die statistische Ermittlung der Deutschen'. *Deutsche Erde* 1(3): 65–68.
Kienemann, Christoph. 2018. *Der koloniale Blick gen Osten: Osteuropa im Diskurs des Deutschen Kaiserreiches von 1871*. Paderborn: Ferdinand Schöningh.
Kiepert, Richard. 1893. *Deutscher Kolonial-Atlas für den amtlichen Gebrauch in den Schutzgebieten*. Berlin: Dietrich Reimer.
Langhans, Paul. 1897. *Deutscher Kolonial-Atlas*. Gotha: Justus Perthes.
———. 1900. *Alldeutscher Atlas*. Gotha: Justus Perthes.
Lerp, Dörte. 2013. 'Farmers to the Frontier: Settler Colonialism in the Eastern Prussian Provinces and German Southwest Africa'. *Journal of Imperial and Commonwealth History* 41(4): 567–83.
Liulevicius, Vejas G. 2009. *The German Myth of the East: 1800 to the Present*. Oxford: Oxford University Press.
Meyer, Philip Julius. 2017. 'Paul Langhans'. In *Handbuch der völkischen Wissenschaften: Akteure, Netzwerke, Forschungsprogramme*, edited by Michael Fahlbusch, Ingo Haar and Alexander Pinwinkler, 2nd edition, 404–7. Oldenburg: de Gruyter.
Mitchell, Timothy. 2000. 'The Stage of Modernity'. In *Questions of Modernity*, edited by Timothy Mitchell, 1–34. Minneapolis: University of Minnesota Press.
Naranch, Bradley. 2005. 'Inventing the Auslandsdeutsche: Emigration, Colonial Fantasy, and German National Identity'. In *Germany's Colonial Pasts*, edited by Eric Ames, Marcia Klotz and Lora Wildenthal, 21–40. Lincoln: University of Nebraska Press.
Naranch, Bradley, and Geoff Eley. 2015. *German Colonialism in a Global Age*. Harrogate: Combined Academic.
O'Donnell, Krista, Renate Bridenthal and Nancy Ruth Reagin, eds. 2005. *The Heimat Abroad: The Boundaries of Germanness*. Ann Arbor: University of Michigan Press.
Partsch, Joseph. 1904. *Mitteleuropa: Die Länder und Völker von den Westalpen und dem Balkan bis an den Kanal und das Kurische Haff*. Gotha: Justus Perthes.
Penny, H. Glenn. 2017. 'Material Connections: German Schools, Things, and Soft Power in Argentina and Chile from the 1880s through the Interwar Period'. *Comparative Studies in Society and History* 59(3): 519–49.
Penny, H. Glenn, and Stefan Rinke. 2015. 'Germans Abroad: Respatializing Historical Narrative'. *Geschichte Und Gesellschaft* 41(2): 173–96.
Perraudin, Michael, and Jürgen Zimmerer, eds. 2011. *German Colonialism and National Identity*. New York: Routledge.
Pickles, John. 2004. *A History of Spaces: Cartographic Reason, Mapping, and the Geo-Coded World*. London: Routledge.
Pitts, Jennifer. 2005. *A Turn to Empire: The Rise of Imperial Liberalism in Britain and France*. Princeton, NJ: Princeton University Press.
Schultz, Hans-Dietrich, and Wolfgang Natter. 2003. 'Imagining *Mitteleuropa*: Conceptualisations of "Its" Space In and Outside German Geography'. *European Review of History: Revue Europeenne d'histoire* 10(2): 273–92.
Seligmann, Matthew S. 1998. *Rivalry in Southern Africa, 1893–99: The Transformation of German Colonial Policy*. Basingstoke: Macmillan.

Sheehan, James J. 1981. 'What Is German History? Reflections on the Role of the Nation in German History and Historiography'. *Journal of Modern History* 53(1): 2–23.

Smith, Woodruff D. 1986. *The Ideological Origins of Nazi Imperialism*. Oxford: Oxford University Press.

Stoler, Ann Laura. 2002. *Carnal Knowledge and Imperial Power: Race and the Intimate in Colonial Rule*. Berkeley: University of California Press.

Sweeney, Dennis. 2014. 'Pan-German Conceptions of Colonial Empire'. In *German Colonialism in a Global Age*, edited by Bradley Naranch and Geoff Eley. Durham, NC: Duke University Press.

Vaughan, Megan. 1991. *Curing Their Ills: Colonial Power and African Illness*. Cambridge: Polity Press.

Walther, Daniel Joseph. 2002. *Creating Germans Abroad: Cultural Policies and National Identity in Namibia*. Athens: Ohio University Press.

Weger, Tobias. 2010. 'Vom "Alldeutschen Atlas" Zu Den "Erzwungen Wegen." Der "Deutsche Osten" im Kartenbild, 1905–2008'. In *Osteuropa Kartiert – Mapping Eastern Europe*, edited by Jörn Happel and Christophe von Werdt, 241–64. Münster: LIT.

Winichakul, Thongchai. 1994. *Siam Mapped: A History of the Geo-Body of a Nation*. Honolulu: University of Hawaii Press.

Zantop, Susanne. 1997. *Colonial Fantasies: Conquest, Family, and Nations in Precolonial Germany, 1770–1870*. Durham, NC: Duke University Press.

CHAPTER SEVEN

~

Friedrich's 'Germany'

Landscape Painting as Imaginary and Experience of Connectivity

Benjamin Tallis

A single, mighty tree bisects the canvas, joining the earth to the sky which, although currently overcast, is lightening. Mountains resembling the Riesengebirge loom in the background to this pastoral valley scene and, if you look closely from your elevated vantage point in the foreground, you can see a shepherd and his sheep. Further back across the lush meadows, in the shadow of the mountains, are the gothic spires of a village from which comes just a wisp of smoke. Once you've seen the shepherd and the spires the tree seems to grow taller still but, despite its rich foliage, is it dead at its tip?

To look at a work by Caspar David Fredrich such as *The Solitary Tree*[1] (1822) is seemingly to gaze at the very archetype of a landscape painting – a beautiful, near symmetrical scene, far removed from controversy – harmless and secure in the artistic pantheon. However, should you sit long enough in the room devoted to Friedrich's work at the Alte Nationalegalerie in Berlin, you might overhear a conversation that goes something like this:

— Beautiful, aren't they? So tranquil, serene – I love the colours and the light.
— Oh sure, they're great – but you know the Nazis loved this stuff, right?

---

1 *The Solitary Tree*, Caspar David Friedrich (1822) – https://en.wikipedia.org/wiki/The_Lonely_Tree#/media/File:Caspar_David_Friedrich_-_Der_einsame_Baum_-_Google_Art_Project.jpg – VgEo9JDzFjfGGg at Google Cultural Institute, zoom level maximum, Public Domain, https://commons.wikimedia.org/w/index.php?curid=13291088.

— Oh really?
— Really. Think about 'blood and soil' – this is the soil.
— Of course – and listen, in the audio guide it says the tree symbolises Germany . . .

Even if you don't, but you do happen to develop a passing interest in Friedrich's work, you'll quickly find critics and historians, both academic and popular, who are keen to show you links between the artist's work and Nazism as well as German nationalism more widely (Koerner, 2009; Schama, 1996). Joseph Leo Koerner, a leading art historian goes as far as to claim that even the small Alder bushes that Friedrich paints, up close, in *Bushes in the Snow*[2] (1828) should be understood as 'fragments of your darkest history' (2009, 283).

In some ways, this is unsurprising as it has long been acknowledged of course that art and culture play a significant role in imagining communities, but the way they do so is more complex and nuanced than is often acknowledged (e.g., Sayer 2000; Shapiro 2004). The fact that Friedrich's art was lauded by the Nazis (and it most certainly was) doesn't necessarily make it Nazi or nationalist art. Indeed, the connections that some art critics and historians make between Friedrich's work and pernicious nationalism need to be problematised, as I do in this chapter.

Too often, such connections are based on instrumental 'readings' of artworks that take paintings as (barely) coded illustrations or emblematic images of the imagined community in question. This tends to minimise art's visual qualities and aesthetic modes of operation in favour of pseudo-textual readings that see the works as mimetic or iconographic representations – mere channels for the production of images as 'correlates of realities' determined elsewhere. Alternately, some scholars engage artworks in a nuanced way but then impose a historical determinism on it so that it seems as if what happened at that time and is represented or alluded to in the artworks must necessarily lead to what we (now) know came after.

These approaches, even in the (slight) caricature I present above, not only overlook the aesthetic qualities of art, they also obscure the often more complex cultural politics at work. In this chapter, I seek to draw out

---

2 *Bushes in the Snow*, Caspar David Friedrich (1828) – https://upload.wikimedia.org/wiki pedia/commons/e/e6/Caspar_David_Friedrich_-_Gebüsch_im_Schnee.jpg—1. Zeno.org, ID number 2000401877X2. akg-images, Public Domain, https://commons.wikimedia.org/w/index. php?curid=18265919.

this politics by looking more closely at the aesthetics of Friedrich's work and analysing the 'imaginary of connectivity' that it presents. I show that, through his revolutionary landscape paintings, Friedrich offers an imaginary of connectivity that not only posits a novel *space* of governance but also subjects – and a subjectivity – of governance. Friedrich imagines Germany as a territorially connected space but in a liberal-nationalist rather than a chauvinistically nationalist way. Moreover, the subjects he imagines are liberal subjects but they are communal, interconnected rather than atomistic ones. I first introduce Friedrich's work in the sociopolitical context of the time it was produced and briefly outline why his approach to landscape was considered so innovative. I then show how his art has often been reductively interpreted before offering an alternative reading by outlining the imaginary of connectivity he proposes. I do this first with regard to the connected space and then the connected subjects of governance he imagines. Finally, I conclude that this interpretation amounts to a 'Romanticisation' of Friedrich and of liberal Germany, which in keeping with the Romantic, liberal ideal, recovers (some of) their original meanings.

Friedrich, 'Germany' and the Revolution in Landscape Painting

At the time they were made, Friedrich's landscapes were seen, by some, as inspiring, revolutionary works, driving art forward and auguring a new way of being in the world. Others, including leading critics, castigated the artist for heresy and for poisoning art with the Romantic mysticism that was spreading through cultures and societies 'like a narcotic vapour' (Ramdohr, quoted in Koerner 2009, 67). Given this controversy and its importance, it is useful to briefly introduce the artist before analysing his imaginary of connectivity. In this section, I situate Friedrich's works in the context of the time and place in which they were produced, with particular regard to the revolution he initiated in landscape affairs.

Friedrich was born in 1774 in Greifswald on the Baltic coast, a city that had been under continuous Swedish rule since the Peace of Westphalia in 1648. During Friedrich's lifetime, the city – and its surrounding region – was transferred to the Kingdom of Prussia by the Congress of Vienna and, after the artist's death (in 1840), became part of the German empire established in 1871. Friedrich left Greifswald to study at the art academy in Copenhagen before moving in 1798 to Dresden – the capital of the Electorate (later Kingdom) of Saxony. It was in Dresden, the 'Florence on the Elbe' with its horde of artistic treasures, surrounding areas of outstanding natural beauty and lively cultural scene, that Friedrich lived for the rest of his life and produced the works for which he became known.

Friedrich's first years in Dresden were characterised by modest if growing renown, including success in a prestigious painting competition organised by Johan Wolfgang von Goethe. In late 1808, however, he sprang to notoriety in Dresden via a controversy which spread throughout the literary and artistic circles of the German-speaking world in the following year. It is perhaps difficult, at this historical remove, to imagine the intensity and stake of the so-called *Ramdohrstreit* that ensued when the Baron Friedrich von Ramdohr, a leading figure in the Dresden art scene, launched a vociferous assault on a painting shown over the Christmas holidays in Friedrich's studio. Ramdohr accused Friedrich's *Cross in the Mountains*[3] (1808) of breaking the 'rules' for landscape painting as well as of having and conveying ideas above its station: 'It is true presumption when landscape painting wants to slink into the church and creep on to the altars' (quoted in Koerner 2009, 58).

Timothy F. Mitchell (1987) emphasises the role that the gilded frame – carved to order and decorated with, *inter alia*, an all-seeing eye of god – played in this controversy as it gave the painting the appearance of a medieval 'retable' (framed) altarpiece. However, as Norbert Wolf (2015, 16–29) and, at length, Joseph Leo Koerner (2009, 56–137) show, the 'damage' was also done by the painting's substance and the very 'system' around which it was composed. To the contemporary eye, the small *Gipfelkreuz* (a 'peak cross', common in the German lands) atop a rocky outcrop, emerging from fir trees against a backdrop of sunbeams and a reddened morning sky may seem innocuous. However, it contravened almost all the conventions of landscape painting laid down by classical theories of art, of which Ramdohr was a leading and conservative exponent. The *Cross* was overtly allegorical and symbolic, endowing this landscape painting with the type of meaning that, in the academic classification, had been reserved for 'History Painting', yet it lacked any of the other characteristics of this genre.

This hierarchical classification of types of painting stemmed from renaissance ideas about the value or nobility of various artistic endeavours and had been institutionalised as universally valid principles by the art academies in the period of classicist dominance. For landscape painting, existing ideas and prejudices were turned into principles drawn from and valorised in, *inter*

---

3 *Cross in the Mountains*, Caspar David Friedrich (1808) – https://en.wikipedia.org/wiki/Cross_in_the_Mountains#/media/File:Friedrich_Tetschener_Altar_1808.jpg – Staatliche Kunstsammlungen Dresden, Public Domain, https://commons.wikimedia.org/w/index.php?curid=27506112.

alia, the work of Claude (Lorrain). In the early nineteenth century, History Painting (of historical or religious scenes, with an allegorical, moral message) still stood above 'Portraiture' (pictures of individuals or groups), 'Genre Painting' (everyday scenes), 'Landscape Painting' (primarily focused on the mimetic or pleasingly beautiful representation of a scenic view) and 'Still Life' (arrangements of domestic objects such as food or flowers). According to the classicist academic tradition, each category should follow certain rules, regarding form (on, e.g., perspective and 'smooth progression into space' for landscape [Koerner 2009, 59]) and content (e.g., a pleasing pastoral scene).

Friedrich's *Cross* systematically violates these dicta. In addition to political symbolism and religious allegory, its charge sheet runs as follows: The foreground is dark and the rocks obscure the horizon as well as whatever 'view' there might be, robbing the painting of depth; the sunbeams rise at a technically impossible angle given what we *can* see and illuminate the cross from below; moreover, it is entirely uncertain where the viewer 'stands' as various aspects of the composition render any single viewpoint either too high or too low for others (Koerner 2009, 59–62, 119). Thus as well as loudly proclaiming inappropriate meanings in inappropriate ways the painting, for Ramdohr, failed on its own terms – and he knew why: because it was infused with 'that mysticism that sells word games instead of concepts, builds principles upon far-fetched analogies, and everywhere seeks to merely *sense* what it should either know and recognize or else modestly be silent about' (quoted in Koerner 2009, 67).

That 'mysticism' was Romanticism, which was fast spreading through the German-speaking cultural world. It sparked heated debate in the influential and popular literary and artistic journals that had been founded on the values of enlightenment and universalist aesthetics and which, for the first time, came under sustained, subjectivist challenge (Koerner 2009, 64). Despite disputing its artistic value, both the critics and the proponents of Friedrich's *Cross* agreed that it had 'introduced something totally new into the history of art' (ibid., 77). It also prefigured 'Expressionism and other modern movements' in going beyond 'approaches to art dominated by a strongly mimetic position', as Roland Bleiker puts it (Bleiker 2009, 29). Significantly for this project, Bleiker argues that non-mimetic approaches bring in

> sensibility and imagination [. . . which . . .] can reorient our thoughts in a way that a mimetic process of recognition cannot. It is in this sense that a work of art can serve as an example of thought that generates productive flows between sensibility and reason, memory and imagination or, as Constantinou puts it, between 'mind, body and soul, thought, power and desire'. (ibid., 44)

The universalist-subjectivist debate would rage in various forms for the next two centuries, but the *Cross* signalled the beginning of the end for the hierarchy of genres as well as ushering in the 'end of iconography' (see next section and Koerner 2009, 172). This cultural upheaval matched the political turmoil of the time following Napoleon's defeat of Prussia, the dissolution of the Holy Roman Empire (HRE) and occupation or subjugation of various parts of the German lands (including Saxony) as well as the religious uncertainty created by the Lutheran revival. The sometimes-despairing introspection and quest for immediacy of meaning brought about by these changes are reflected in the art of the time. Friedrich's first acknowledged masterpiece, the *The Monk by the Sea*[4] (1810), showcases these themes and combines them with longer-standing Romantic concerns and expressions.

A near-abstract 'moodscape' (Wolf 2015, 8) shrouded in the fog of uncertainty, yet replete with the longing of the sublime sea and sky, the Monk is alone on the dunes; and we too are alone – not *with* him so much *as* him. Like the *Cross*, the *Monk* 'breaks with all traditions' (ibid., 33). Its abandonment of depth caused contemporary writers to emphasise its 'boundlessness' and 'apocalyptic featurelessness' (ibid.). The writer Heinrich von Kleist described the experience of seeing it as if 'one's eyelids had been removed' (ibid., 34). Yet, the *Monk* also appealed beyond the Romantic hard core: The painting was purchased, along with its 'pendant' (or companion) canvas, by King Friedrich Wilhelm III of Prussia and the artist was elected to the Berlin academy.

Friedrich's 'epochal invention of the emptied landscape' – neither moralising history painting nor mere pretty view – was matched by his innovative use of the *Rückenfigur*, the figure with their back turned to the viewer, of which the Monk by the sea is an early example (Koerner 2009, 145). Several paintings featuring such *Rückenfiguren* are linked to the Napoleonic subjugation of the German lands and the subsequent 'Liberation War' (e.g., *The Chasseur in the Forest*,[5] 1814) and others refer to resistance to the illiberal

---

4 *The Monk by the Sea*, Caspar David Friedrich (1810) – https://en.wikipedia.org/wiki/The_Monk_by_the_Sea#/media/File:Caspar_David_Friedrich_-_Der_Mönch_am_Meer_-_Google_Art_Project.jpg – KwEv_TMiJhn5kA at Google Cultural Institute, zoom level maximum, Public Domain, https://commons.wikimedia.org/w/index.php?curid=13266070.

5 *The Chasseur in the Forest*, Caspar David Friedrich (1814) – https://commons.wikimedia.org/wiki/File:Caspar_David_Friedrich_-_The_Chasseur_in_the_Forest_-_WGA8247.jpg#/media/File:Caspar_David_Friedrich_-_The_Chasseur_in_the_Forest_-_WGA8247.jpg – Web Gallery of Art: Image Info about artwork, Public Domain, https://commons.wikimedia.org/w/index.php?curid=15393852.

governance that followed the 1815 Congress of Vienna (*Two Men Contemplating the Moon*,[6] 1820). Despite the decline of Romanticism as a driving force in German culture and new trends towards historical and classicist revivals in landscape, Friedrich continued to paint what are now recognised as masterpieces well into the 1830s, albeit to decreasing contemporaneous acclaim.

By the time of his death in 1840, Friedrich had largely faded from public view to the extent that he worried about leaving his family in penury. The failure of the 1848 revolutions in the German lands and the rise of Prussia culminated in the founding of the Prussian-dominated German empire in 1871. In 1876, when a 'national gallery' for 'German art' opened in the now imperial capital of Berlin, the names of great icons of German art were prominently displayed on its exterior – without that of Caspar David Friedrich. There was later, however, a revival of interest in his work, signalled by the 1906 exhibition at the national gallery and which peaked in the febrile atmosphere of National Socialism's death cult of blood and soil (Koerner 2009, 78). Despite being repeatedly tarred with the brush of Nazism by critics, scholars and artists, the recuperation of the beauty of Friedrich's work and excavation of its myriad other meanings gathered pace in the last quarter of the twentieth century, particularly after the fall of the Berlin wall in 1989 and the German reunification in 1990.

Today, Friedrich's paintings are the pride of the Alte Nationalegalerie in Berlin, and he is recognised as an artistic revolutionary as well as the creator of some of the most beautiful and arresting images ever made. Nonetheless, as we will see in the next section, reductive political readings of his work still hold currency – and thus obscure the imaginaries of connectivity he envisioned as well as their political implications.

A 'German' Landscape: Imagining a Connected Germany – and Its Politics

They are plotting demagogic intrigues.

—Caspar David Friedrich, describing the figures
in *Two Men Contemplating the Moon* (1820)

---

6 *Two Men Contemplating the Moon*, Caspar David Friedrich (1820) – https://en.wikipedia.org/wiki/Two_Men_Contemplating_the_Moon#/media/File:Caspar_David_Friedrich_-_Two_Men_Contemplating_the_Moon_-_Google_Art_Project.jpg – Google Cultural Institute, Public Domain, https://commons.wikimedia.org/w/index.php?curid=21847087.

Caspar David Friedrich's revolutionary landscape paintings constitute an imaginary of German connectivity. They connect places and people across space and time to envision a 'German' space of governance. Yet, as noted above, when interpreting Friedrich's work politically it has thus been tempting for historians, art historians, artists and critics to make direct links between Friedrich's work and the rise of German nationalism. Many have also linked Friedrich's work to the pernicious kind of nationalist politics that seemed, in their telling, to chart a linear course from the liberation wars and the quest for Germany unity through Prussian militarism and the founding of the German empire to Nazi atrocities. Simon Schama and others have, however, tended to reach this conclusion through (quasi-)iconographic 'readings' of Friedrich's works but, as the analysis in the previous section showed, this is precisely how these works should not be interpreted. Koerner, on the other hand, provides a sophisticated and insightful engagement with Friedrich's aesthetics but then collapses it into a retrospectively applied and unsustainable historical determinism.

In this section, I show how popular and influential analyses of Friedrich's landscapes have often fallen into these traps. Not only do such readings elide Friedrich's art in all its beauty and nuance, they also obscure the ways in which Friedrich *does* offer an imaginary of German connectivity that also implies a novel space of governance. I therefore go on to show how Friedrich's paintings connect people and places through time and space and why this was important politically as well as artistically.

Reductive Readings of Friedrich's Landscapes and Politics

Andrew Graham Dixon's popular (2010) BBC television series, *The Art of Germany*, promises to take us, the viewers on a journey, through the story of German Art: 'from the radiant landscapes of Caspar David Friedrich to thrusting Prussian spires and the abyss of the third Reich'. The second episode (of three) begins with Graham Dixon continuing a theme from the first ('A Divided Land') (2010a) by emphasising the consequences of German weakness and vulnerability but, 'Dream and Machine' (Dixon 2010b) purports to show 'how artists were at the forefront of Germany's drive to become a single nation'. The second quarter of the hour-long show is largely devoted to Friedrich, beginning with the *Wanderer above the Sea of Fog*[7] (1818) and moving

---

7 *Wanderer above the Sea of Fog*, Caspar David Friedrich (1818) – https://en.wikipedia.org/wiki/Wanderer_above_the_Sea_of_Fog#/media/File:Caspar_David_Friedrich_-_Wanderer_above_the_sea_of_fog.jpg – the photographic reproduction was done by Cybershot800i. (Diff), Public Domain, https://commons.wikimedia.org/w/index.php?curid=1020146.

through the *Monk by the Sea* (1810), the *Abbey in the Oakwood*[8] (1810) and several other paintings including the *Ruins of Eldena in the Giant Mountains*[9] (1834). While noting that there are many possible interpretations, Graham Dixon sees in the *Wanderer* a 'rallying cry for incipient German nationalism' and, possibly, a 'celebration of the purification of the German lands'. Despite the odd choice of words, he refers here to the liberation from Napoleonic occupation, but this again shows the difficulties that some critics have in interpreting German art.

Looking at *On the Sailing Boat*[10] (1818), Graham Dixon, 'reads' the painting's elements, in his typically iconographic fashion, piecing together its meanings. Although he allows for some uncertainty or polysemicity in his decoding, he nonetheless wonders whether the city in the distance may in fact symbolise the dream of a new, united Germany to which the couple on the boat are being borne on the winds of hope – and history. Despite describing Friedrich's works as 'moving monuments to an age of anxiety', Graham Dixon claims that 'enshrined in Friedrich's sunnier pictures there was also a dream of nationhood'. After panning across several of Friedrich's landscapes, we then cut to a striking shot of Schinkel's iron victory column in Berlin, which, to a militaristic soundtrack, we are told symbolises Prussian military might – and determination to use it to forge a united Germany. Such combinations of iconographic analysis and sweeping association are not, however, limited to televised treatments for a general audience.

Simon Schama (1996), from whom Graham-Dixon occasionally borrows, lists in detail the nationalist elements of (some of) Friedrich's paintings. In the Chasseur in the Forest (1814), he notes 'the heavy load of patriotic symbols carried by the painting: the raven, perched on the felled fir stumps (signifying martyred soldiers), singing its song of death to the isolated French chasseur' (ibid., 106–7). Schama claims that 'Friedrich's composition was much more than a mechanical inventory of such inspirational emblems',

---

8 *The Abbey in the Oakwood*, Caspar David Friedrich (1810) – https://en.wikipedia.org/wiki/The_Abbey_in_the_Oakwood#/media/File:Caspar_David_Friedrich_-_Abtei_im_Eichwald_-_Google_Art_Project.jpg – UAEmmuxqtNUt-g at Google Cultural Institute, zoom level maximum, Public Domain, https://commons.wikimedia.org/w/index.php?curid=13265468.

9 *Ruins of Eldena in the Giant Mountains*, Caspar David Friedrich (1834) – https://commons.wikimedia.org/wiki/File:Klosterruine_Eldena_und_Riesengebirge_(C_D_Friedrich).jpg#/media/File:Klosterruine_Eldena_und_Riesengebirge_(C_D_Friedrich).jpg – Digitale Bibliothek MV, Public Domain, https://commons.wikimedia.org/w/index.php?curid=2695093.

10 *On the Sailing Boat*, Caspar David Friedrich (1818) – https://commons.wikimedia.org/wiki/File:Caspar_David_Friedrich_-_On_the_Sailing_Boat_-_WGA8255.jpg#/media/File:Caspar_David_Friedrich_-_On_the_Sailing_Boat_-_WGA8255.jpg – Web Gallery of Art: Image Info about artwork, Public Domain, https://commons.wikimedia.org/w/index.php?curid=15393861.

yet this is precisely how his account presents it, as does his reading of *Von Hutten's Grave*[11] (1823) (ibid., 120). Moreover, he ignores contemporaneous works by Friedrich, which do not have overtly patriotic or nationalist aspects.

Schama then explores one of Anselm Kiefer's 'Occupations', which sees the contemporary artist substitute himself, giving a Nazi salute, for Friedrich's Rückenfigur. Schama also showcases Kiefer's stinging parody of the Chasseur in the Forest and joins the artist in broadening this into a wider critique of the German forest myth and history of militaristic nationalism (1996, 120–34). Neil MacGregor (2014, 148) implicates the Romantics, including Friedrich, in the creation of the forest myth and notes that Friedrich also 'suffered from the admiration of the Nazis' (ibid.). As Joseph Koerner (2009, 78) writes, it was 'at this nadir of Western civilisation' that 'Friedrich's art is represented as having achieved its moment of greatest renown'.

It is clear that Friedrich incorporated symbols of the quest for German nationhood in his work. What is less clear – and certainly less clear than in analyses such as those of Graham Dixon or Schama – are the connections between these symbols, as well as the type of nationalism they symbolised, and the chauvinistic nationalism that begat the German empire and the horrors of National Socialism. These 'Nationhood-to-Nazism' arguments not only rely on a unilinear historical determinism, which would be questioned by genealogical approaches, but also on the elision of the multiple meanings – and ways of meaning – in Friedrich's work, despite often paying lip service to such polysemicity. The way such arguments are framed and contextualised also plays a role – such as cutting from Friedrich to Prussian militarism or jumping to Kiefer's tarring of Friedrich with the Nazi brush in his own, less reflexive phase as an artist. Moreover, the iconographic readings of the content of Friedrich's work that underpin such analyses take insufficient account of the artistic and aesthetic innovation in his painting – and obscures the nuanced nature of the artist's politics.

This is particularly vexing in Koerner's case as the first eleven chapters of his (2009) study guide the reader through Friedrich's revolutionary compositions, foregrounding his insistence on ambiguity and indeterminacy as well as his passionately historicist and subjectivist aesthetics. Indeed, the analysis I present in this chapter is indebted to Koerner's book, which is the most

---

11 *Von Hutten's Grave*, Caspar David Friedrich (1823) – https://commons.wikimedia.org/wiki/File:Caspar_David_Friedrich_-_Huttens_Grab.jpg#/media/File:Caspar_David_Friedrich_-_Huttens_Grab.jpg –Zeno.org, ID number 20004019156, Public Domain, https://commons.wikimedia.org/w/index.php?curid=8961708.

theoretically sophisticated and daring yet rigorous treatment of Friedrich's work to date. It is thus especially disappointing that the final chapter of his book builds to the conclusion that every detail of Friedrich's work is tarred with Nazism or its malign nationalist underpinnings: 'what you thought were just alders in the snow are fragments of your darkest history' (Koerner 2009, 283).

Moreover, interpretations of this kind impose a unitary historical determinism on the movements for German unity and statehood – which sought to politically and territorially forge the disconnected German lands into a coherent, contiguous space of government – as necessarily leading to empire and, ultimately, to genocide. Such narrow and totalising readings contradict Koerner's injunctions to the multiplicity of meanings in Friedrich's works – and those of other scholars (e.g., Vaughan 1972; Wolf 2015). They also ignore the numerous contingencies and alternate paths (even if they were not taken) on the road from the liberal nationalism of the first half of the nineteenth century to the Nazi abyss (see, e.g., MacMillan 2003 on the 1919–1933 period alone).

In the remainder of this section and in the next section, I focus on Friedrich's imaginary of connectivity through landscape. By doing so, I show that while he does indeed envision a Germany as a united space of governance, this was not necessarily the chauvinistically nationalist or totalitarian Germany that is presented in more reductive political interpretations of his work.

A Different Politics: 'German' Landscape as Imaginary of Connectivity

Friedrich's imagination of united Germany involved a high degree of spatial connectivity, bringing together many of the disaggregated and diversely ruled territories where the German language was spoken and which had been part of the HRE of the German Nation, which was dissolved in 1806. Koerner's approach (but not his conclusion) is instructive in discerning this connectivity in Friedrich's work, as he encourages and demonstrates the value of reading across and between different paintings, rather than limiting analysis to single paintings within Friedrich's oeuvre. Koerner also shows how the artist insisted on the particularity of the fragments from which he composed his landscapes. Thus, the places, which are symbiotically connected to their subjects (see next section) matter for the meanings which are evoked not only symbolically and allegorically but also compositionally and cumulatively across Friedrich's oeuvre.

Friedrich paintings feature fragments of landscapes from urban Saxony, particularly the cities of Dresden and Halle, as well as the Saxon countryside, particularly the Elbe valley and the mountains of the 'Saxon Switzerland' and Harzgebirge; North Bohemia and the Middle Bohemian mountains; Silesia and the Giant Mountains (Riesengebirge); Prussia, particularly the Baltic cities of Greifswald and Stralsund, coastal views and other aspects of the island of Rugen but also the city of Neubrandenburg; and also, although only once, the Watzmann – one of the highest peaks in the Bavarian alps. Some paintings, such as the views of named places (e.g., *Neubrandenburg*,[12] 1817) or the *Wanderer* (Saxon Switzerland) show these fragments in isolation while others, such as the *Sisters on the Balcony*[13] (1820) combine details from many different places. The viewer is thus called upon to organise and make sense of these fragments (a typical Romantic trope) across and within paintings and even to form a sensible whole from them that relates to their own existence and experience.

Friedrich thus painted over the political divisions of the German lands in his work, which connects Saxony to Prussia, including Baltic Pomerania and the Northern Hanseatic ports, but also to Silesia and Bohemia, encompassing what later became infamous as the Sudetenland. The Watzmann aside, Friedrich did not, however, tend to paint the Catholic areas of the German-speaking lands – Austria, the Rhineland or (what is now) Baden-Wurttemberg. Yet it is important to note that there was mutual sympathy between Friedrich and 'Rhineland romantics' such as Joseph von Goerres and Friedrich's work was also widely written about, discussed and considered relevant in these areas too (Koerner 2009, 65). In *Imagining the Nation in Nature*, a book focused on the Rhineland, Thomas Lekan goes as far as to label Friedrich himself a 'Rhine Romantic' (Lekan 2004, 9) and credits the nineteenth-century saturation of the landscape in Germany with symbolic meanings to Friedrich's art as much as to 'the poetry of Heinrich Heine, the philosophy of Gottfried Herder . . . and the music of Richard Wagner' (ibid.).

There were, however, also longer-standing connections at work in Friedrich's paintings, which he combined to considerable effect with newer

---

12 *Neubrandenburg*, Caspar David Friedrich (1817) – https://de.wikipedia.org/wiki/Neubrandenburg_(Gemälde)#/media/Datei:Caspar_David_Friedrich_036.jpg—Friedrich – The Yorck Project (2002) 10.000 Meisterwerke der Malerei (DVD-ROM), distributed by DIRECTMEDIA Publishing GmbH. ISBN: 3936122202., Public Domain, https://commons.wikimedia.org/w/index.php?curid=151083.

13 *Sisters on the Balcony* (1820) – https://commons.wikimedia.org/wiki/File:Caspar_David_Friedrich_-_The_Sisters_on_the_Balcony_-_WGA8258.jpg#/media/File:Caspar_David_Friedrich_-_The_Sisters_on_the_Balcony_-_WGA8258.jpg—1. Web Gallery of Art: Image Info about artwork2. arthermitage.org3. The Hermitage, St. Petersburg, Public Domain, https://commons.wikimedia.org/w/index.php?curid=15393864.

currents of German connectivity. The repeated use of gothic cathedrals and fragments of ruined gothic buildings, such as the abbey at Eldena (near Greifswald), bridged the sectarian divide. This harked back to the building of the Strasbourg and Cologne cathedrals, begun in the twelfth and thirteenth centuries, respectively, and thus before the reformation and the schism in the church. Moreover, thanks in part to Goethe who described Strasbourg cathedral as both a 'sublimely towering, wide-spreading tree of God' and as properly 'German architecture', the gothic had come to be seen as a particularly national style (Koerner 2009, 85–86, 100; Wolf 2015, 40). This national style was partly seen as such because it recalled the supposed (and supposedly lost) German golden age when, united in the HRE, the German lands had prospered and flourished culturally, despite also being frequently ravaged by war. This nostalgia was also apparent in Friedrich's stylistic echoing of the medieval artist Albrecht Durer, which was noted by Ramdohr. Koerner also sees a further submerged compositional echo of the religious art of the lost golden age in Fredrich's rigorous use of symmetry, which had not previously been a significant feature of landscape painting (ibid., 139, 277).

The Liberation wars had stirred feelings of patriotic unity as those who had fought alongside each other began to feel kinship beyond their own princedoms. The emergence of university societies, with names such as Teutonia and Germania, in place of the old 'Landmannschaften' that were exclusive to natives of particular provinces was accompanied by the adoption of so-called *altdeutsch* clothing. This was a style that consciously mimicked but updated the clothes of the urban bourgeoisie of the lost 'golden age' and the combination of the black velvet Biretta hat, long dark coat and wide collar shirt can be seen on several of Friedrich's *Rückenfiguren*. Most famously, he described the *Two Men Contemplating the Moon* (1820), who are dressed in *altdeutsch*, as 'plotting demagogic intrigues' (Wolf 2015, 58).

'Demagogue' was a specific term used in the hardline 'Karlsbad decrees' introduced in 1819 by Prince Metternich and referred to someone who 'espoused the ideal of a unified German state established by constitution and governed with the consent of its citizens' (Koerner, 2009: 279). The Karlsbad decrees marked the formalisation – and intensification – of the oppressive, anti-liberal governance that had been practised since the restoration of monarchic rule following the Congress of Vienna in 1815 (Rewald and Monrad 2001). Friedrich's use of and explicit avowal of these figures – advocates for German unity but also for liberal government – is thus significant. However, the artist's use of figures dressed in *altdeutsch* also signalled other forms of connectivity at work. In a number of works, such as *Moonrise Over the Sea*[14] (1822), they are situated in countryside or coastal settings, yet the figures are (by their dress) city dwellers. Friedrich pictures them finding wonder, fascination and sublimity in nature, which makes a connection between the urban and the rural: This is *their* landscape too and it can be as beautiful and meaningful as any exotic or antique scene (Dixon 2010b; Lekan, 2004). Here, participation is required on behalf of viewers, putting themselves in the place of the urbanites in the picture, feeling themselves as being in these landscapes, as enjoying them or even feeling that they too belong there, albeit for temporary leisure.

In forging this imaginary, Friedrich revived and adapted the tradition of the 'world-landscape' which, prior to the dominance of the classical hierarchy of genres, was a type of painting that brought together disparate elements to make an imaginary, 'ideal' landscape. Thought to have been initiated by the Netherlandish painter Joachim Patinir in the fifteenth century, Pieter Bruegel and Albrecht Altdorfer are among its more famous exponents (e.g., Gibson 1989). Rather than a world landscape however, Friedrich specifically creates a 'German landscape' and he does so across his oeuvre rather than in a single painting. This not only prevents the incontestable ascription of single, dominant meanings to his individual works (as they also depend on other works) but also requires the participation of the viewer in linking them together – jumping or bridging gaps between the frames. As the next section shows, participation and relationality are other crucial aspects of Friedrich's imaginary of connectivity. Friedrich's creation of this 'German landscape', allied to participation of the viewing subject also has considerable political significance for the type of rule that was imagined in this Germany as a space of governance. Rather than the oppressive and chauvinistic governance imposed through the type of nationalism that the iconographic readings of Friedrich's works imply, it was more likely a romantically form of liberal nationalism.

Envisioned Community: Imagining and Experiencing German Connectivity

A picture must not be invented but felt.

—Caspar David Friedrich

---

14 *Moonrise Over the Sea*, Caspar David Friedrich (1822) – https://en.wikipedia.org/wiki/Moonrise_by_the_Sea#/media/File:Caspar_David_Friedrich_-_Mondaufgang_am_Meer_-_Google_Art_Project.jpg – mwFGGdzKbfGMkg at Google Cultural Institute, zoom level maximum, Public Domain, https://commons.wikimedia.org/w/index.php?curid=13290421.

To understand how Friedrich's landscapes work as imaginaries of German connectivity and how they augur a new space of governance, it is essential to understand their symbiotic relation with the subjects of those landscapes. John Wylie (2007, 3) notes the phenomenologist Maurice Merleau-Ponty's observations that self and landscape also seem intertwined in the paintings of Paul Cezanne from the late nineteenth century. Significantly for this chapter Merleau-Ponty argues that this 'enlaced' relation 'precedes and preconditions rationality' (ibid.). Engaging Friedrich's works through the 'lived and embodied experience' of subjectivity in landscape thus adds a further, extra-rational dimension to the current analysis (ibid.). This resonates not only with the subjective aesthetics of Romanticism but also with Kantian understandings of the sublime, which is seen to reside in the subject's reactions (to, e.g., landscape – or landscape painting) rather than in any objective quality of these 'things' in 'themselves' (Koerner 2009, 212). This section now looks how Friedrich produces a particular, individual romantic-modern subjectivity (which I see as a subjectivity of liberal governance) through the connections he imagines between people and landscape but also between people and their selves.

Friedrich's interest in and political commitment to the emancipation of individuals from monarchic rule as well as from oppressive occupying forces is well documented – as in his comment, noted above, to the artists Foerster and Cornelius that the Moonwatchers were 'plotting demagogic intrigues' as well as in his written statement that 'as long as we remain serfs to Princes nothing great will ever happen. Where the people have no voice, they are not allowed to have any sense of themselves' (Wolf 2015, 45). Politically, this commitment was manifest in the artist's support for a unified, self-determining German state that would be constitutionally established. The desire to be rid of the French occupying forces can be clearly seen in paintings such as the Chasseur in the Forest. However, beyond explicit allegorical and symbolic elements in his paintings, Friedrich advances a highly particular and, at the time, groundbreaking aesthetics of subjectivity across his oeuvre. As Neil MacGregor put it in his recent (and influential) *Germany: Memories of a Nation*, Friedrich 'used landscape as an external vision of being German' and 'spent his life painting wild, sublime landscapes in which the individual discovers his potential and the nation does the same' (MacGregor 2014, 121). Despite finding particular expression in the German context, Friedrich's imaginary of connectivity between person and landscape, between subject and self, is more universal with regard to experience of nature, culture, individual and society.

In the introductory chapter, Lobo-Guerrero et al. emphasise that 'connectivity is not "aprioristic" – what makes it possible is an *experience* of connecting' (emphasis added). This foregrounding of experience resonates with the aesthetics of the Romantics, who sought specifically to create *erlebniskunst* – experience art or the art of experience. As I showed earlier, the Romantics and especially Friedrich challenged the rule-bound hierarchies for the 'proper' form, substance and content of particular types of painting, including landscape painting. Significantly, Romantic art also moved away from overly 'literary' art where only those with the correct training and erudition could 'read' paintings in order to understand their meaning correctly. Instead, in search of 'immediacy' they focused on the visual and aesthetic, rather than 'textual' or literary facets of art, in order to evoke *feelings* rather than just thoughts – and to make the viewing of art an experience as well as to better represent experience itself. The ways in which Friedrich sought to make the viewing of art an experience – by interpellating the particular individual looking at the work and in seeking to provoke or enlist their participation in meaning-making – are outlined below.

Particularity and Participation

Friedrich's landscape paintings are good examples of how the Romantic movement introduced new ways of both representing and provoking experience, which was entangled with specific understandings of subjectivity. In this section, I look at experience with regard to *particularity* (of both people and nature) and *participation* or the *relationality* between painting and person as well as between person and landscape. Particularity and relationality play significant roles in Friedrich's production of a specific yet potentially universal subjectivity, grounded in experience, and which implies an imaginary of connectivity: The participation of individuals connects their particular singularities through and to the various elements of the 'common' landscape outlined in the previous section.

Taking particularity first, it is important to note that despite the symbolic and allegorical qualities noted above, the elements of Friedrich's landscapes are never generic. It is, for example, never just any old oak tree or any mountain or valley that he painted but, rather, *particular* oak trees, mountains, valleys, rivers, streams and people. In his book-length study of the topic, Joseph Leo Koerner argues that (together with other innovations in his painting) this specificity thus produces a particular 'subject of landscape' (2009). Koerner builds out from a close viewing of some of Friedrich's smaller canvases – a thicket of alder branches and a grove of fir trees – all the way to Friedrich's most sweeping canvasses. He shows convincingly how this particularity fixes YOU, the viewer of the painting as a particular individual, by situating you in front of a particular fragment of nature that can be no other – and nor can you. This interpellation of the viewer entangles us in a relationship with the painting, which dramatises the landscape and its multiple meanings but which also depends on our involvement as an engaged, feeling subject. Koerner situates this within Romanticism's historical project to 'activate us as individuals' (2009, 28).

As Koerner (2009) and Norbert Wolf (2015) note, such subjective activation was a reaction against atomistic rationalism and aimed instead to provoke 'authentic emotion' in the viewer. This was part of a wider quest to provoke deep, reflexively felt connections between people and nature as well as between people and themselves, creating a relational aesthetic, which also charges the viewer with a 'duty' (Koerner 2009, 33) to supplement the work with their own input, their own meanings. As Jacques Derrida (Derrida 1998, 141–52) famously noted, the supplement can often overwhelm the character of the supplemented. And so it is with Friedrich's paintings, as the particular viewer is required not only to participate and interpret but also to organise and make sense of the particular fragments from which the artist has composed the landscape. As noted above, this can be within a single painting but also between and across different paintings. Moreover, the provocation of overwhelming, multiple and contestable meanings, to be reflected on by individuals but also discussed among them, is very much the goal – as Heinrich von Kleist and his co-authors already noted in their review of the *Monk by the Sea* in 1810.

As Koerner shows, Friedrich's approach is in keeping with the Romantic principle of *Eigentümlichkeit*, which in this case implies that 'truth' is the 'property of the unique, particular, experiencing and radically autonomous Self' (2009, 69). The philosopher and theologian Friedrich Schleiermacher was influential for the Romantics – including Friedrich – and tried to reconcile the enlightenment with Protestant spirituality, arguing that 'every man must represent humanity in his own way' and 'create his own picture of the world'. Indeed, Friedrich himself wrote that 'the spirit of nature reveals itself differently to each individual' (Koerner 2009, 70). The artist achieves this effect through the combination of particularity and participation with which he interpellates the viewer to create an *experience* of connection as well as the ways he interrelates the viewer with nature and with her or his own self, through the experience of connecting with the painting.

Envisioned Community: 'Between You and the Painting'

Yet, with Friedrich there is connectivity at work as well as the individuation described above. There is a commonality that is provoked between viewers as they relate to the painting but also in the relation that is advanced between person and landscape and person and self. This creates a potential community of people with similar subjectivities – autonomous yet interrelated individuals situated in landscape, which is itself a particular imaginary of spatial and temporal connectivity between them. Moreover, the importance of stirring feelings and emotional connections in the viewer, as opposed to merely fulfilling learned, rational, ahistorical criteria (as Ramdohr would advocate), leads Koerner to argue that Friedrich, as a Romantic, 'democratizes' aesthetics (2009, 73). For Koerner, Friedrich 'aspires to make meaning appear not as the artist's constructed invention but the outcome of the individual viewer's own ordering and interpretive labour' (2009, 102). This interpretive labour, through feeling as well as thinking, also distinguishes Koerner's analysis from that of, for example, Schama or others who simply list the signs to be read or decoded by the viewer.

Friedrich's ways of achieving this participatory, emotional connection encompassed a number of formal innovations including the use of unusual, partial and multiple perspectives within one picture, causing the viewer to continually try and retry to situate themselves; disconnected foregrounds and backgrounds with any way between them blocked or obscured, leading the viewer to pause and question rather than simply flow affably through the scene. Another of Friedrich's ways is the use of haze and fog which, as Koerner and Kant note, offers a reflexive way into the sublime which lurks within the viewer and their reactions to nature, but which also leads again to questioning and uncertainty. This sublime fogginess often contrasts, however, with another of Friedrich's innovations – the radiant illumination he achieves through new uses of glaze, often for moonlight, and which along with a mastery of colour and composition is one of the many ways in which Friedrich uses beauty (but not easy, inoffensive beauty) to draw the particular viewer into engaging with the work. Friedrich also frequently set his paintings in twilight, whether dawn or dusk (and sometimes it's hard to tell), which plays on uncertainty but also on temporality and cyclical rhythms of nature that go beyond human life and to which people must adapt but which they also seek to harness or control, even if they will be outlasted by them; similarly, this notion of smallness, yet boundless possibility (another trope of the sublime), is clear in Friedrich's use of infinite horizontals, including unbroken horizons (reaching both sides of the canvas), and in the inclusion of one (or more) *Rückenfigur(en)* – the figures used so often by Friedrich with their backs turned to the viewer, putting us viewers in their place, *in the landscape*.

The effect was electric. If the *Cross in the Mountains* scandalised conservative critics like Ramdohr who recognised the scale of the challenge to his world, *The Monk by the Sea* (1810) reached a far wider audience with similar impact. It was recognised as a masterpiece from its first showing at the Berlin Academy, after which it was purchased by the King of Prussia. In addition to his earlier-noted comment that the experience of seeing the painting was as if 'one's eyelids had been removed', Heinrich von Kleist, then editing the *Berliner Abendblatter*, emphasised the relationality that is such a key aspect of Friedrich's art: 'What one expects to happen within the painting, happens between you and the painting' (quoted in Koerner, 2009, 247).

The stark, infinite yearning of this near-abstract canvas, in which the solitary figure is the only vertical, expresses much of what made Friedrich's art so revolutionary – and so affecting (e.g., Dixon, 2010b). Kleist, together with leading Romantics Clemens Brentano and Ludwig Achim von Arnim, presented a cacophony of reactions to the piece, many of the speakers of which put themselves in the place of the Monk despite his back-turned unknowability. It is this diversity, the provocation of such transversal discourse, that signals the paintings' dual effect of individuation and connectivity – Romanticism's double-edged sword of 'fragmentation' and 'community creating' as Hans-Georg Gadamer put it (cited in Koerner 2009, 157).

Over time, however, Friedrich's use of the *Rückenfigur* evolved, and these figures who gaze *into* his own canvasses tended to take on both literally and metaphorically bigger roles. The most iconic of his *Rückenfiguren* features is the *Wanderer above the Sea of Fog* (1818), which Andrew Graham Dixon has called 'the most famous German painting of the entire Nineteenth Century' (2010b). In the *Wanderer* and the *Woman before the Setting Sun*[15] (1818), the *Rückenfigur* acts as a 'reflective foil of both the artist and the viewer' (Koerner 2009, 194). This not only dramatises the experience that inspired the painting and the relational gaze between the viewer and the painting but also (and again drawing on Merleau-Ponty) the double nature of the act of seeing – *to see is also to be seen* – and the *Rückenfigur* is an explicit reminder of this (ibid., 277). Friedrich achieves a similar effect in *Evening Star*[16] (1835) by showing his family walking home across fields at dusk.

Koerner argues that this relational gaze (a spur to participation by the viewer) is another key aspect of Friedrich's conception of landscape and is also palpable in paintings without *Rückenfiguren* such as *The Solitary Tree*

---

15 *Woman before the Setting Sun*, Caspar David Friedrich (1820) – https://commons.wikimedia.org/wiki/File:Caspar_David_Friedrich_-_Woman_before_the_Rising_Sun_(Woman_before_the_Setting_Sun)_-_WGA08253.jpg#/media/File:Caspar_David_Friedrich_-_Woman_before_the_Rising_Sun_(Woman_before_the_Setting_Sun)_-_WGA08253.jpg – Web Gallery of Art: Image Info about artwork, Public Domain, https://commons.wikimedia.org/w/index.php?curid=15453489.

16 *Evening Star*, Caspar David Friedrich (1835) – https://commons.wikimedia.org/wiki/File:Caspar_David_Friedrich_-_Der_Abendstern_(ca.1830).jpg#/media/File:Caspar_David_Friedrich_-_Der_Abendstern_(ca.1830).jpg – akg-images, Public Domain, https://commons.wikimedia.org/w/index.php?curid=35127634.

(1822) and *The Great Enclosure*[17] (1832), both of which draw the viewer in and precariously emplace us *in the landscape*. Koerner argues compellingly that it is the relational gaze that produces the dual vision of the encounter between (I) subject and world and (II) subject and self (ibid., although this is really the 'subject' of the whole book). He also notes the appropriateness in this regard of the double meaning of the term 'vision' as both the faculty of sight and that which is seen or, indeed, foreseen (ibid.). I would go further and say this multiple, relational duality (seeing and being seen, subject-world and subject-self, vision as both sight *and* what is seen) is how Friedrich's art produces an *envisioned community* of connected subjects: subjects who are connected in similar ways to landscape as well as to themselves and thus, potentially, to each other.

In his revolutionary landscape paintings, Caspar David Friedrich offers us an imaginary of connectivity that implies not only a space of governance but also subjects of governance. The subjectivity that is inherent to his landscapes envisions us as reflexive and highly agential individuals, yet also as communal and intersubjective rather than atomised or discrete. In this imaginary we are thus connected, through landscape, to nature but also to our Selves and to each other. This vision is very much in keeping with Friedrich's liberal nationalist politics as well as his Romantic aesthetics – mediated through newly and thoroughly relational representation of the experience of being in the world.

Conclusion: Romanticising Friedrich, Romanticising 'Germany'

The world must become romanticized. That way one finds again the original meaning.

—Novalis, 'Preliminary Studies' (Vorarbeiten), 1798 (Koerner 2009, 7)

This chapter has shown how the landscape paintings of Caspar David Friedrich constitute an imaginary of 'German' connectivity. Friedrich's

---

17 *The Great Enclosure*, Caspar David Friedrich (1832) – https://commons.wikimedia.org/wiki/File:Caspar_David_Friedrich_007.jpg#/media/File:Caspar_David_Friedrich_007.jpg – The Yorck Project (2002) 10.000 Meisterwerke der Malerei (DVD-ROM), distributed by DIRECTMEDIA Publishing GmbH. ISBN: 3936122202., Public Domain, https://commons.wikimedia.org/w/index.php?curid=151055.

revolutionary approach brought about a sea change in landscape painting, both reflecting and generating cultural and social currents at a particular historical moment, to suggest how disconnected German territories could be connected as a space of governance. This space of governance arises from an imaginary of connectivity that not only links territories to each other but also connects people to this common territory through shared histories and also through common contemporary experience. Moreover, Friedrich's landscapes imagine new connections between individuals and their 'Selves', envisioning a newly reflexive, autonomous and individual, yet also communal subjectivity that combines nature and culture. This imaginary of connectivity encompasses the emplacement of body in landscape and the embodiment of self as well as individual strivings for personal and spiritual as well as political and social meaning.

Friedrich, like other Romantics, questioned – and provided new answers to – some of the more problematic elements of 'enlightened' views of people and the way they can be governed (in the broadest sense) as well as of relations between culture and nature. They provided new ways and means of understanding and achieving the (often-connected) projects of collective and individual self-determination. Moreover, this 'filling out' (or filling in) of the outlines of the modern state suggested at Augsburg and Westphalia was supplemented by a new imaginary of the connection of people and government to territory (Mukerji 1997) – via the elevation of territory to 'nationally significant landscape' (e.g., Lekan 2004; Shapiro 2004; Wylie 2007). This landscape governance helped cement the role of the state as the sole source of authority on a territory – or posited the idea that this was an ideal state of affairs. By corollary, it saw the nation, imbued with a particular and special connection to that land as the ideal collective subject to inhabit it and be governed through it (see also, Mukerji 1997 on the making of the French territorial nation-state). How it should be governed, however, remained an open question as did the kind of individual and collective subjectivity beyond nationality.

This imaginary of connectivity and the related space of government it implies holds the possibility – but not the certainty – of oppressive, exclusive and chauvinistic nationalism. It is important to note, in this light, that several of those who are linked to Friedrich's work espoused odiously chauvinistic views. Ernst Moritz Arndt, whose name appears on the humanist Ulrich *von Hutten's Grave* in Friedrich's painting of the same name, designed and popularised the *altdeutsch* costume and gained initial acclaim for advocating a linguistic-based German nationalism (e.g., Evans 2017, 75–76). Friedrich may have shared this linguistic view of the nation, given his aforementioned bridging of sectarian divides and similar honouring of the reforming Hanoverian/Prussian General Scharnhorst and the Catholic 'Rhineland Romantic' Joseph von Goerres in the same painting (Koerner 2009; Lekan 2004). Arndt, however, was also notorious as an anti-Semite, and he inspired the ceremonial burning of anti-German texts in Wartburg in 1817, which is often seen as a fore-echo of the repugnant practices of National Socialism (Evans 2017, 75–76; Koerner 2009). There is, however, no suggestion that Friedrich himself held anti-Semitic views nor that he was chauvinistically nationalist.

Turning the Romantics' gaze back on themselves, the 'night side' of nationalism, is nonetheless an issue which anyone engaging with Friedrich has to contend – and seriously reflect upon. Yet, if (as above) we reject the unilinear historical determinism that sees a straight and necessary path from nineteenth-century German liberal nationalism, through militaristic Prussia and the German empire to Nazi atrocities and, moreover, if we look at Friedrich's imaginary of connectivity, then a different and more progressive politics emerges. Where Friedrich can be faulted with regard to nationalism it is regarding nationalism in general rather than German nationalism in particular, nor the especially pernicious form German nationalism would later take. Where Friedrich's nationalism is particularly German, it is the nationalism of the liberation struggle and the liberal-nationalist politics that were common in the nineteenth century. Friedrich's imaginary of German connectivity that unites territories, but also connects individuals to their own subjectivity and agency, neither prefigures nor promotes authoritarian or imperial nationalism and rather opens plural and potentially progressive possibilities for governance (and subjectivity).

Most obviously, Friedrich's imaginary resembles the liberal subjectivity and governance that was pioneered in the nineteenth century and which has been realised (to a significant degree) in a united Germany after 1989. The emphasis on the feeling, experiencing subject in the landscape, with the agency to affect individual as well as collective destiny could even, at only a slight stretch, also be interpreted as suggesting a performative and thus potentially inclusive mode of being. Limiting Friedrich's paintings and, indeed, his innovative imaginary, by imposing particular (oppressive) political views on them, overlook the sublime artistry and revolutionary aesthetics of his work as well as his cultural, social and political intent, not to mention his expressed faith in the individual and hope in the collective as well as the constitution. Looking at connectivity, rather than relying on instrumental, emblematic or quasi-iconographic 'readings' of Fredrich's work, also mitigates against the imposition of a reductive politics. However, such reductive politics has also simply been retrospectively applied from later vantage points, dominated by the memory of the holocaust. The political intent in such cases (Koerner, Kiefer) is undoubtedly good, but these interpretations do not stand up to sustained analysis of Friedrich's work and his imaginary of connectivity, as I have shown in this chapter.

Koerner repeatedly quotes Novalis on the need to 'Romanticise the world' in order that its original meaning may be recovered. This piece has attempted to do something similar for Friedrich's own work with regard to its political context and significance. It also attempts to recover the polysemicity and nuance that characterises Koerner's otherwise inspiring and perceptive study of Friedrich but which at the end of his book succumbs to his singular view of Friedrich through the prism of the holocaust. By contrast, the present chapter 'Romanticises' Friedrich's connected, Liberal Germany, which died in 1848 only to be reborn in 1989. In so doing, it shows the importance of landscape, through experience and feeling as well as rational thought, to the creation of spaces and subjects of governance, through the notion of an *envisioned community*.

Bibliography

Bleiker, Roland. 2009. *Aesthetics and World Politics*. Basingstoke: Palgrave Macmillan. http://public.eblib.com/choice/publicfullrecord.aspx?p=555449.

Derrida, Jacques. 1998. *Of Grammatology*. Corrected ed. Baltimore, MD: Johns Hopkins University Press.

Evans, Richard J. 2017. *The Pursuit of Power: Europe 1815–1914*. The Penguin History of Europe. London: Penguin.

Gibson, Walter S. 1989. *Mirror of the Earth: The World Landscape in Sixteenth-Century Flemish Painting*. Princeton, NJ: Princeton University Press.

Graham Dixon, Andrew. 2010a. 'Art of Germany'. *A Divided Land*. BBC.

———. 2010b. 'Art of Germany'. *Dream and Machine*. BBC.

Koerner, Joseph Leo. 2009. *Caspar David Friedrich: And the Subject of Landscape*. London: Reaktion Books.

Lekan, Thomas M. 2004. *Imagining the Nation in Nature: Landscape Preservation and German Identity, 1885–1945*. Cambridge, MA: Harvard University Press.

MacGregor, Neil. 2014. *Germany: Memories of a Nation*. London: Allen Lane.

MacMillan, Margaret. 2003. *Peacemakers: The Paris Peace Conference of 1919 and Its Attempt to End War*. London: Murray.

Mitchell, Timothy, F. 1987. 'What Mad Pride! Tradition and Innovation in the Ramdohrstreit'. *Art History* 10(3): 315–27.

Mukerji, Chandra. 1997. *Territorial Ambitions and the Gardens of Versailles*. Cambridge Cultural Social Studies. Cambridge: Cambridge University Press.

Rewald, Sabine, and Kasper Monrad. 2001. *Caspar David Friedrich: Moonwatchers*. New York; New Haven, CT: Metropolitan Museum of Art; Yale University Press.

Sayer, Derek. 2000. *The Coasts of Bohemia: A Czech History*. Princeton, NJ: Princeton University Press.
Schama, Simon. 1996. *Landscape and Memory*. 1. Vintage Books ed. New York: Vintage Books.
Shapiro, Michael J. 2004. *Methods and Nations: Cultural Governance and the Indigenous Subject*. New York: Routledge.
Vaughan, William, ed. 1972. *Caspar David Friedrich: 1774–1840; Romantic Landscape Painting in Dresden*. London: Tate.
Wolf, Norbert. 2015. *Caspar David Friedrich 1774–1840: The Painter of Stillness*. Cologne, Germany: Taschen.
Wylie, John. 2007. *Landscape*. Key Ideas in Geography. London: Routledge.

CHAPTER EIGHT

Cultivating Disconnection

Imaginaries of Rurality in the Catalan Pyrenees

Camila del Mármol

In this chapter, I analyze how disconnection as a representation of place is cultivated in order to foster a new service economy in a district of the Catalan Pyrenees, the Alt Urgell. The production of imaginaries of rurality is a common theme in advertising for rural tourism in Europe. Many scholars have studied the social construction of rurality and the variety of values that have become associated with rural life (Bunce 2003; Cloke 2003; Halfacree 1993; Urry 1995). The consumption of the countryside is widely promoted by governments and local administrations aiming to co-opt visitors from big cities. Moreover, it is fostered and sponsored by national and international policies (Wilson 2007). Tourism and heritage have been evolving as fundamental development strategies in rural regions (Bell and Jayne 2010), as can be seen in crucial documents from the European Union such as the report on the Future of Rural Society (European Commission 1988; see also del Mármol 2012). Scholars analyzing the European policies for rural areas, such as the Common Agricultural Policy (CAP) directives or the Leader Programme, argued that they were clearly directed at supporting post-productivist measures (Buller, Wilson, and Höll 2000; Wilson 2001). In the Alt Urgell, tourism and heritage (both natural and cultural) have become a necessary alternative for promoting rural development.

The Alt Urgell district is located in the northwestern section of Spain, in the Catalan Pyrenees. The steep slopes of its mountains and the lack of roads explain its late entry into broader national markets (Arqué, Garcia, and Mateu 1982; Tulla 1994). The region experienced drastic changes throughout the twentieth century, bringing on several waves of depopulation from the end of the nineteenth century to the 1980s (Guirado 2007). The beginning of the twentieth century brought about a new production system based on specialization in dairy farming that was to replace the old production profile of the district: an economic system based on subsistence agriculture and livestock farming (Arqué et al. 1982; Pallarés-Blanch, Tulla, and Martín 2013). Many changes were still to come; at the end of the twentieth century, following European Union directives, restrictive quotas were applied to milk production, driving the sector to major restructuring and even to the collapse of the smaller farms in the upper valleys. Later on, new economic paths were opened and promoted in line with contemporary European trends: A new conceptualization of rural spaces led to the emergence of a new service economy designed to attract and accommodate rural tourism (López i Gelat, Feliu, and Bartolomé 2008; Vlès 2014).

The emergence of a new production model in the Alt Urgell focused on the implementation of a service economy came hand in hand with the development of heritage processes (del Mármol and Vaccaro 2015). The commoditization of rural space is a common trend within Western countries at the turn of the century (Halfacree 1999; Wilson 2001) and allowed for the development of new values and uses of the territory leading to a new rural modernity (Collantes 2009). Leisure, tourism, and heritage as integral aspects of these transformations influenced the evolution of the region. Many authors studying the impact of heritage processes in the Pyrenees and related areas (Grasseni 2009; Roigé and Frigolé 2010; Vaccaro and Beltran 2010) have emphasized the strong influence of these new discourses within the transformation of rural areas. Heritage discourses gained importance in the 1980s, promoting an array of new ideas that revalorized elements from the past that had been discarded due to the earlier crises in farming and agricultural models (see Kirshenblatt-Gimblett 1998). While the old production system was being questioned, rural museums were flourishing everywhere, retrieving old crafts and trades, and natural areas and parks seemed to dominate the landscape. New discourses revalorizing the past thrived throughout the valleys and mountains of the Catalan Pyrenees (Frigolé 2007; Vaccaro and Beltran 2010). Many of these discourses were mediated by specific imaginaries of disconnection that have shaped the social representations of place. Tourist brochures, advertising, as well as the main discourses legitimating heritage activations (such as museums, natural parks, and many other venues) were based on a romantic image of the district as an isolated refuge of natural beauty, old values, and traditions.

The fantasies promoted within heritage discourses are about being unconnected, as Ferguson (2002) specified: an original condition of isolation. But these representations allow for concealing the political and economic history experienced by the local population. The complex history of the area must be better thought of as a tale of connections and disconnections (Ferguson 2002). A long experience of failure of economic strategies together with the strong depopulation of the region due to the attraction of the major cities resulted in a local feeling of being thrown aside or forgotten. In the following sections, I will explore the production of imaginaries of disconnection and their counterpart: a complex history of connection and disconnection not only in economic and political terms but also within symbolic discourses of the past.

This study is based on long-term ethnographic research conducted in the area from 2006 to 2012. The qualitative approach based on participant observation techniques and several interviews conducted over the years was complemented by quantitative data on rural transition (population indexes, transformation of the labor market, development of economic sectors, etc.).

Imagining the Rural

Imaginaries of rurality are usually built in opposition to urban life (Cloke 2006, 19). The countryside is thus conceptualized in a generally positive manner, as a symbolic vessel containing the secret to a better and more authentic existence. Raymond Williams (1980) analyzes Western representations of rural society as a myth that conceals historical and local specificities and that takes on the shape of an ancient way of life that is lost forever. This representation of rurality embodying more authentic lifestyles and values is still at work and results in specific imaginaries that are prone to be mobilized for the needs of tourism economies. This revaluation of the past does not just refer to a concrete historical moment but rather to a timeless reality. In this symbolic way, it has become imbued with moral values, in opposition to contemporary societies.

The Catalan Pyrenees have been imagined and reimagined by different schools of thought throughout recent history. This mountain range played an important role during the *Renaixença*[1] (Jiménez and Prats 2006) and was represented in a romantic vision provided by famous writers and intellectuals

---

1 Renaixença: Romantic literary movement interested in the revival of Catalan language and culture that developed in Catalonia at the beginning of the nineteenth century.

(e.g., Balaguer 1968; Verdaguer 1945). From the perspective of this movement, the Pyrenees were seen as the cradle of Catalan identity, the purity of the mountains reflecting a transcendent strength that was to inform the Catalan character. The valleys and mountains were seen as a haven of old values and ancient traditions. These imaginaries also affected the perceptions projected upon local inhabitants: Once regarded as provincial and narrow-minded, they were gradually seen in a new light, which was closer to that of the "noble savage" (see Roma 2004). An idealized image of nature in its pristine form has been a structural component in the shaping of the Pyrenean imaginaries ever since.

The region was already seen as a tourist destination at the end of the nineteenth century with the creation of Hiking Clubs (Jiménez and Prats 2006), influenced by similar processes occurring in the Alps (Briffaud 1994). However, not until the twentieth century did tourist development reach the whole area. Mostly from the 1980s on, the tragic reality of depopulation was turned into an idyllic representation of seclusion that was thought to be attractive to visiting urban dwellers. Incentives to develop tourism in the Catalan Pyrenees were part of local government plans and measures and EU structural development funds (del Mármol 2014). Many actions were implemented, including the creation of natural parks and ski stations, a series of town planning measures to preserve the landscape, the improvement of transport infrastructure, the recovery of old paths, the creation of ethnographic heritage such as ethnographic museums, greater appreciation of local festivals and celebrations, and the restoration of churches and monuments that were considered of historical interest (see Frigolé 2007; Roigé and Frigolé 2010; Vaccaro and Beltran 2010). Development plans, specific laws concerning mountain areas, and other similar documents stemming from the national and Catalan governments spread a clear discourse of revalorization of what were literally considered the new resources of the region: natural and cultural heritage.

Tourism imaginaries have been extensively analyzed as a crucial aspect for the promotion of places (Salazar 2012; Urry 1995). The production of images and imaginaries of places are hardly new: In fact, they have constituted a pervasive feature of the human imagination (Hopkins 1998). What is relatively new is the use of these imaginaries and its conscious production for marketing and promoting localities under the auspices of neoliberal politics (Ashworth and Voogd 1994). The current state of Western economies, dominated by a new neoliberal order that has changed the previous articulation of power (Harvey 2005; Treanor 2005), relies on a new configuration of ideas and values. This prevailing economic logic involves constant market expansion (Treanor 2005), throwing people and places into a pervasive need for growth and competition (see Santamarina and del Mármol 2017). Place promotion is thus part of development plans, which are partly implemented by producing tourism imaginaries.

Durkheim has established that imagination is a social fact that impacts human life, having acute effects on identity building. Current approaches note the relevance of the social work of imagination as a constitutive feature of modern subjectivity (Appadurai 1996; Ricoeur 1994). As an organized field of social practice (Appadurai 1996, 31), it is constituted by the negotiation of images produced by different agents and is permeated with power relations. The study of social imaginaries raises impending problems, such as the malleability and changing nature of the subject matter, a characteristic that can be found in every field where cultural meaning is being produced. Many questions can be posed regarding the analysis of tourism imaginaries, such as the following: How are they produced? Is it an orchestrated process? From which levels of political administration it is organized? How is power playing a role in this production? How are these imaginaries disseminated? How do they impact local populations? Here I will address the production of narratives of disconnection within imaginaries in the Alt Urgell, focusing on the values and ideas on which they are based. Salazar (2012, 866) recommends grasping the intangibility of imaginaries by focusing on the conduits through which they become visible as images or discourses. I will trace the production of these narratives in tourist advertising, brochures and leaflets distributed locally, as well as in museographic discourses.

Cultivating Disconnection

"Relaxation, excitement, getting away from it all." These wishful words open up the official website of *Visit Pirineus*, a coordinated effort to publicize the range of destinations within the Catalan Pyrenees. The project is led by the Catalan government (*Generalitat de Catalunya*, specifically its Tourist Department) together with local administrations. The idea of disconnection present in the concept of "getting away from it all" is shared by many tourism imaginaries, as the tourism narrative is usually based on the idea of escape (MacCannell 1999; Turner and Turner 1978). The website goes on to describe the Catalan Pyrenees as follows:

> A place where you and nature are in perfect harmony, making you feel beautiful and good inside. A land marked by soaring mountains, a rich cultural heritage and exceptional cuisine. Unspoiled nature surrounds you as you enjoy sports activities, visits to natural parks and a culture stretching back to ancient

times. A cradle of cultures where ancient customs and traditions have been preserved. Calmly savour the essence of a life that retains its authenticity. Let this incredible land inspire you. Do you know the Catalan Pyrenees? Discover and experience an inland paradise.[2]

This quote illustrates the recurrence of several tropes widely disseminated throughout tourism imaginaries around the world. The overarching role of nature is repeatedly stressed—a pure, genuine nature that reaches out and permeates the visitor's inner self. A land frozen in an "ancient time" that stands for "authenticity." In other words, the image of paradise. According to Fabian (2002, xi), "Time belongs to the political economy of relations between individuals, classes, and nations." For this author, the affirmation of difference as distance is a temporal device used within the construction of complex relationships with the Other (ibid., 16). The specific "Other" in this narrative is to be found in the Pyrenees as a cradle of cultures, a land of old traditions and customs without specific references to its current population.

The ancient time referred to in the quote above, as well as in similar discourses found in printed brochures distributed throughout the region, is not a concrete period in the local past. Moreover, the specificities of the region's recent history remain disregarded and neglected by this vague and imprecise myth referring to a utopic past. Only in some cases, these veiled allusions turn into a specific appraisal of a concrete historical period. An official brochure distributed by *Aralleida*, the brand of the *Diputació de Lleida* (the provincial Government) for promoting tourism, refers to the Alt Urgell primarily as a historical region with a rich architectural heritage, specifically stressing its Romanesque architecture (La Seu d'Urgell Cathedral and several smaller churches scattered across its valleys). This longstanding heritage is favored over the recent experiences of past decades that remain alive in the minds of elderly inhabitants. What is being disregarded are the local population's ceaseless efforts to keep up with current times and be accepted as something more than a remnant of a better past. Endless pamphlets, catalogues, and advertisements strive to place local populations in this ambiguous time frame, as is the case of a recent promotional campaign called *Fogons de l'Alt Urgell*, a gastronomic guide compiled by several governmental and local administrations. In it, the local population is described as follows:

---

2 Visit Pirineus, Generalitat de Catalunya. Available from: http://www.visitpirineus.com/ca/pirineus. Last accessed August 13, 2017.

Over the years, the people of the Pyrenees have lived in harmony with their immediate surroundings of earth, water and livestock; in short, with nature. This bond gave rise to ways of life that remained virtually unaltered until the mid-twentieth century. Although the mountain regions thereafter changed a great deal, new generations of Pyrenean people have nonetheless inherited that ancestral popular culture which, luckily, is reluctant to disappear.[3]

In the *Visit Pirineus* website, the panegyric goes on as follows:

Natural parks and reserves in which you will find total paradise. Rich and varied flora and fauna right from the easternmost side, next to the Mediterranean, to the westernmost point. Places where it is even possible to find species such as the bear, and where its prints may have been the only ones left there before your own. The Pyrenees are first and foremost beauty, a unique area where nature has spared no effort in scattering the charms of paradise.

Once again, nature is the principal theme of the narrative, a natural world that is conceived as stripped of any human trace (Figure 8.1). Not just stripped, it is in fact genuinely original, authentic, pristine. Natural parks and protected areas proliferated in the Pyrenees long ago but especially from the 1980s on with the new legislative framework emerging after Franco's dictatorship and the influence of the European Union environmental programs (Vaccaro and Beltran 2010). As an example, 46.6 percent of the Alt Pirineu and the region of Aran (encompassing most of territory of the Catalan Pyrenees) is currently located within some type of natural protection area.[4] The reference to an intact landscape erases centuries of human presence, a complex history that inhabits the memory of the local population. Vaccaro and Beltran (2010, 17) have already referred to a recent "naturalization of rural landscape" in the form of an environmental recovery occurring after the decrease in agricultural pressure on the land. It was a deliberate project driven by the creation of natural parks and protected spaces, under the auspices of the state and in the context of European laws. This naturalization was carried out at the expense of a deeper knowledge of the complex relations of the local society with its surroundings. As many informants have expressed in similar words, "animals are more protected than people." In some way, this falls under what Rosaldo (1989, 107) has referred to as "imperialist nostalgia": the mourning for what one has destroyed.

---

3 "Fogons de l'Alt Urgell." Gastronomic Guide. Available at: http://www.alturgell.cat/sites/default/files/turisme_gastronomia_GUIA%20ANGLES.pdf.

4 Source: Departament de Territori i Sostenibilitat, Generalitat de Catalunya. Idescat, 2013.

Figure 8.1 La vall de la Vansa i Fórnols, Alt Urgell, 2016. Author: Camila del Mármol

Similar tropes and idealizations are to be found in local museums. I will specifically examine the Turpentine-makers Museum (*Museu de les Trementinaires*), a small ethnographic institution created in the town of Tuixent in 1998 (see Frigolé 2005). It is part of an initiative of the *Consell Comarcal de l'Alt Urgell* (the regional government): The Trade of the Past Route (*Ruta dels oficis d'Ahir*), involving a series of museums that revive different trades that are considered "traditional" and which all disappeared during the twentieth century.[5] The Turpentine-makers Museum is a perfect example of the idealization of past activities. In it, the visitor can find long accounts of women turpentine makers, their efforts and knowledge in the process of gathering herbs and producing turpentine, as well as the accounts of their long trips across the mountains to sell their products in other regions of Catalonia. These women are presented as hallmarks of an ancient peasant society in which courage, solidarity, and an ethic of hard work were prevalent. The

---

5 The rest of the museums that make up this route are *The Loggers Museum* (*Museu dels Raiers*), the *Oliana's Ice well* (*Pou de Gel d'Oliana*), the *Flourmill of Trobada* (*Farinera de la Trobada*), the *Mountain Vine and Wine Museum* (*Museu de la Vinya i del Vi de Muntanya*), and the *Wool Fabric* (*Fàbrica de Llanes d'Arsèguel*).

romanticized version of old rural society allows for a moral account of its features.

The idea for setting up the Turpentine-makers museum stemmed from a couple of neorurals (Chevalier 1981), newcomers from nearby cities who arrived in the valley in the late 1980s. The *Generalitat de Catalunya* was promoting the creation of learning centers in remote country villages aimed at fostering place promotion. The teachers from the Tuixent school, together with some other people from outside the valley, led the way in searching for an original topic, in a race for differentiation that was already affecting the promotion of places. They came up with turpentine making, an activity led in the past by some women from the poorest houses. They were locally known as the "women who went around the world," in a clear reference to their long unsupervised travels. What can be viewed as a positive connotation in today's global, mobile society was not a prized aspect of women's lives, being mostly a cause for shame and embarrassment. The revalorization of this element of the past and its rise as a cultural heritage trademark of the village of Tuixent was a complex process.

The museum celebrates the bravery of the turpentine makers, their wisdom and expertise in preparing natural remedies and treating patients, to the point of turning these women into a heroic myth. Even though the narrative behind the "women who went around the world" could also be read in terms of an effort to make a connection with the past (Frigolé 2005), the magnification of past trades, the knowledge of the environment, and the quaint representation of "Turpentine-maker cuisine" to be found in the museum refer to a better, idealized past, a celebration of a timeless, disconnected memory. The complexity of past social relations is absent from the museographic discourse, as is a critical reading of contemporary social conflicts. Beyond the original objections of local inhabitants to accept the celebration of what was remembered as superficial and even shameful venture of some women, the main unrest was expressed by many old residents who experienced the end of agriculture and cattle breeding as a progressive loss that drastically changed their lived environment. In this context of loss and disorientation, why is such a concrete aspect of the past so firmly celebrated? And how does it relate to the town's current state of abandonment and depopulation?

Disconnection is to be found twice in these discourses. First, in the idea of "getting away from it all," reaching a natural paradise that will change the visitor from within. The idea of travel as a self-realization experience is at work here (Fabian 2002, 7): Disconnection from the routine will reveal the secret to the authentic self. When leisure displaces work as the structural framework of contemporary society (Maccannell 1999), a break away from the everyday is essential for experiencing authenticity. Second, the production of ideas of disconnection is present in what Echtner and Prasad (2003) referred to as "the myth of the unchanged," the assumption that some elements from the past—social relations and traditions, as well as an archaic natural setting unspoiled by human action—are somehow conserved in the present. Accordingly, the region is disconnected in temporal terms and offers visitors a timeless cultural and natural environment. The following quote from *Visit Pirineus* clearly illustrates this point:

> There are places at the foot of the mountains where time passes with no clock marking the hours and minutes, places that do not figure on tourist guides or hotel brochures. Romanesque hermitages, mountain paths, solitary forests, rural accommodation, and small villages where people still celebrate traditional festivals, relish genuine cuisine, and maintain time-honoured trades.[6]

A History of Connections and Disconnections

The imaginaries of disconnection discussed above are set against a complex backdrop made of connections and disconnections. The reference to an idealized isolation obscures a critical perspective on the history of peripheries in Western countries. Current global economies have deeply affected social and ecological landscapes around the globe (Sivaramakrishnan and Vaccaro 2006). As Ferguson (2002, 14) claims, "Disconnection or abjection occurs inside capitalism and not outside of it, making a global second class." The recent history of the Alt Urgell district is made up of changes and disruptions and includes numerous efforts to fight against the local dynamic of depopulation and abandonment. I will offer a general overview of the transformations in the past century to provide a deeper context within which the imaginaries of disconnection acquire new meanings.

The productivity of agriculture and livestock in the Alt Urgell was always restricted by the severe climate conditions and the extreme topography of the region. At the beginning of the twentieth century, the local economy was based on subsistence agriculture and livestock farming run by extended families occupying self-sufficient farms (Arqué et al. 1982; Pallarés-Blanch et al. 2013). In the late nineteenth century, a regional market grew slowly based on the exchange of wine, livestock, and occasional agricultural surplus (Gascón 2015). However, it was followed by a progressive population decline (Guirado 2007) due in part to Spain's entry into global markets, causing

---

6 Webpage Visit Pirineus. Available at http://www.visitpirineus.com/en/blog/hidden-pyrenees.

the decline of agricultural prices and intensifying permanent migration to industrial cities or foreign countries (Nistal 2010). The late arrival of the phylloxera to the Southern side of the Pyrenees was also a relevant aspect leading to the demographic recession.

In 1915, a group of local landowners created the *Cooperativa del Cadí*, a venture that shifted the focus to intensive cattle farms oriented to milk production (Escribà et al. 2001; Gascón 2010, 2015). Seizing the opportunity of the new roads built to connect La Seu d'Urgell with cities like Lleida or Barcelona, which made it easier to reach wider markets, these private landlords started an in-depth effort to renew the livestock farming system. From the beginning, the *Cooperativa* produced butter and cheese aimed to supply the national markets. It was a fundamental innovation in the history of the Catalan Pyrenees, greatly transforming the previously limited regional commerce. The district became one of the largest dairy production centers in the country (Tulla 1994) and a well-connected hub of diary product manufacturing.

The recession brought about by the Spanish Civil War paused the expansion of this new production system, taking around forty years for it to be fully implemented. Tulla (1994) identified the shift to the capitalist integration of the farming and livestock breeding system in the region as beginning in the early 1950s, when even the smaller farms located in distant villages far from the capital turned to milk production; the change reached its peak at the end of the 1980s. By the end of the century, however, it all changed. With the entry of Spain into the European Economic Community (EEC) in 1986, the local milk industry was shattered by the imposition of the EEC production restrictions. Quotas per region were imposed in order to balance European production. The restrictions came along at a moment in which the larger farms were pressuring the local market, increasing their production margins and expanding their technological means to compete with high-quality milk from abroad. This, alongside other issues that were complicating the viability of smaller and less mechanized farms, such as the lack of generational replacement, increasing bureaucracy, and cumbersome quality and hygiene controls, caused many farms to close. Most farms faced a choice between specialization and abandonment. The ones with better land conditions, close to the factories in the district capital, and with generational replacement followed the path of hyper-specialization and technological development. For the Alt Urgell, Tulla (1994, 246) argues that productivity became the key word that articulated the restructuring of the milk industry and resulted in a complete disregard of the beneficial aspects of traditional farming and herding activities in the area. While by 1950 there were 1,373 dairy farms, by

1980 the number had dropped to 821 and was down to 90 in 2009 (Pallarés-Blanch et al. 2013).

Thereafter, an economic shift toward the development of a service and tourism economy took place. Agricultural and farming activities were no longer the main economic sector (Hinojosa 2008). While some old farms turned to rural tourism, profiting from the European subsidies such as the Leader program, others were left without activity due to the owners' old age and lack of descendants. Many houses were just closed and sold or are still in the hands of an old proprietor living from a pension. Beyond the remaining intensive milk production, in a few cases the dairy farmers headed in another direction also favored by EU support: extensive bovine livestock breeding (Aldomà-i-Buixadé 2003; Fillat 2003). New population also arrived, mostly from the 1980s on, younger inhabitants from other parts of Catalonia or Europe, searching for a new life in closer contact with nature.

This general overview summarizes a complex development that goes way beyond the simplistic picture of the imaginaries of disconnection. If anything, we must refer to a history of multifaceted efforts and failures, risky attempts, and ventures as much as breakdowns and collapses that were greatly biased by national and transnational dynamics and political agendas. But not only is the political and economic history of the region much more than the widespread images of disconnection. There are also local representations, narratives, and discourses that intend to place the district in complex symbolic conceptions of the past beyond the idealized and timeless imaginaries depicted in previous pages. To close this text, I will go through what I refer to as imaginaries of connection—specific uses of the past (Bensa and Fabre 2001; Kaneef 2004; Trouillot 1995) that were mobilized by different actors in order to place the region in a broader context and bring it into dialogue with global dynamics.

Social representation of the past creates a sense of continuity with former times (Halbwachs 1967; Macdonald 2013). However, it is not just about remembering: The production of narratives about the past can be expressed in the idiom of oblivion and social indifference (Cole 1998). Forgetting and remembering are integral aspects of the social representation of the past. The production of traditions might work as a defense strategy in order to sustain ways of living and modes of existence, turning them into a political right (Sahlins 1994). It can be described as a new cultural consciousness, as a tool to control local relations with the dominant society. In the Catalan Pyrenees, Ros I Fontana (1997) analyzes a movement of revalorization of mountain society that developed during the 1980s. The recovery of the medieval past by restoring ancient monuments and other ruins, but mainly by producing narratives about a glorious past in the region, allows the social imagination to bring forth positive images to counter the reality of abandonment. According to this author, it was about the need of legitimizing a culture that was about to disappear due to the strong depopulation and successive agricultural crises. The regeneration of a rural identity, struck by the weight of modernity during the 1950s and 1960s, found an alternative shelter in these narratives.

The use of the Cathar history in the region is an example of this process. The Albigensian Crusade was a critical moment in the history of Occitania, widely known and represented in France (Biget 1979; Soula 2005). Pomian (1980) notes that in this country the Cathars acted as a "screen through which future generations can project their own contradictions and conflicts"[7] (quoted in Soula 2005, 225). But that was not the case in Catalonia, where the implications of the Cathar heresy were not widely discussed (Gascón 2003). In 1960, though, the work of Ventura led the way for future reinterpretation of this past in the Catalan Pyrenees. The annihilation of the Christian heretics in Occitania, according to this author, was a political scheme to block the creation of a Catalan-Occitan nation on both sides of the mountain range, a new nation that could have eclipsed the power of the French monarchy and the Papacy. Shortly thereafter, the Alt Urgell witnessed the local success of a literary work influenced by these ideas: *Cercamón*, by Lluís Racionero (1982). The novel, which follows the life of well-known medieval characters, both fictional and historical, seized the romantic appeal of Catharism to project an alternative imagination in which the region became the center of a possible future that had never arrived. A celebration of Pyrenean identity, the book sketches the portrait of a sophisticated and enlightened culture that popped up from the mountains and was devastated by the royalist powers. According to the book, what would become the origin of Catalan identity evolved in the Pyrenees, in a well-suited parallelism with the national narratives of defeat against the Spanish Crown:

> A Pyrenean country: the heart in the mountains, the plain being the back and, as arms, the huge rivers Rhône and Ebro. . . . This is rejected both by the Franc and the Pope, they do not want it because we represent a different world. Occitania flourishes with a political freedom that allows for the communal organization of towns, with representatives elected by the people and popular militia to defend their freedom.[8] (Racionero 1982, 94)

---

7 My translation from French.
8 My translation from Catalan.

In this romantic representation, the Pyrenees are depicted as the center of the Catalan-Occitan nation that would have illuminated the darkness of medieval Europe. Placing the Pyrenees in a complex history that establishes a dialogue with contemporary national narratives helps build strategies of symbolic connections, claiming a role in the present. For many local inhabitants, these narratives were a way of connecting their place with wider narratives and different temporalities, considered as crucial for the development of European history. In this way, the account of the Pyrenees portrayed as a forgotten country is counterweighted by epic narratives that intend to render the depopulated spaces relevant and meaningful. The fictional framework allows for the building of new connections, metaphorically in many ways but also concretely in particular experiences. The Cathars are the founders of a modern and developed society, showcased as the forebears of European grandeur. At the same time, they are presented as the founders of the Pyrenean population, the promise of a refined society that could have made its way across the continent but was beheaded by the despotic whims of brutal monarchies. The Cathars convey the Pyrenean connection to Europe, struggling to outline an alternative positive perception that would counter negative representations.

Moreover, these imaginaries of connection can develop into specific practices that seek novel experiences of connectivity. Concretely, I will refer to the Cathar markets held in the Alt Urgell county, festivities made up in the past twenty or thirty years that seek to attract tourists and visitors to small and depopulated mountain hamlets that are striving for survival within the competitive tourist markets. Two villages in the region hold events related to the Cathar past in which several aspects of medieval history are celebrated. The Cathar festival of Josa de Cadí (Figure 8.2), a small hamlet that was abandoned during the 1980s and later became occupied mostly during the summer (with the exception of a handful of year-round residents), is one of these examples. A strong solidarity has emerged in the past years between the summer community, consisting primarily of descendants of former villagers, and Catalans from different areas of the country who were looking for a place to go during the scorching summers in the cities. During the 1990s, the local mayor found out that the local medieval lord of Josa de Cadí had been a supporter of the Albigensian heresy and decided to recover this forgotten history in order to establish new connections. He organized the first "Cathar meeting," to which the *Centre d'Agermanament Català-Occità*, an association that promoted Catalan-Occitan relations, was invited. The idea was to present the Cathar history of the village to its former residents (living mostly in nearby cities), while stretching the connections with the other side of the mountain range. Even though the evolution of the celebration is complicated and must be analyzed in the light of local conflicts (del Mármol 2012), the truth is that the celebration outlived its original motives and has become the most attended celebration of the hamlet to date, attracting visitors and tourists from all around.

Imaginaries of connection, or as Khalvashi (2018), following Crapanzano, describes as "imaginative horizons," afford a specific population "the ability to act on its present and imagine the future" (ibid., 4). She refers to the political cosmologies and everyday imagination revolving around the mythology of Medea in Georgia, which helps conceptualize contemporary realities while simultaneously displaying conflicting views and social experiences of inequality and dispossession. The negative and disdainful images of Spanish rural areas built during decades dominated by the influential discourse of modernization left their mark on the social construction of local identities (see Collier 1997). The Cathar past embodies a social experience made of abandonment and contempt, while also offering some redemption in a new narrative that offers the promise of a better future. But the connection not only stretches toward Europe; by identifying the Cathars as a cornerstone of Catalan identity, the Pyrenees acquire a central role in the history of Catalonia, which is currently being reconfigured in novel ways (see Clua 2014).

Figure 8.2 Josa de Cadí, Alt Urgell, 2014. Author: Camila del Mármol

During the 1980s, when this medieval past was unearthed, it also offered the chance of containing and displaying the memories of the Franco repression, the experiences of political persecution and the strict control of local identities and regional languages. The length of the Franco dictatorship hindered the development of mechanisms for coping with the social dislocation of the Civil War, which was not expressed beyond the official narrative of the glorious victory over communism and the enemies of the fatherland. The history of the Albigensian Crusade offers an analogy of the Franco repression, which did not have the benefit of better channels of expression since the political regime of the Transition (*la Transición*), the new democratic government, decided to put history aside in order to achieve political stability integrating the Franco technocrats and some key figures within the new government. The Cathar past provided a lens through which to reflect about repression, persecution, migration, and resilience, while also offering new perspectives for the future. The future that should had been turns into a promise of redemption, a possibility of an accomplished reality.

Imaginaries of connection and their will to offer alternative ground for the production of local identities express the will of keeping up with the present. For a better understanding of the imaginaries of disconnection, they need to be contextualized within wider uses of the past, within local strategies to create a continuity with former times. Disconnection, thus, is just a narrative that works within the new economic shift, and it is deliberately unfolded within the local promotion and marketing of the region. In this sense, it is also a connection strategy, a symbolic mechanism for being placed in the world.

Conclusion

This chapter deals with a variety of social imaginaries that, in different ways, have an impact on the political, social, and economic organization of a region in the Catalan Pyrenees. Strategic objectives defined within different developmental plans and a new legal setting[9] were crucial in the definitive transformation of the Pyrenees into a tourist attraction at the end of the twentieth century. The region was placed on a new political agenda that coordinated a series of common ideas and directives for the future of

---

9 Such as the *Law 2/1983, from the 9th of March, of high mountain areas* (DOGC 312, de 16/03/1983), or the ordinances creating several natural parks in the region.

European rural areas (Vaccaro and Beltran 2010). As a result, the region is integrated into a major social representation model that promotes rural areas as remnants of ancestral traditions, pristine nature, and immanent identities.

Imaginaries of disconnection play a key role in the production of this representation model and are firmly produced and reproduced in tourism brochures, leaflets, museum exhibitions, and advertising campaigns. This powerful ensemble is aimed at attracting visitors and selling them not just products but a general overview of the place, a moral representation of rurality. Behind this attractive screen lies a complex history of economic and production collapses, rural abandonment, depopulation, and, again, new initiatives and programs intended to develop the area. Far from the picture of isolation that tourism narratives provide, the complex history of the region emerges as a contrasting backdrop that turns out to be less appealing than the romantic images of isolation and idealized nature. Here the idiom of disconnection is the means to launch a new chapter of the recent history of the Catalan Pyrenees, while also producing distortions and blatant omissions with rampant disregards. Similar to the previous ones, this new chapter of local history will probably be fraught with new experiences of connection and disconnection.

As an alternative to the imaginaries of disconnection, a variety of sectors in the local population engage in the production of diverse narratives of connection that build bridges with alternative representations and promote the social imagination of novel paths of connection. At the same time, they enable alternative forms of producing regional subjectivity and identity. By engaging imaginatively with the local past, they offer new ways of reflecting on Pyrenean identities more broadly.

Imaginaries of connection and disconnection are an integral part of social consciousness. They structure tales of redemption and disenchantment, forecast hopes and anguishes, and express wishful thinking while reflecting on different and even contradictory pasts. Dissimilarly deployed by different actors, they both show the will to produce specific strategies of connection, either by fostering tourism or by rethinking the local past under the prism of complex connections. In this chapter, I did not refer to these imaginaries as false consciousnesses or mere ideologies but considered them as active players in the production of networks to which the region is connected. I outlined a mapping of social imaginaries of connection and disconnection in the Catalan Pyrenees in order to explore the complex interlinkages established within the social production of discourses and imaginaries and the political and economic development of the region.

Bibliography

Aldomà-i-Buixadé, Ignaci. 2003. "Evolució del model econòmic de la muntanya." *Espais Etnogràfics, La muntanya a Catalunya, Revista del Departament de Política Territorial i Obres Públiques* 49: 66–73.
Appadurai, Arjun. 1996. *Modernity at Large. Cultural Dimensions of Globalization.* Minneapolis: University of Minnesota Press.
Arqué, Maite, Angela Garcia, and Xavier Mateu. 1982. "La penetració del capitalisme a les comarques de l'Alt Pirineu." *Documents d'Anàlisi Geogràfica* 1: 9–67.
Ashworth, Gregory, and Hendrik Voogd. 1994. "Marketing and Place Promotion." In *Place Promotion: The Use of Publicity and Marketing to Sell Towns and Regions*, edited by John Gold and Stephen Ward, 39–52. Chichester: John Wiley.
Balaguer, Victor. 1968. *Les esposalles de la morta. Raig de lluna.* Barcelona: Edicions 62.
Bell, David, and Mark Jayne. 2010. "The Creative Countryside: Policy and Practice in the UK Rural Cultural Economy." *Journal of Rural Studies* 26: 209–18.
Bensa, Alban, and Daniel Fabre, eds. 2001. *Une histoire à soi. Figurations du passé et localités.* Paris: Éditions de la Maison des sciences de l'homme.
Biget, Jean-Louis. 1979. "Mythographie du Catharisme (1870–1960)." *Historiographie du Catharisme, Cahiers de Fanjeaux* 14: 271–342.
Briffaud, Serge. 1994. *Naissance d'un paysage.* Toulouse: Université de Toulouse.
Buller, Henry, Geoff Wilson, and Andreas Höll, eds. 2000. *Agri-Environmental Policy in the European Union.* Aldershot: Ashgate.
Bunce, Michael. 2003. "Reproducing Country Idylls." In *Country Visions*, edited by Paul Cloke, 14–30. Harlow: Pearson.
Chevalier, Michel. 1981. "Les phénomenes néo-ruraux." *L'Espace Géographique* 1: 33–47.
Cloke, Paul. 2003. *Country Visions.* Harlow: Pearson.
———. 2006. "Conceptualizing rurality." In *Handbook of Rural Studies*, edited by Paul Cloke, Terry Marsden, and Patrick Mooney, 18–28. London: Sage.
Clua, Montserrat. 2014. "Identidad y Política En Cataluña: El Auge Del Independentismo En El Nacionalismo Catalán Actual." *Quaderns de l'Institut Catala d'Antropologia* 19(2): 79–99.
Cole, Jennifer. 1998. "The Work of Memory in Madagascar." *American Ethnologist* 25(4): 610–33.
Collantes, Fernando. 2009. "Rural Europe Reshaped: The Economic Transformation of Upland Regions, 1850–2001." *Economic History Review* 62(2): 306–23.
Collier, Jane. 1997. *From Duty to Desire : Remaking Families in a Spanish Village.* Princeton, NJ: Princeton University Press.
del Mármol, Camila. 2012. *Pasados locales, políticas globales. Procesos de patrimonialización en un valle del Pirineo catalán* [Local Pasts, Global Politics. Heritagisation Processes in a Valley of the Catalonian Pyrenees]. Valencia: Germanias.
———. 2014. "Through Other Times: The Politics of Heritage and the Past in the Catalan Pyrenees." In *Tourism and the Power of Otherness: Seduction of Difference*, edited by David Picard and Michael Di Giovane, 31–51. Bristol: Channel View Publications.

del Mármol, Camila, and Ismael Vaccaro. 2015. "Changing Ruralities: Between Abandonment and Redefinition in the Catalan Pyrenees." *Anthropological Forum* 25(1): 21–41.

Echtner, Charlotte M., and Pushkala Prasad. 2003. "The context of Third World Tourism Marketing." *Annals of Tourism Research* 30(3): 660–82.

Escribà, Gemma, Pilar Pérez, Jordi Nistal, Ricardo Calvo, and Rosa Bullich. 2001. *L'Alt Urgell. Una visió de conjunt.* Vol. 1. La Seu d'Urgell: Institut d'Estudis Ilerdencs.

European Commission. 1988. "Future of the Rural Society." Commission communication transmitted to the Council and to the European Parliament on July 29, 1988. COM (88) 501 final 1988. Bulletin of the European Communities Supplement 4/88.

Fabian, Johannes. 2002. *Time and the Other. How Anthropology Makes Its Object.* New York: Columbia University Press.

Ferguson, James. 2002. "Global Disconnect; Abjection and the Aftermath of Modernism." In *The Anthropology of Globalization. A Reader*, edited by Jonathan Inda and Renato Rosaldo, 270–85. Londres: Blackwell.

Fillat, Frederic. 2003. "La intensificació ramadera i l'abandó, dues tendències dels Pirineus espanyols al començament del s. XXI." *Espais Monogràfics, La Muntanya a Catalunya, Revista del departament de Política territorial i Obres Públiques* 49: 8–14.

Frigolé, Joan. 2005. *Dones que anaven pel món. Estudi etnogràfic de les trementinaires de la Vall de la Vansa i Tuixent (Alt Urgell).* Barcelona: Generalitat de Catalunya.

———. 2007. "Producció cultural de lloc, memòria i terciarització de l'economia en una vall del Prepirineu." *Revista d'Etnologia de Catalunya* 30: 70–80.

Gascón Chopo, Carles. 2003. *Càtars al Pirineu Català.* Lleida: Pagès Editors.

———. 2010. *Comarques oblidades. Josep Zulueta i el Pirineu l'any 1890.* La Seu d'Urgell: Edicions Salòria.

———. 2015. *Cadí: 100 anys de Cooperativa.* La Seu d'Urgell: Cadí Societat Cooperativa Cat. Ltda.

Grasseni, Cristina. 2009. *Developing Skill, Developing Vision: Practices of Locality at the Foot of the Alps.* Oxford: Berghahn Books.

Guirado, Carles. 2007. "Del despoblament a la revitalització demogràfica: canvis en el comportament de la població al Pirineu català (1860–2006). El cas de l'Urgellet i el Baridà (Alt Urgell-Cerdanya)." Master diss., Universitat Autònoma de Barcelona.

Halbwachs, Maurice. 1967. *La mémoire collective.* París: Les Presses universitaires de France.

Halfacree, Keith. 1993. "Locality and Social Representation: Space, Discourse and Alternative Definitions of the Rural." *Journal of Rural Studies* 9(1): 23–37.

———. 1999. "A New Space or Spatial Effacement? Alternative Futures for the Postproductivist Countryside." In *Reshaping the Countryside: Perceptions and Processes of Rural Change*, edited by Nigel Walford, John Everitt, and Darrell Napton, 67–76. Wallingford, CT: CAB International.

Harvey, David. 2005. *A Brief History of Neoliberalism.* Oxford: Oxford University Press.

Hinojosa, Alberto. 2008. *Estudi estadístic dels municipis de l'Alt Urgell.* Barcelona: Universitat Politècnica de Catalunya.

Hopkins, Jeffrey. 1998. "Signs of the Post-Rural: Marketing Myths of a Symbolic Countryside." *Geografiska Annaler* 80(2): 65–81.
Jiménez, Sole, and Llorenç Prats. 2006. "El turismo en Catalunya: evolución histórica y retos de futuro." *Pasos. Revista de Turismo y Patrimonio Cultural* 42: 153–74.
Kaneef, Deema. 2004. *Who Owns the Past? The Politics of Time in a "Model" Bulgarian Village.* New York: Berghahn Books.
Khalvashi, Tamta. 2018. "The Horizons of Medea: Economies and Cosmologies of Dispossession in Georgia." *Journal of the Royal Anthropological Institute* 24(4): 804–25.
Kirshenblatt-Gimblett, Barbara. 1998. *Destination Culture. Tourism, Museums, and Heritage.* Berkeley: University of California Press.
López i Gelat, Jordi Tàbara Feliu, and Joan Bartolomé. 2009. "The Rural in Dispute: Discourses of Rurality in the Pyrenees." *Geoforum* 40 (2008): 602–12.
Maccannell, Dean. 1999. *The Tourist: A New Theory of the Leisure Class.* Berkeley: University of California Press.
MacDonald, Susan. 2013. *Memorylands: Heritage and Identity in Europe Today.* London: Routledge.
Nistal, Jordi. 2010. "Crisi agrària i moviments cooperativistes a l'Alt Urgell (1890–1920)." *Dovella* 104: 28–38.
Pallarés-Blanch, Marta, Antoni Tulla, and Ana Vera Martín. 2013. "Reintegración de un territorio entre fronteras: el Alt Segre, Pirineos." *Geographicallia* 63–64: 121–56.
Pomian, Krzysztof. 1980. "Les avatars de l'identité historique." *Le Débat*, n° 3, 114–18.
Racionero, Lluís. 1982. *Cercamón.* Barcelona: Caixa d'Estalvis de Catalunya.
Ricoeur, Paul. 1994. "Imagination in Discourse and in Action." In *Rethinking Imagination: Culture and Creativity*, edited by Gillian Robinson and John F. Rundell, 87–117. London: Routledge.
Roigé, Xavier, and Joan Frigolé, eds. 2010. *Constructing Cultural and Natural Heritage: Parks, Museums and Rural Heritage.* Girona: ICRPC Llibres (4).
Roma, Francesc. 2004. *Del Paradís a la Nació. La muntanya a Catalunya.* Valls: Cossetania.
Ros i Fontana, Ignasi. 1997. *Aquelles muntanyes se n'han anat al cel. La memòria col·lectiva a la vall de Castellbò (Alt Urgell).* Tremp: Garsineu Edicions.
Rosaldo, Renato. 1989. "Imperialist Nostalgia." *Representations*, no. 26, Special Issue: Memory and Counter-Memory: 107–22.
Sahlins, Marshall. 1994. "Good-Bye to Tristes Tropes: Ethnography in the Context of Modern World History." In *Assessing Cultural Anthropology*, edited by Robert Borofsky, 377–98. New York: McGraw-Hill.
Salazar, Noel. 2012. "Tourism Imaginaries: A Conceptual Approach." *Annals of Tourism Research* 39(2): 863–82.
Santamarina, Beatriz, and Camila del Mármol. 2017. "Ciudades creativas y pueblos con encanto." *Revista de dialectología y tradiciones populares* 72(2): 359–77.
Sivaramakrishnan, Kalyanakrishna, and Ismael Vaccaro. 2006. "Postindustrial Natures: Hyper-Mobility and Place Attachments." *Journal of Social Anthropology* 14(3): 301–17.
Soula, René. 2005. *Les Cathares: Entre légende et histoire. La mémoire de l'albigéisme du XIX siècle à nos jours.* Toulouse: Institut d'Études Occitanes.

Treanor, Paul. 2005. *Neoliberalism: Origins, Theory, Definition.* http://web.inter.nl.net/users/Paul.Treanor/neoliberalism.html. Accessed December 12, 2018.

Trouillot, Michel-Rolp. 1995. *Silencing the Past: Power and the Production of History.* Boston, MA: Beacon Press.

Tulla, Antoni. 1994. *Procés de transformació agrària en àrees de muntanya. Les explotacions de producció lletera com a motor de canvi a les comarques de la Cerdanya, el Capcir, l'Alt Urgell i el Principat d'Andorra.* Barcelona: Institut Cartogràfic de Catalunya (col. Tesis doctorals).

Turner, Victor, and Edith Turner. 1978. *Image and Pilgrimage in Christian Culture: Anthropological Perspectives.* New York: Columbia University Press.

Urry, John. 1995. *Consuming Places.* New York: Routledge.

Vaccaro, Ismael, and Oriol Beltran, eds. 2010. *Social and Ecological History of the Pyrenees: State, Market, and Landscape.* Walnut Creek, CA: Left Coast Press.

Ventura, Jordi. 1960. *El catarismo en Cataluña.* Barcelona: Boletín de la Real Academia de Buenas Letras de Barcelona, XXVIII.

Verdaguer, Jacint. 1945. *Canigó.* Vic: Llibreria Sala.

Vlès, Vincent. 2014. *Métastations: Mutations urbaines des stations de montagne—Un regard pyrénéen.* Bourdeaux: Presses Universitaires Bourdeaux.

Williams, Raymond. 1980. "Ideas of Nature." *Problems in Materialism and Culture.* London: Verso.

Wilson, Gerald. 2001. "From Productivism to Post-Productivism . . . and Back Again? Exploring the (Un)changed Natural and Mental Landscapes of European Agriculture." *Transactions of the Institute of British Geographers* 26(1): 77–102.

———. 2007. *Multifunctional Agriculture: A Transition Theory Perspective.* Trowbridge: Cromwell Press.

CHAPTER NINE

Organisms, Nodes and Networks
Paolo Palladino

> Only connect the prose and the passion, and both will be exalted, and human love will be seen at its highest. Live in fragments no longer.
>
> —E. M. Forster, *Howards End*

The following reflections on "connectivity" are precipitated by my long-standing interest in understanding the status of the organism in contemporary post-structuralist theory. According to this theory, things in themselves are meaningless, and they only acquire their distinctive meaning as they are connected with yet other, equally meaningless things. Over the course of a recent project, I have sought to test the limits of this construction of things and their meaning by examining the role that sheep play in contemporary endeavors to regenerate declining rural communities.[1] While the sheep mediate the integration of these communities into global networks of trade and consumption, their role has involved a complex play of connection and disconnection, not only between the sheep and the places in which they are sometimes found, but also in the relations of care that are invested in these sheep. Against this background, the notion that the organism might

---

1 I am grateful to the European Union's Horizon 2020 research and innovation program for its award of a Marie Sklodowska-Curie Individual Fellowship (657750), which enabled the research on which this paper is based. I am equally grateful to Luis Lobo-Guerrero and colleagues in the Department of History and Theory of International Relations for the home they provided during the tenure of this fellowship.

be situated between and betwixt node and network, as neither one nor the other, seems to me important to our understanding of connectivity.

This chapter will focus on the Pecora Sambucana and the Oveja Xisqueta, the first being a breed of sheep native to the Maritime Alps and the second being a native of the Catalan Pyrenees. The forms of life that have developed around these two breeds are particularly interesting because, in their different ways, they illustrate very usefully the complex relations between space, time, and bodies out of which "heritage breeds" emerge. Despite the attention I will pay to these relations, however, I am not interested in establishing their importance to a wider understanding of the historical conditions of possibility for the emergence of a discourse of connectivity.[2] Though interested in these matters, I wish instead to approach connectivity as a formal feature of networks, and my line of inquiry into this feature will focus on the nodes in these networks once the latter take on the attributes of an organism. To be more precise, it seems to me that the forms of life that have developed around the Sambucana and the Xisqueta pose a number of questions with regard to the understanding that seems to emerge from contemporary convergence of thinking about bodies and the media that the organic body is no more than a "fleshless envelope" (Franklin 2012, 461; see also Wegenstein 2006).[3] Paraphrasing Forster's resonant injunction, I want to ask how one is to understand the relationship between love and its object if the latter is no more than the relationship itself (see also Kirsch 2010). The discussion of this question will be structured around bodies' material constitution, the topological arrangement of components parts, and the temporal structure of these composite arrangements, particularly as it relates to mortality and loss. The discussion will also move from Deleuzian perspectives on the body, which call into question the status of the organism as any singularity (Deleuze 1992), through related questions about the relationship between human and nonhuman animals, to Nancean understanding of multiplicity (Nancy 2000) and touch (Nancy 2008). Usefully, Deleuze and Nancy both spatialize the body, but their different configuration of that spatialization is important to understanding what a politics and ethics of connectivity might

---

[2] For an introduction to the conditions of historical possibility from which a discourse of "connectivity" first emerges, see Kittler (1992, 1999). For an equally useful introduction to the ways in which sheep might be said to figure in this same field of possibilities, see instead Woods (2017).

[3] Wegenstein (2006) offers a useful review of a long-standing debate over the fate of the body within modernity, dividing the literature between those who regard this as a process of fragmentation and those who hold onto some form of somatic holism. Wegenstein's argument is that, despite their differences, the two perspectives share a separation of flesh and representation that hinders the understanding of contemporary forms of embodiment.

Figure 9.1 Jean Luc Cornec, "TribuT," 1991. Copyrighted and reproduced with permission. © DACS 2018

entail (see also Dejanovic 2016; Esposito 2010). My conclusion is that the production of the mortal body wholly transforms the relationship between nodes and networks. It then seems to me that the contraposition of Forster's injunction and Jean-Luc Cornec's witty construction of a bleating flock of sheep out of coiling cord and ringing telephones captures very effectively what I want to say about nodes, networks, and connectivity (Figure 9.1). Whence the drive to "connect"?

In sum, I propose to take connectivity as my organizing theme and to examine its implications by considering the relationship between nodes and networks where these take organic form and mortality becomes a matter of concern. Finally and by way of the briefest methodological consideration, it is not my intention to offer some unmediated exercise in philosophical exegesis and confrontation. My approach instead takes the form of an ethnographic reflection, involving thinking about nodes, networks, and connectivity with the aid of sheep and their associated forms of life (Cronon 2009).

Materiality: What Are Bodies Capable Of?

Deleuze (1992) discusses how a body is to be understood as a nexus of forces such that no traditional, purely organic definition can serve as a model for a body's capacities. According to Deleuze, these capacities cannot be known in advance because they are dependent on the contingencies of encounters with other bodies. As a result, the individuality of any particular body is to be understood as the outcome of a process of becoming, of "bodying" (Buchanan 1997). As Deleuze and Guattari (1988) put it pithily,

> We know nothing about a body until we know what it can do, in other words, what its affects are, how they can or cannot enter into composition with other affects, with the affects of another body, either to destroy that body or to be destroyed by it, either to exchange actions and passions with it or to join with it in composing a more powerful body. (257)

Since the ontology sustaining this understanding of the body has to be taken at face value, the test of its merits must rest with its productivity, with its capacity to let us see the world differently. As a result, I will deploy this Deleuzian understanding to articulate how the processes of connection that are involved in the production of one particular organic body, that of the Sambucana, come to order the spatial and temporal coordinates structuring the lives of yet other bodies, namely the consumers of the Sambucana rendered into meat, cheese, and wool.

The Sambucana plays a pivotal role in the endeavor to revitalize the Valle Stura, in the Maritime Alps. This sheep is the product of a complex breeding operation aimed at recovering a breed that is presumed to have been lost through crossing with sheep from many regions outside the Valle Stura (Lebaudy 2011). While interesting in themselves, the technical details of this operation are not as important as a number of other things to be said about the Sambucana.[4]

First, the Sambucana is best understood as a site of cultural construction. The Ecomuseo della Pastorizia, a local ecomuseum, sustains the recovery of the Sambucana as a vehicle to commemorate the Valle Stura's former historical importance. Yet, while the Sambucana serves very usefully to integrate the trajectories of contemporary, local trade in wool, cheese, and meat,

---

4 Despite the absence of all the outward signs associated with modern genetic enterprises, the development of the Sambucana rests on the integration of long-established agricultural practices and an understanding of the animal body as a complex, genetic composite (see Luparia 2000).

sheep were only important to the Valle Stura for a brief moment in time, when they contributed to the erstwhile Kingdom of Savoy's participation in a global trade in wool (Ambrosoli 2000).[5] Furthermore, once the market for wool dwindled into insignificance, the sheep's flesh and milk provided no viable, alternative source of income for those who had staked their livelihood upon sheep because the sheep's flesh was consumed very rarely and only by the poorest members of society, and the cheeses most sought out were made from cow's, not sheep's milk. Instead the valley became renowned as a source of manpower to manage the commercial flocks of the Languedoc and dairy cattle in the Montferrat. Consequently, if the Sambucana serves to evoke a once integrated alpine community, distinct and self-contained, it also lends another axis to Aime, Allovio, and Viazzo's (2001) study of transhumant shepherding in a valley neighboring the Valle Stura. By charting patterns of mobility, the authors contest a common perspective on alpine communities, which regards these communities as once integrated and self-sustaining but eventually falling victim to the corrosive progress of modernity (see also Rosenberg 1988). In the Valle Stura, this questionable organic perspective is reproduced by the contemporary materialization and commodification of the past as "living" past (Lowenthal 1998) (see also Graham, Ashworth, and Tunbridge 2000).

Second, if the Sambucana is to be understood as an "invented tradition" (Hobsbawm 1983), it is important to take note of the work that such invention does. According to Legg's (2005) reading of Nora's *Lieux de Mémoire*, Nora regarded the body as a site of counter-memory, real and resistive to the state's appropriation of the past. As Nora puts it:

> We should be aware of the difference between true memory, which has taken refuge in gestures and habits, in skills passed down by unspoken traditions, in the body's inherent self-knowledge, in unstudied reflexes and ingrained memories, and memory transformed by its passage through history. (1989, 13)

In other words, unlike history, the body does not lie. Here, however, the body is no such thing. The Sambucana is better understood as the contemporary monument, working in a different economy of political signification to that

---

5 Despite wool having long been one of the principal commodities traded across the globe, there is no single, comprehensive analysis of sheep, wool, and their historical importance. There is nothing comparable to Riello's (2013) study of cotton apart from Fontana and Gayot's (2004) collection of disparate essays on the history of markets for wool. On the sheep that have sustained these markets, see Ryder (2007) and also Armstrong (2016).

of the state but an economy of political signification nonetheless. Reprising Shukin's (2009) critical dissection of the animal's body and the formation of capital, but moving in the opposite direction to Shukin's attention on dismemberment, the Sambucana produces exchange value by enabling the integration of otherwise disparate and centrifugal economic, social, and cultural processes into an idealized, single commemorative structure. This alters qualitatively the understanding of the past and in a manner such that it also enables the development of new markets and new forms of consumption. Not only does the production of the Sambucana respond to the growing importance attached today to the preservation of genetic resources (Evans and Yarwood 2000) but also to a related yearning for the authenticity of the food eaten and the clothes worn (see Craig and Parkins 2006; Gwilt and Rissanen 2011; Pike 2015). Usefully, Jordan (2015) discussed the phenomenon as involving the consumption of "edible memory." Furthermore, insofar as contemporary biopolitical governmental formations tie power and bodies together, here the binding would appear to operate by means of our choices with regard to what we eat and wear (see Evans and Miele 2012; Goodman 2016; Shamir 2008). In so doing, the production of the Sambucana might be said to partake in a more general bioeconomic and biopolitical turn, operating in a comparable, structurally significant mode, the mode of "bio-heritage" (see Houlbrook 2017; Lowenthal 2005; Roigé and Frigolé 2014).

In sum, the development of the Sambucana illustrates how the organism forges connections across time and space, to create a place, its history, and the exchange value of the commodities exported. Place, history, and economic value are not, in other words, primary but are instead produced, and they are produced as part of a process of folding, refolding, and crumpling (see Bennett and Connolly 2012; Patton 2012; Sauvagnargues 2016). From this perspective, there also is little need to equate bodies and organisms, the machine being an equally well-suited figure for the body's connective capacities, so lending weight to Cornec's substitution of coiling cord for the sheep's fleece (see also Smith 2017).

Topology: Configuring Bodies and Networks

While Deleuze powerfully subverts critical understanding of the body, otherwise sympathetic feminist responses have highlighted the need to retain something of the agency invested in the sexual body, albeit on terms that might prove immune to charges of naturalism (Marrati 2006). Grosz (1994) has sought to forge a way forward by mobilizing the Möbius band to conjure an understanding of the body as both a discursive product and an autonomous material agent. The Möbius band is a complex topological figure whereby a two-dimensional, rectangular surface is twisted and closed on itself so that the resulting three-dimensional band's inner and outer surfaces flow seamlessly into one another, while still remaining visibly distinct. My second case enables an exploration of such complexity and its significance to the understanding of the relationship between nodes, networks, and connectivity.

Like the Sambucana in the Valle Stura, the Xisqueta plays an important role in the renewal of communities in the Pallars Sobirà, in the Catalan Pyrenees (see also Mármol and Vaccaro 2015). The Associació Rurbans (hereafter Rurbans), a local voluntary organization, together with Obrador Xisqueta, an equally local association of sheep owners, operate the Escola de Pastors de Catalunya (hereafter EPC) (Ahumada 2013). The latter offers young people from across Spain, from both urban and rural backgrounds, an opportunity to learn the business of shepherding and to secure employment not just as shepherds but also in a whole range of related and ancillary occupations. Furthermore, Rurbans seeks to rebalance the contemporary, dominant association of ovine production with meat consumption by developing supplementary markets, including the renewal of markets for wool and woolen textiles whose production and trade once drove local shepherding to the margins of the global agricultural economy.

Significantly, the enterprise evolving around the Xisqueta rests on ambitions to reorder the movement of global capital. As Ploeg (2008) observes, the difficulties confronting contemporary agricultural producers worldwide have led many to either abandon production or to minimize their engagement with the market. The latter response effectively returns the producers to the status of peasants. Some have actively embraced this process of global repeasantization, aiming to reappropriate the agro-ecological commons and forge a new "bio-civilization" (Goodman and Salleh 2013). Rurbans seeks to follow in these steps, sometimes employing the phrase "som pagès," Catalan for "we are peasants," as its slogan (see Monllor 2013a, 2013b). Admittedly, policies privileging large landowners and corporate forms of agricultural production have proven a major hurdle. As interviews with graduates of the EPC document reflect (Ahumada 2013), limited access to land is a major constraint upon the successful integration of new agricultural producers and upon the consequent renewal of local communities (see also interview with local community organizer, August 15, 2015). At the same time, however, a still experimental blending of wool from the Xisqueta with wool of the Merina Negra, which is produced by the members of Laneras, a cooperative located in distant Extremadura, promises to multiply the political leverage and transformative ambitions of Big Brother Bio Farming, the latter being an umbrella for social enterprises such as Rurbans and Laneras (interview with local community organizer, August 14, 2015). In other words, by managing the relationship between sheep breed and provenance, the wool and woolen garments that the Xisqueta cooperative retails, either directly or through supportive metropolitan retailers, act as networking devices, connecting not just a new generation of ethical consumers but also social enterprises across Spain, France, and, increasingly, the entire European Union (see also Lang 2010; Marsden and Murdoch 2006).

This said, while the processes involved in the Xisqueta's construction then echo those associated with the Sambucana and also suggest that these two organisms are best characterized as networking technologies, interviews with the EPC's graduates reflect a countercultural, affective investment in the work of shepherding that calls for closer attention. This is how two graduates summarize the nature of shepherding as a distinctive form of work, involving an equally distinctive relationship between humans, sheep, and the landscape:

> It is another life!
> ...
> You get to know each sheep, you see how they grow and you become attached to them. It's different.
> ...
> It's a very strange kind of connection because you suddenly start to feel as if you, the sheep and the landscape are one. (Ahumada 2013, 25, 30)

Furthermore, the following exchange between two other graduates conveys the difficulties involved in the functional nature of this otherwise intimate relationship:

> Seeing them entering the slaughterhouse was traumatic. That was when I said "I have had enough and want to do it my way"
> ...
> You cannot invest too much affection in animals who you will have to sell or sacrifice. Since they ultimately are commodities, all that you can offer them is the best life possible, feeding them well, being patient and not making them bear the brunt of your own limitations.
> ...
> I know all this, but when you identify one animal in particular and you put a name to it. (Ahumada 2013, 76–78)

The halted, incomplete nature of the closing statement, conveyed by the conventional use of ellipsis, "i li posis un nom . . ." in the Catalan original, recalls Agamben's (1999) discussion of Deleuzian understanding of existence and the singularity of the named, lived life. There are a number of things that can then be said about EPC's graduates investment in the work of shepherding.

First, Agamben draws on Deleuze's "Immanence: A life" (2001) to argue that the conjunction of the act of naming and its suspension is the signature of "life itself," this being a form of life beyond the grasp of power and knowledge. There are good reasons to eschew Agamben's neo-vitalist assumptions about an immanent, self-moving power.[6] It bears noting, however, how Derrida's (2008) reflections on Adam's naming of the animals in the mythical Garden of Eden associate this act and the exercise of sovereignty over animal existence, but they also point to God's surrender of sovereignty over Adam. As such, the naming of animals is a free act. Viewed from this perspective, naming can then be regarded as an ambiguous exercise, pivotal to objective classification but also individuating and so opening onto responsibility to the "creature" named. The ellipsis signals this relationship that exceeds the capacities of language to capture its full meaning. On this understanding, it is important not to overlook how, even when destined for slaughter, each named animal has its story and how this individuating, singularizing story is fundamentally important to the relationship between the like of shepherd and his or her sheep (Fontana 2004) (see also Aime, Allovio, and Viazzo 2001; Despret and Meuret 2016). At the very least, such intimate relationship is vitally important to the investment of labor that the renewal of the peasant mode of production requires (Porcher 2017).[7]

Second, if Rurbans can be regarded as acting as a vector of global political transformation, its gains would seem to stem from the grounding of the enterprise in the specificities of the particular form of life that the conjunction of name and ellipsis signals. Thus, for example, Rurbans' organizers deploy the notion of iconic representation reflexively, rejecting any disproportionate insistence on a distinctive genetic identity of the Xisqueta (interviews with

---

6 Agamben argues that Deleuze's (2001) mobilization of the ellipsis to characterize the singularity of a lived life offers a wholly different way of understanding human existence. Focusing on Deleuze's formative reading of Spinoza, as well as their shared interest in those situations where existence is suspended between life and death, Agamben proposes that the hesitation conveyed by ellipsis bears witness to Spinoza's understanding of life as immanent cause. Cooper (2009) disputes Agamben's reading of Deleuze and Spinoza. On the related notion of linguistic vitalism, see Chiesa and Ruda (2011).

7 Yi-Fu Tuan (2004) argues that naming and affection are never far removed from dominance. The point here, however, is not to dispute the importance of power but to draw attention to fissures within its fabric.

community organizer and local sheep owner, August 15, 2015).[8] To Rurbans' members and the EPC's graduates, their enterprise is about the reproduction and renewal of a local and distinctive form of life, which, simultaneously, calls on them to move outside themselves, connecting with others, not just consumers, but also the nonhuman animals on whom the enterprise depends. This comportment resonates with Porcher's (2017) reflections on life and death in the modern slaughterhouse. Porcher attends to the complex ties between the lives of nonhuman animals, the work of raising and eventually slaughtering these animals, and the consumers who would reject the forms of life dependent on the slaughter. Drawing on Mauss to displace Marx's understanding of value, Porcher proposes that the slaughtered animal should be regarded as enabling the continuation of life by donating their own. As Porcher puts it, "The tie means more than the commodity . . . the value of the tie is of more importance than the value of the usage and the value of the exchange" (104). In other words, the affective ties between human and nonhuman animal that are built up over the course of the working lives lived together, from birth to death, are a source of value beyond the abstract calculations on which use value and exchange value are predicated. Returning to Rurbans, it is openness to these ties, to the obligations which they and their interruption entail, that makes each and every member of the collective part of a lively and insurgent "form-of-life," the lived life that "can never be separated from its form, a life in which it is never possible to isolate something such as naked life" (Agamben 1996, 2–3) (cf. Oliver 2008; Wadiwel 2015).

As a result, the body of the animal to which the phrase "i li posis un nom . . ." points would seem to operate in a manner that resonates with Grosz's distinctive understanding of subjectivity. Grosz turns to the Möbius band to articulate how power, the body, and subjectivity are intertwined, writing of this topological figure:

> It enables subjectivity to be understood not as a combination of psychic depth and a corporeal superficiality but as a surface whose inscriptions and rotations in three-dimensional space produce all the effects of depth. It enables subjectivity to be understood as fully material and for materiality to be extended and to include and explain the operations of language, desire, and significance. (210)

On this understanding, which derives as much from Lacanian psychoanalysis and its account of the co-constitution of seemingly antithetical features of

---

[8] The genetic status of the Xisqueta would appear to be as complicated as that of the Sambucana (see Ainhoa et al. 2014; Vidal 2004).

the subject's psychic structure, as it does from Deleuzian, if not Bergsonian, flattening of spatiotemporal relations, the body and power flow into one another so seamlessly that the two are indiscernible and yet remain distinct. While Grosz mobilizes this insight to understand the production of desire, particularly in relation to heterosexual norms and the possibility of their subversion, here the emphasis is on the manner in which this understanding holds out the possibility of an unmediated, immediate connection with an authentic, original body, which binds, on the one hand, the assemblages of shepherds, sheep, and landscape, and, on the other hand, the geopolitical order evolving out of these same assemblages (see also Grosz 1995, 2004).

In sum, while the processes involved in the Xisqueta's construction echo those associated with the Sambucana, the connections between pastoral existence and the global transformations which the Xisqueta enacts call into question Cornec's clothing of his sheep in the winding cord of a now antiquated analogue technology because the Xisqueta displays all the attributes of an actor-network technology and its distinctive dispersal of agency (see also Law and Mol 2008). Yet, there remains something about this understanding of the relationship between nodes, networks, and connectivity that seems insufficient to capture the full thrust of Forster's injunction.

Temporality: What of the Organism's Mortality?

While helpful, Grosz's recourse to the topology of the Möbius band, which is poised precariously between the certainties of mathematical, axiomatic thought, and the ambiguities of poetic expression, also testifies to a difficulty and interruption in the articulation of nodes, networks, and connectivity.[9] The nature and source of this difficulty is perhaps better understood by returning to the exchange between the two graduates of the EPC quoted earlier. As the first shepherd puts it, "Seeing [the animals] entering the slaughterhouse was traumatic." In other words, the exchange between the two graduates and its disclosure of the singularity of the life lived are precipitated by the confrontation with mortality, with the temporality of existence. This detail is of some importance.

In a discussion of the human, the animal and the possibility of understanding these two terms in a manner that transcends all anthropocentrism, but

---

9 Lacan, from whom Grosz borrows the understanding of subjectivity as a Möbius band, insists that its mobilization is strictly mathematical, rather than metaphorical. On the difficulties involved in maintaining the distinction, see Martin and Secor (2014). For a useful discussion of the theoretical significance of Lacan's turn to this topological figure, see Palombi (2009).

will also acknowledge the differences in kind that motivate Grosz's analysis of corporeal existence, Cimatti (2013) argues that, for all the references to animals, most reflections on the constitution of the subject have been about the human and what it means to be human. In and of itself, Cimatti argues, the animal does not exist. The animal is instead the imagined figure of the other, in whom the subject invests all hope of securing possession of itself, elusive as this may be since all markers available hitherto have proved inadequate to the task of differentiation that goes with the subject's proper and distinctive name. As Cimatti also observes, the confrontation with mortality is a pivotal moment in the constitution of this subject, disclosing as it does the inextricable link between naming and the impossibility of securing the identity of the subject named, on the one hand, and, on the other hand, the inevitability of this same named subject's eventual dissolution, in death. As a result, the desire for the communion of all animals, human and nonhuman, should be understood as the expression of this subject's alienation from itself and from the world in which it is immersed inescapably. Viewed from this perspective, the desire for connection to which some of the EPC graduates would seem to speak, also points to a desire to overcome mortality that comes with the naming of the animal, by embracing the flow of life itself. Yet, as long as one holds to any notion of individuation and subjectivity, such embrace of absolute immanence is bound to be self-defeating. Cimatti argues that this embrace, if it is at all possible, calls for a complete exit from the symbolic order and becoming animal. In other words, one can only become immanent by ceasing to be altogether, but the desire for such annihilation emerges from the very symbolic order one wishes to escape. The alternative is to embrace this understanding of human subjectivity, as precarious and forever alienated, and begin instead to explore the limits of the symbolic order, seeking the chinks through which human animality reveals itself, perhaps in the work of poetry.[10]

Just as the ontology underlying Deleuzian understanding of corporeality has to be taken at face value and the test of its merits lies in its productivity, the same should be said of Cimatti's heterological understanding of the subject and its constitution. From this point of view, Cimatti's concluding turn to poetry, as witness to the work of traversal and the disclosure of the real,

---

10 Cimatti's analysis might be regarded as a Lacanian response to Derrida's reflections on the relationship between the human and the animal, which can also be read as primarily a critique of Lacan and Lacanian understanding of language; see also (Oliver 2008).

seems retrograde. By retrograde, I mean that poetry is invested here with the power to disclose something already existent, rather than the power to bring into being something unprecedented. It may be more productive instead to note how the impasse over the possibility of any connection between different forms of corporeal existence, which Cimatti identifies, also leads to some convergence between himself and Nancy, though its implications remain unexplored. It seems to me that a Nancean understanding of the dependence of all sense of singularity on a body that is not one's own, but is instead the nexus of relationships to others, offers greater scope to combine understanding of existence advanced so far, that is, as wholly relational, and yet allow not only for discontinuity between self and other but also for care about fragility and mortality (see also Dejanovic 2016; Watkin 2015).

Nancy (2000) seeks to decenter and spatialize existence. Revisiting Heidegger's understanding of existence, Nancy proposes that existence takes the form of irreducible plurality such that the unfolding of being must be understood as taking place in the opening of the gap separating self and other. On this understanding, loss is the discovery of self to which the transformative words "seeing them [the animals] entering the slaughterhouse was traumatic" would seem to speak. It bears stressing that these are transformative words out of which emerges something different, if not unprecedented. The fuller implications of this understanding of existence is nowhere exhibited more clearly than in Nancy's (2008) account of touch. Nancy employs Christological imagery to articulate his distinctive thinking about the act. Following this imagery, one is called to distinguish between the notion of touch at stake in Thomas' relationship to Christ's body, whereby the real is guaranteed by the possibility of touch, and the relationship between Christ and Mary Magdalen, whereby the real is produced by detachment and the denial of touch in the famed *noli me tangere* scene. The opening up of a gap in the fabric of the world, in other words, is both the condition of possibility of touch and its denial, as well as productive of all that flows from the consequent, dynamic play of connection and disconnection. Returning to the questions about connectivity that this essay seeks to raise, if meaning arises out of the relationality of networked nodes, the condition of possibility of such relationality is the action of separation, the opening of the gap between the diverse nodes that constitute the network. Admittedly, the ontology of this understanding is as unsettling as any neo-vitalist attribution of intrinsic meaning, but it also enables a shift from questions of identity to questions of process and the differential temporalities characterizing the life and times of nodal conjunctions (Colebrook 2012) (see also Dejanovic 2016; Esposito 2010; Esposito and Nancy 2001).[11] This is perhaps the very stuff of crumpling, as distinct from crumpled, topologies to which the Sambucana's own complex relationship to the times and spaces of the Valle Stura would seem to speak (see also Bennett and Connolly 2012).

To conclude, post-structuralist theory proposes that meaning arises out of relational networks. The above reflections on networks, nodes, and connectivity have sought to examine the nature of the nodal points, focusing particularly on their materiality as well as associated topologies and temporalities of existence. The discussion was articulated around the development of two breeds of sheep, the Sambucana and the Xisqueta, drawing on more-than-human geographies to articulate the relations between space, time, and bodies out of which these breeds have emerged. While much of the literature on contemporary forms of life has drawn attention to the fragmentation of the organism and the role of such fragmentation in the production of value, the development of the Sambucana has moved in the opposite direction, illustrating how, by reconfiguring spatiotemporal connections, the organism serves to create place, history, and value. Viewed from this perspective, there is no reason to draw any distinction between organisms and machines, both being composite, nodal points whose historical significance derives from the networks out of which they emerge. Cornec's installation captures the point very effectively. On the other hand, the development of the Xisqueta also draws attention to agency of the emergent nodes. To the EPC's organizers and graduates, the importance of the Xisqueta resides in its enabling the reproduction and renewal of a local and distinctive "form-of-life," which, simultaneously, calls on them to move outside themselves, connecting with others, including nonhuman, animal others. Every good shepherd knows one sheep from the next. As such, the body of the named animal, whether on the upland pastures in the Maritime Alps or the Catalan Pyrenees, would seem to exemplify Grosz's understanding of subjectivity as resembling a Möbius band, which Grosz has mobilized in response to Deleuzian perspectives on the body

---

11 Esposito and Nancy have been involved in a protracted debate over the relationship between the body and the flesh. Nancy rejects the language of the flesh because he regards it as part and parcel of Christian onto-theology, preferring instead to think about the possibility of community by imagining a plurality of copresent bodies. Esposito takes the opposite view, arguing that the language of the flesh provides a better model for the constitution of the community because bodies entail closure and exclusion. Tellingly, Esposito also suggests that the language of the flesh opens the discussion to engagement with Deleuze and his notion of the "body without organs," which he understands as a configuration of the flesh that does not coincide with the body. It seems to me that what is at issue in this debate is the relationship between bodies and organisms, terms that this paper seeks to distinguish by reference to the latter's mortality.

and their calling into question the status of the organism as any singularity. Nodal points are both effects and transformative agents.

This said, the understanding of the relationship between nodes and networks advanced so far would seem to overlook the role of disconnection in the constitution of these nodes, the disconnection that has figured in this paper as the confrontation with mortality, with questions about who or what dies and how. As a result, the analysis offered here has also moved progressively from Deleuzian perspectives to a Nancean understanding of corporeal existence, drawing on both their shared understanding of existence as emerging out of spatial relations between multiple bodies, and what would appear to be a divergent understanding of temporality. Viewed from this vantage point, the desire for connection across space, time, and phylum, to which some of the EPC graduates would seem to speak when they evoke a "strange kind of connection [such that] you suddenly start to feel as if you, the sheep and the landscape are one," might be understood as also speaking to a desire to overcome mortality by embracing absolute immanence, by embracing the ultimate medium, life itself. The more important point, which this essay has sought to articulate, is however that meaning arises out of the relationality of networks, but the condition of possibility of such relationality is the act of separation, the becoming "fragment." The act of separation constitutes the material bodies sustaining network, meaning and perhaps even love. As such, existence might be said to take place betwixt and between the materiality of the nodes and the immateriality of the networks out of which the nodes emerge. This, I think, is the meaning of Forster's injunction to "connect."

Bibliography

Agamben, Giorgio. 1996. *Means without End: Notes on Politics*. Minneapolis: University of Minnesota Press.
———. 1999. "Absolute immanence." In *Potentialities: Collected Essays in Philosophy*, 220–39. Stanford, CA: Stanford University Press.
Ahumada, Laia de. 2013. *A Cel Ras: Converses amb Joves Pastors*. Lleida: Pagès Editors.
Aime, Marco, Stefano Allovio, and Pier Paolo Viazzo. 2001. *Sapersi Muovere: Pastori Transumanti di Roaschia*. Roma: Meltemi.
Ainhoa, Ferrando, Félix Goyache, Pere-Miquel Parés, Carlos Carrió, Jordi Miró, and Jordi Jordana. 2014. "Genetic Relationships between Six Eastern Pyrenean Sheep Breeds Assessed Using Microsatellites." *Spanish Journal of Agricultural Research* 12(4): 1029–37.
Ambrosoli, Mauro. 2000. "The Market for Textile Industry in Eighteenth Century Piedmont: Quality Control and Economic Policy." *Rivista di Storia Economica* 16: 343–63.
Armstrong, Philip. 2016. *Sheep*. London: Reaktion.

Avellanet, Rosa, Jose Aranguren-Méndez, and Jordi Jordana. 2005. "La Raza Ovina Xisqueta en España: Caracterización Estructural de las Explotaciones." *Animal Genetic Resources Information* 37 (April): 21–29.

Bennett, Jane, and William Connolly. 2012. "The Crumpled Handkerchief." In *Time and History in Deleuze and Serres*, edited by Bernd Herzogenrath, 153–71. London: Continuum.

Buchanan, Ian. 1997. "The Problem of the Body in Deleuze and Guattari, or, What Can a Body Do?" *Body & Society* 3(3): 73–91.

Chiesa, Lorenzo, and Frank Ruda. 2011. "The Event of Language as Form of Life: Agamben's Linguistic Vitalism." *Angelaki: Journal of the Theoretical Humanities* 16(3): 163–80.

Cimatti, Felice. 2013. *Filosofia dell'Animalità*. Roma: Laterza.

Colebrook, Claire. 2012. "Post-Human Humanities." In *Time and History in Deleuze and Serres*, edited by Bernd Herzogenrath, 103–26. London: Continuum.

Cooper, Melinda. 2009. "The Silent Scream: Agamben, Deleuze and the Politics of the Unborn." In *Deleuze and Law: Forensic Futures*, edited by Rosi Braidotti, Claire Colebrook, and Patrick Hanafin, 142–62. London: Palgrave Macmillan.

Craig, Geoffrey, and Wendy Parkins. 2006. *Slow Living*. Oxford: Berg.

Cronon, William. 2009. "Foreword." In *Dreaming of Sheep in Navajo Country*, edited by Marsha Weisiger, ix–xiii. Seattle: University of Washington Press.

Dejanovic, Sanja. 2016. "Through the Fold: A Jointure of Gilles Deleuze and Jean-Luc Nancy." *Philosophy Today* 60(2): 325–45.

Deleuze, Gilles. 1992. *Expressionism in Philosophy: Spinoza*. New York: Zone Books.

———. 2001. "Immanence: A Life . . ." In *Pure Immanence: Essays on A Life*, 25–33. New York: Zone Books.

Deleuze, Gilles, and Félix Guattari. 1988. *A Thousand Plateaus: Capitalism & Schizophrenia*. London: Athlone.

Derrida, Jacques. 2008. *The Animal That Therefore I Am*. Edited by Marie-Louise Mallett. New York: Fordham University Press.

Despret, Vinciane, and Michel Meuret. 2016. *Composer avec le Moutons: Lorsque des Brebis Apprennent à leurs Bergers à leur Apprendre*. Avignon: Cardère Éditeur.

Esposito, Roberto. 2010. "Flesh and Body in the Deconstruction of Christianity." *Minnesota Review* 75: 89–99.

Esposito, Roberto, and Jean-Luc Nancy. 2001. "Dialogo sulla filosofia a venire." In *Essere Singolare Plurale*, edited by Jean-Luc Nancy, vii–xxix. Torino: Einaudi.

Evans, Adrian Bruce, and Mara Miele. 2012. "Between Food and Flesh: How Animals Are Made to Matter (or Not to Matter) within Food Consumption Practices." *Environment and Planning D: Society and Space* 30(2): 298–314.

Evans, Nicholas, and Richard Yarwood. 2000. "The Politicization of Livestock: Rare Breeds and Countryside Conservation." *Sociologia Ruralis* 40(2): 228–48.

Fontana, Giovanni Luigi, and Gérard Gayot. 2004. "Les villes lainières d'Europe entre histoire et patrimoine." In *Wool: Products and Markets (13th–20th Century)*, edited by Giovanni Luigi Fontana and Gérard Gayot, 11–15. Padova: Università degli Studi di Padova.

Fontana, Ignasi Ros. 2004. *La Transhumància Andorrana al llarg del Segle XX*. Barcelona: Alta Fulla.
Franklin, Seb. 2012. "Cloud Control, or the Network as Medium." *Cultural Politics* 8(3): 443–64.
Goodman, James, and Ariel Salleh. 2013. "The 'Green Economy': Class Hegemony and Counter-Hegemony." *Globalizations* 10(3): 411–24.
Goodman, Michael K. 2016. "Food Geographies I: Relational Foodscapes and the Busy-Ness of Being More-Than-Food." *Progress in Human Geography* 40(2): 257–66.
Graham, Brian, G. J. Ashworth, and J. E. Tunbridge. 2000. *A Geography of Heritage: Power, Culture & Economy*. London: Arnold.
Grosz, Elizabeth. 1994. *Volatile Bodies: Toward a Corporeal Feminism*. Bloomington: Indiana University Press.
———. 1995. *Space, Time and Perversion: Essays on the Politics of Bodies*. New York: Routledge.
———. 2004. *The Nick of Time: Politics, Evolution, and the Untimely*. Durham, NC: Duke University Press.
Gwilt, Alison, and Timo Rissanen. 2011. "Introduction from the Editors." In *Shaping Sustainable Fashion: Changing the Way We Make and Use Clothes*, edited by Alison Gwilt and Timo Rissanen, 13–14. London: Earthscan.
Hobsbawm, Eric. 1983. "Inventing Traditions." In *The Invention of Tradition*, edited by Eric Hobsbawm and Terence Ranger, 1–14. Cambridge: Cambridge University Press.
Houlbrook, Ceri. 2017. "Constructing Cultural and Natural Heritage: Parks, Museums and Rural Heritage." *International Journal of Heritage Studies* 24(4): 443–44.
Jordan, Jennifer A. 2015. *Edible Memory: The Lure of Heirloom Tomatoes and Other Forgotten Foods*. Chicago, IL: University of Chicago Press.
Kirsch, Adam. 2010. "The Prose and the Passion." *The New Republic*, July 13.
Kittler, Friedrich A. 1992. *Discourse Networks 1800/1900*. Stanford, CA: Stanford University Press.
———. 1999. *Gramophone, Film, Typewriter*. Stanford, CA: Stanford University Press.
Lang, Tim. 2010. "From 'Value-for-Money' to 'Values-for-Money'? Ethical Food and Policy in Europe." *Environment and Planning A: Economy and Space* 42(8): 1814–32.
Law, John, and Annemarie Mol. 2008. "The Actor-Enacted: Cumbrian Sheep in 2001." In *Material Agency: Towards a Non-Anthropocentric Approach*, edited by Carl Knappett and Lambros Malafouris, 57–78. Dusseldorf: Springer.
Lebaudy, Guillaume. 2011. "De la Demontine a la Sambucana." *Ethnozootechnie* 91: 73–85.
Legg, Stephen. 2005. "Contesting and Surviving Memory: Space, Nation, and Nostalgia in Les Lieux de Mémoire." *Environment and Planning D: Society and Space* 23: 481–504.
Lowenthal, David. 1998. *The Heritage Crusade and the Spoils of History*. Cambridge: Cambridge University Press.
———. "Natural and Cultural Heritage." *International Journal of Heritage Studies* 11(1): 81–92.
Luparia, Simona. 2000. "The Sambucana Sheep: A Project to Save a Valley." *Animal Genetic Resources Information* 27: 27–33.

Mármol, Camila, and Ismael Vaccaro. 2015. "Changing Ruralities: Between Abandonment and Redefinition in the Catalan Pyrenees." *Anthropological Forum* 25(1): 21–41.

Marrati, Paola. 2006. "Time and Affects: Deleuze on Gender and Sexual Difference." *Australian Feminist Studies* 21(51): 313–25.

Marsden, Terry, and Jonathan Murdoch. 2006. "Between the Local and the Global: Confronting Complexity in the Contemporary Agri-Food sector." In *Between the Local and the Global: Confronting Complexity in the Contemporary Agri-Food Sector*, edited by Terry Marsden and Jonathan Murdoch, 1–8. Amsterdam: JAI Press.

Martin, Lauren, and Anna J. Secor. 2014. "Towards a Post-Mathematical Topology." *Progress in Human Geography* 38(3): 420–38.

Monllor, Neus Rico. 2013a. "Introducció." In *A Cel Ras: Converses amb Joves Pastors*. Edited by Laia de Ahumada, 15–20. Lleida: Pagès Editors.

Monllor, Neus Rico. 2013b. "La nova pagesia: Vers un nou model agrosocial." *Quaderns Agraris* 35: 7–24.

Nancy, Jean-Luc. 2000. *Being Singular Plural*. Stanford, CA: Stanford University Press.

———. 2008. *Noli Me Tangere: On the Raising of the Body*. New York: Fordham University Press.

Nora, Pierre. 1989. "Between Memory and History: Les Lieux de Mémoire." *Representations* 26: 7–25.

Oliver, Kelly. 2008. *Animal Lessons: How They Teach Us to Be Human*. New York: Columbia University Press.

Palombi, Maurizio. 2009. "Neither Inside, nor Outside: Considerations on the Structure of the Subject and of Language in Jacques Lacan." *Etica & Politica/Ethics & Politics* 11(1): 351–60.

Patton, Paul. 2012. "Deleuze, Foucault and History." In *Time and History in Deleuze and Serres*, edited by Bernd Herzogenrath, 69–84. London: Continuum.

Pike, Andy. 2015. *Origination: The Geographies of Brands and Branding*. Malden, MA: Wiley.

Ploeg, Jan Douwe van der. 2008. *The New Peasantries: Struggles for Autonomy and Sustainability in an Era of Empire and Globalization*. Abingdon: Earthscan.

Porcher, Joceyline. 2017. *The Ethics of Animal Labor: A Collaborative Utopia*. Cham: Palgrave Macmillan.

Riello, Giorgio. 2013. *Cotton: The Fabric That Made the Modern World*. Cambridge: Cambridge University Press.

Roigé, Xavier, and Joan Frigolé. 2014. "Intrducción: La patrimonialización de la cultura y la naturaleza." In *Construyendo el Patrimonio Cultural y Natural: Parques, Museos y Patrimonio Rural*, edited by Xavier Roigé, Joan Frigolé, and Camila del Mármol, 9–28. Valencia: Germania.

Rosenberg, Harriet G. 1988. *A Negotiated World: Three Centuries of Change in a French Alpine Community*. Toronto: University of Toronto Press.

Ryder, Michael Lawson. 2007. *Sheep and Man*. London: Duckworth.

Sauvagnargues, Anne. 2016. "Becoming and History: Deleuze's Reading of Foucault." In *between Deleuze and Foucault*, edited by Nicolae Morar, Thomas Nail, and Daniel W. Smith, 174–99. Edinburgh: Edinburgh University Press.

Shamir, Ronen. 2008. "The Age of Responsibilization: On Market-Embedded Morality." *Economy and Society* 37(1): 1–19.
Shukin, Nicole. 2009. *Animal Capital: Rendering Life in Biopolitical Times*. Minneapolis: University of Minnesota Press.
Smith, Daniel W. 2017. "What Is the Body without Organs? Machine and Organism in Deleuze and Guattari." *Continental Philosophy Review* 51(1): 95–110.
Tuan, Yi-Fu. 2004. *Dominance and Affection: The Making of Pets*. New Haven, CT: Yale University Press.
Wadiwel, Dinesh. 2015. *The War against Animals*. Leiden: Brill.
Watkin, Christopher. 2015. "Badiou and Nancy: Political Animals." In *Nancy and the Political*, edited by Sanja Dejanovic, 43–65. Edinburgh: Edinburgh University Press.
Wegenstein, Bernadette. 2006. *Getting under the Skin: Body and Media Theory*. Cambridge: MIT Press.
Woods, Rebecca J. H. 2017. *The Herds Shot Round the World: Native Breeds and the British Empire, 1800–1900*. Chapel Hill: University of North Carolina Press.

CHAPTER TEN

Conclusions

Luis Lobo-Guerrero, Suvi Alt and Maarten Meijer

The project of thinking about imaginaries of connectivity and the creation of novel spaces of governance was originally posed as a provocation for authors to explore how ideas and practices of connectivity, novelty and governance materialised in spatial orders, and how could these orders be explored through the imaginaries that could, in principle, reveal them. Connectivity, as suggested in the introduction, does not render itself as a transcendental category of thought through which meaning can be stabilised and governed. Its relational character demands from the observer attention to the processes that make it possible, a focus on the effects that betray connectedness and, most importantly, an emphasis on analysing the terms under which something is made to connect or disconnect.

Why bother with thinking about connectivity and its effects as suggested here? The simple answer, as has been explored throughout the chapters in more or less explicit form, is that it reveals the operation of orders of governance. Orders of governance are understood here as the result of the relationality between agents, ideas, objects, beliefs and contexts which materialise in different forms which shape and influence conduct, spaces being the ones explored in this book. Governance, in this respect, is taken to be an effect of ordering practices. A connection is a revelation of order.

In a similar way, novelty was introduced in this book, thinking with Blumenberg, as the human ability 'to introduce absolute beginnings into reality' (Blumenberg 1985, 169). Here again, novelty is taken to betray an agency which manifests itself in an almost existential (modern) angst to create *ad infinitum*. As a creative claim, novelty performs an epistemological role. It operates as condition for emerging orders. As condition for emerging orders, novelty reveals itself as a connectivity effect. The connectivity effect, however, is not traceable to a sum of interacting components in time. It needs to be understood, instead, as an emerging event that does not relate to a logical sequence based on causal events. Emergence is not foreseen; it is not the result of prognosis. Emergence takes place and needs to be understood in relation to the very particular epistemological context upon which it occurs. In this respect, the pervasive claim to novelty in the modern age relates to an emphasis on events that perform a continuous and intense present.

The intellectual challenge is then how to approach novelty as the condition for emerging orders. The strategy explored in this book has been to approach imaginaries as empirical spaces where relationships between connectivity, governance and novelty can be explored. This is not a simple empirical approach that assumes phenomena to be out there waiting to be found. It is rather an approach that constitutes the imaginary as a site where intellectual experimentation and creativity takes place. It assumes the imaginary as a space where a creative experience, the experience of creating ways of being in the world, takes place.

Through the discussions, writing, editing and intellectual interactions out of which this book has resulted, it has become evident that such a creative experience invites creative reflection. In what follows, we reflect on the imaginary of connectivity presented in the chapters and the experience it reveals.

Experiences of Order, Power and Governance

In different ways, the chapters speak of experiences that are not fixed or stable but which can become so through their being incorporated into a particular order of governance. Yet, many of the chapters also suggest that there is something about the way in which things connect that retains the possibility of destabilising the established order and serving as the basis for an emerging one. As such, the possibility of experience that escapes its enframing is always there but, conversely, experience is also always vulnerable to being productive of an order of governance. Connectivity thus carries a double character. This tension between the production of order and that which exceeds it is at the heart of many of the chapters in this book.

Carina Huessy examines the face as a site of connecting that, in a time of biometric and behavioural profiling, is deemed to require governing and securing. The imaginary of connectivity that can be located in the face reveals an experience of bordering and governance. The experience of the border entails the separation of the safe from the unsafe, the good from the bad. Huessy argues that especially during the 'war on terror', this border was conceived as shifting and mobile. Instead of being located between geographical entities, the face becomes the site where this separation takes place and the uniqueness of each individual face is what enables the separation. The specific connectivities that constitute each individual face make possible its identification. The face, quite concretely, operates as one's passport and one's boarding pass as airports, for example, become increasingly 'smart'. Yet, new technology aims not only at identifying the face but also at identifying specific forms of behaviour, such as lying. As such, the experience of the border that the face reveals is not based only on what the face is but also on what it does.

The face, however, is also unpredictable due to its inherent ability to change. Huessy highlights the way in which increasingly sophisticated machine learning and data processing are used to try to capture the face regardless of its unpredictability. This incessant potential for emergence is nevertheless, Huessy argues, the way in which the face always exceeds its biopolitical governance. According to Huessy, the unpredictability of the face harbours 'potent fields of resistances'. As such, the experience of the face is double – Janusian – as there is a continuous tension between its stability and its unpredictability. Huessy, nevertheless, does not explore further the forms that these potential resistances might take. The face is conceptualised as free, yet always vulnerable to being captured by apparatuses of governance. It thus remains unclear whether or in what form the face could ever escape the fundamental tension between freedom and governance at the heart of biopolitics.

Barry Ryan examines the sea as an imaginary of connectivity that engenders both zones of governance and human zones of experience. The zones of governance emerge from human experience and their purpose is to regulate the movement of things and people. In Ryan's discussion, the state operates as that sphere of political existence that seeks to control and operate upon that which passes through or inhabits it. Yet, Ryan argues that zones of governance at sea are much more flexible and fluid than the zones of governance that states institute on land. Maritime zonation requires the state to adapt its operations of governance to the materiality that it is seeking to control.

Yet, according to Ryan, such zones of governance can never fully capture the human experience of space. Existential zones are informal and dynamic, holding the possibility of escaping the governance, or 'zonation', of territorialising entities such as the state. Through what he calls a 'phenomenology of zonation', Ryan identifies the properties that characterise human experience of spatial organisation. One such property is (a)roundness, which he perceives as a primordial way of relating to and organising space. Whereas the state tries to capture (a)roundness by regularising it, the human experience of (a)roundness nevertheless always exceeds and complicates the regularity that the state aims to institute. The zones of governance, such as cartographic expressions or symbols on a GPS system, are also experienced but only through experiencing the policing that maintains them. Ultimately, Ryan argues, similarly to Huessy, that the technologies of governance that aim to capture human experience or identity are never able to do so fully. While the study of international relations has focused extensively on these practices of state zonation, it has often neglected the spaces of human and, especially, of non-human experience. Ryan suggests that the zones of governance are always in tension with human and non-human zones of experience, and this tension is where we should direct our attention. Human imagination and non-human experience are, for Ryan, the spaces where we ought to look in order to move beyond a mere critique of practices of governance.

The imaginary of connectivity explored by Luis Lobo-Guerrero is that of the European cosmographic imaginary of the world in the sixteenth century. This imaginary reveals a particular way of experiencing life and space. Lobo-Guerrero emphasises, furthermore, that particular ways of experiencing world are infused with forms of power relations and, thus, orders of governance. The specific experience of interest here is the experience of knowing and of creating knowledge. As a consequence of the discoveries of the sixteenth century, Lobo-Guerrero argues, preceding conceptions of knowledge and experience became unsatisfactory because they were not able to adequately grapple with the problem of novelty that emerged with the discoveries. New empirical observations led to the questioning of the foundations of existing knowledge. More specifically, the tension at the heart of Lobo-Guerrero's examination is constituted between the Ancients' resort to a conception of knowledge as the revelation of something already known and the conception of knowledge emerging in the Renaissance whereby it is an experience of knowing that reveals itself. In the Renaissance, the notion of invention transformed from the discovery of something that already existed to the idea that it is possible to create something with no prior existence as a result of experience. Knowledge is experienced through creating it as opposed to revealing it.

Lobo-Guerrero emphasises that the discoveries and inventions of the fifteenth and sixteenth centuries expressed a form of creating knowledge through experience that is different from method-driven empiricism. Rather, what is at stake here is 'an openness to the strange, a capacity to marvel, and an extraordinary empirical resourcefulness in action and thought' (Lobo-Guerrero, 25). Whereas a pre-constituted method always orders experience, what Lobo-Guerrero calls 'empirical dexterity' is rather the ability to engage with that which exists in 'the absence of a road' (Agamben 2007a, 32). This also means that the subject of such knowing does not pre-exist the experience of knowledge production. Rather, the subject of knowledge is constituted by an encounter with a novel experience that cannot be comprehended through pre-existing ways of making sense of reality. Like Ryan, Lobo-Guerrero is suggesting that we turn our attention to the spheres of human experience that can reveal forms of existence that are not reducible to orders of governance. Whereas Ryan suggests that the discipline of international relations has focused on state and other institutional practices at the expense of the spheres of human imagination and experience, Lobo-Guerrero argues that the issue is not only the neglect of such spheres as objects of analysis. Rather, he takes issue with the form of empiricism that is at the centre of international relations specifically and social sciences more generally. The predominance of method-driven empiricism means that there is very little space for the kind of experience of knowing that Lobo-Guerrero associates with 'empirical dexterity'. In other words, the limits of our engagement with the constitution of novel spaces of governance concern not only *what* is known but also *how* it is known.

Camila del Marmól discusses the imaginary of the Art Urgell region and problematizes the governance of rural Catalonia through touristic development. Approaching tourism as constituting an imaginary of connectivity, she observes an underlying tension between historical pressures of political and economic centralization and the experiences of communities inhabiting the Art Urgell as they struggle to preserve and produce their autonomy and identity. In doing so, del Marmól argues that the imaginary of rural disconnectivity that results from the tourism discourse is an integral part of the socio-economic regimes through which the Art Urgell is governed. Like so many rural spaces inside and outside Europe, the Art Urgell is envisaged to be a space outside the hectic and rushed temporality of the city, a space where one can truly experience an authentic life sheltered from modernity through its disconnected nature. The imaginary of the Art Urgell is analysed by del Marmol as a disconnected space deeply implicated with the production of a touristic experience of 'being disconnected' as well as being complicit in the governance and ordering of the Art Urgell through a regime of touristic regional development.

As argued by del Marmol, touristic experiences and their discourse of authenticity should not by any means be taken at face value. For Agamben, tourism represents the loss of experience that characterizes late capitalism. Thus, he writes in *Profanations* that 'everything today can become a Museum, because this term simply designates the exhibition of an impossibility of using, of dwelling, of experiencing' (2007b, 84) In a similar way, the significance of modern touristic 'experience' is noted by Baudrillard when he discusses tourist attractions as a waste treatment plant to regenerate an imaginary and save the experience of reality in the world without. 'The imaginary of Disneyland is neither true nor false', he writes in *Simulacra and Simulation*, 'it is a deterrence machine set up in order to rejuvenate the fiction of the real in the opposite camp' (1994, 13).

Whereas del Marmól does not go as far as Agamben or Baudrillard in her critique of touristic imaginaries that foreclose the Art Urgell as a disconnected space, her problematisation concerns the way in which such imaginaries present an experience as untainted, natural and authentic. She shows how touristic experiences and touristic imaginaries of rural disconnectivity presuppose particular constellations and histories of connections – markets, national projects of socio-economic development, as well as EU agricultural and regional policies – and in turn constitute 'active players in the production of networks to which the region is connected' (del Marmól 2019, 16). Thus, this imaginary of disconnectivity influences the interpretation of the complex history of the region and feeds into local historical experiences of religious, political and economic conflict between the communities inhabiting the Art Urgell and broader Spanish communities. In this way, touristic discourses become part of the history of Catalan autonomous regional identity and reinforce a political imaginary that portrays the belief that community-building efforts of the Art Urgell have been suppressed and frustrated by centralisation and nation-building efforts within Spain. Though presenting itself as an authentic and concrete experience of rural life, the touristic experience of the Art Urgell is abstract and should be understood as such. It can only truly be appreciated by situating it within the broader constellations that enable it and the local histories it violates by forgetting and concealing.

Paolo Palladino, on the other hand, argues that histories that seek to understand the present as produced by power relations, operating within loosely post-structuralist understandings of the body, themselves fail to take note of the depth and singularity of mortal experience as surfacing in the event of touching and being touched. The central tension organising Palladino's discussion problematises connectivity, as understood through the relational ontologies of Gilles Deleuze and his followers, by taking serious note of existential experience insofar as it disconnects from the constellations in which it emerges. Through this tension, Palladino grapples with the double character of connectivity – of being productive of a governmental order and yet eluding or even potentially resisting such a constellation – as he explores the relation between the biotechnical production of sheep bodies and their mortal alterity.

On the face of it, the Deleuzian likening of bodies to machines seems to be highly productive for problematising the discourse of authenticity surrounding projects to resuscitate Alpine and Catalan regional identity through the introduction of the region's sheep: the Pecora Sambucana and Oveja Xisqueta. These specific breeds of sheep and their supposed intimate connection with 'authentic life' of the Maritime Alps and Catalan Pyrenees are constructed within the biopolitics and bioeconomics of regional development. A striking artistic rendering of the artificiality of these sheep – as testified by the gene-technological apparatuses through which these 'authentic organisms' are constructed – is provided by Cornec's sheep statues, which are made wholly out of telephones and their coiling cords.

Yet, Palladino's careful analysis moves beyond this initial reading. The Pecora Sambucana sheep, genetically modified through careful breeding practices, are most certainly produced and thereby inseparable from the historical constellation of genetic technology and economic interests tied to the project of constructing ostensibly 'historically authentic' ways of life in the Catalan Pyrenees, as critically discussed by del Marmól. Nonetheless, a key existential experience is missed if the understanding of these sheep is reduced to Deleuzian or Latourian analyses of historico-governmental constellations of power. Where such analyses reduce bodies to surfaces, thereby making them ontologically indistinguishable from machines, Palladino implores us to consider the existential depth of mortal bodies as it withdraws from these histories.

The experience of touch that Palladino draws from the experiences of 'rurban' students working with these animals signifies an irreducible depth of the encounter between human and sheep. Students are confronted with their own mortality and the singular and mortal existence of their others. Rather than ontologies that understand the body as being reducible to relations, assemblages or actor-networks, Palladino points to the importance of the work of Cimatti and Nancy to understand the existential particularity at play here: an existence that is 'wholly relational, and yet allows not only for discontinuity between self and other, but also for care about fragility and mortality' (Palladino 2019, 15). Whereas del Marmól critically displaces touristic experiences of 'authentic rural disconnectivity' by situating them within the region's wider history of connectivity, Palladino argues how disconnectivity – now understood in ontological terms – is key to understanding the interaction between mortal bodies, as it withdraws from such histories while being produced within them. If touristic experience is best understood through the constellations that enable it, the experience of touch cannot be appreciated by blindly subsuming it under the latter. Rather, Palladino argues, the '[o]*pening up of a gap in the fabric of the world* ... is both the condition of possibility of touch and its denial, as well as productive of all that flows from the consequent dynamic play of connection and disconnection' (Palladino 2019, 15–16, emphasis added).

In a similar way, Benjamin Tallis' analysis of the work of Caspar David Friedrich in terms of the way it envisages the German landscape and affects its viewers generates a discussion of art and its experience through a problematisation of the tension between art and its context. Thus, Tallis highlights experiences of connectivity on the level of content and form of Friedrich's works, while implicitly moving to an understanding of an artwork's disconnectivity with regard to the question of interpretation and political context.

Although contemporary critics tend to subsume Friedrich's works under the heading of 'proto-fascist art', Tallis suggests that the quality and innovativeness of his works be appreciated through its art-historical context and by engaging with the visual aesthetics of his paintings. During Friedrich's own life, his works provoked the German artistic establishment through his rejection of the prevailing Renaissance doctrine that centred on the hierarchisation and separation of art genres. Where this tradition prescribed strict rules on content and form to be used in landscape painting, iconography or portraiture, Friedrich employed unusual perspectives, compositions and colours in order to create a novel type of painting: the romantic landscape. Rather than representing quiet pastoral scenes devoid of humans, Friedrich's landscapes evoke and express emotions – the sublime of nature. The creation of a landscape painting, for Friedrich, takes place when observation and emotion meet, which is why he advices to 'close your bodily eye so that you may see your picture first with the spiritual eye' (Chilvers 2009, 230).

To this end, Friedrich's paintings operate on a logic of theatricality that draws viewers into the artwork rather than into the logic of mimetic representation that characterises pre-romantic art. Friedrich's landscapes do something and thereby activate the observer, in other words, rather than passively emulate what is seen by the artist's 'bodily eye'. By employing techniques such as unusual perspectives and the *Rückenfigur*, Friedrich creates paintings that invite the viewer to actively participate in its expression, by affectively realising or feeling what this particular landscape shows and provokes. Thus,

Tallis argues, we are best to see Friedrich's landscape as a particular imaginary of connectivity: It generates a novel connection between different German regions and between the German peoples and their landscapes by forging a connection between the artwork and its viewer. It is this connectivity that we experience when looking at a Friedrich painting.

Yet, in arguing for the connectivity effect of Friedrich's paintings, Tallis inevitably complicates the politico-artistic question of interpretation. On the one hand, he argues with passion that Friedrich's critics in the twentieth and twenty-first century misinterpret his works when they reduce his works to (proto-)Nazi art. On the other hand, he suggests that we will 'experience' Friedrich's paintings truly when we just go and view them for ourselves and put them in the context of their creation. Is Tallis suggesting that an art critic like Koerner, whose otherwise careful analyses Tallis clearly appreciates, has never seriously looked at a landscape by Caspar David Friedrich? Or that Nazi art censors were themselves simply mistaken when they saw in Friedrich's works somewhat of an ode to the *Blut und Boden*? Rather than settling for one interpretation over the other, a reframing of the issue is possible by separating the theatricality of Friedrich's works from the idea that they can be understood literally. The crucial innovation and novelty of Friedrich's landscapes, as Tallis suggests, is their theatricality, the connectivity effect they achieve with and through the viewer. Yet, just because viewers hereby become part of the artwork does not mean that they therefore have a privileged epistemological position that enables them to understand everything that a Friedrich painting has to offer. Following Heidegger, Greenberg and Harman, we might say that an artwork always holds an ontological independence from both artist and viewer (e.g., Harman 2016, 198–224; Heidegger 2011, 90, 131). Like Palladino's articulation of the experience of touch, the experience of an artwork withdraws from any context in which it is posited and any particular direct political interpretation or *Erlebnis* we may have of it: It always remains there to challenge us, to offer something new. In addition to its historical involvement in the production of orders of governance by generating particular connections between Germans and the German landscape, the experience of Friedrich's art is also always an experience of an other who continues to elude our attempts at grasping its hidden depths.

Moving on to a different spatial imaginary, Sujin Eom presents and engages with the tensions at play in constituting a new transpacific space in the nineteenth century. This spatial construction was premised on the mutually constitutive categories of race and space, which framed a very particular form of mobility, of migrant populations, of urban dwelling and of governance. The establishment of Yokohama in Japan and Incheon in

Korea as treaty ports widened the port network opened to foreign trade and commerce in East Asia and attracted Euro-American entrepreneurs and Chinese migrants and labourers. Migration brought along concerns on security and health through the cohabitation of populations, but it also contributed towards creating the physical, cultural and political contexts of the new transpacific space.

An enabling element of this experience relates to the introduction of a propulsion technology, steam ships, which allowed for the establishment of relatively stable transport routes improving on the unpredictability and time lengths of the age of sail. Steamships and the new shipping lines required the introduction of a different understanding of connectivity which involved physical elements such as dedicated infrastructure and supply chains to provide for coal and maintenance of the fleets, human resource in the form of specialist services and labour, organisational elements in the form of logistical operations and, very importantly, a chronological element which involved the coordination of time and processes between ports.

This technological and organisational change, which was far from simple, affected the kind of labour required and made available in the port cities and the conditions under which it operated. As Eom analyses, the concentration of populations from diverse cultural, social and economic backgrounds became visible in the urban built space, in the segregation between groups and the forms of governance implemented for managing interaction and productivity. Because the development of the treaty port economy operated upon the increased mobility and concentration of merchants and labourers, the resulting mix of permanent and transit populations brought health and security concerns for the authorities in unprecedented forms. Treaty port cities were governed as trading outposts with colonial-like characteristics based on the laws and institutions of Euro-American traders and governors. Governance operated upon racial discrimination and commercial principles that shaped a transpacific trading space.

Continuing with a similar regional context but addressing imaginaries in a different form, Ariel Shangguan engages with the problem of a globalising order through the contentious idea of sovereignty. Shangguan builds on the tension that arose between a Confucian worldview, the Chinese idea of world order, *tian xia* (all under heaven), that prevailed for millennia until China was forcefully introduced into the international realm during the Opium Wars in the nineteenth century. For Shangguan, both *tian xia* and the Western modern conception of sovereignty reveal two understandings of connectivity which are not compatible. Whereas the latter has enabled China to contest Western imperialism and become a player within the international system, the former has led to forms of essentialism in Chinese intellectual discourse.

The experience of connectivity in the idea of *tian xia* contrasts starkly with that of Western sovereignty. *Tian xia* entails a borderless world where the middle kingdom, a centre of civilizational superiority, is surrounded by barbarians. These are allowed to enjoy the order provided by the power of the monarch if they willingly submit to him and the knowledge of his authority. Western sovereignty entails the existence of an international system premised upon the recognition of sovereignty between states and the operation of a system of international law where states are considered equal. The borderless space of world government of *tian xia* rivals with the bordered spaces of the international. Whereas for Western sovereignty it is the recognition of states as actors and entities which enables forms of connectivity and disconnectivity, for *tian xia* it is the recognition of the authority and law of the monarch of the middle kingdom which allows things to connect.

In Shangguan's argument the experience of connectivity that results from the two ideas of *tian xia* and Western sovereignty is in sum one which results from two contested forms of authority and governance. The terms under which people, goods and polities are to connect depend very much on the rationality, the principles of formation upon which order is conceived. The experience of connecting within *tian xia* is one of subsuming order under a dictated law. That of connecting under Western sovereignty is one that results from the interaction between international entities through force, cooperation or law.

Çapan and dos Reis' chapter provides a case of imagined spaces of connectivity in relation to the idea of Germanness in the context of the recently created empire in the late nineteenth century. Maps produced by the leading cartographic publishing house Justus Perthes are used to reveal a tension between an imagined German population spread across the globe, an extended German territory encompassing the location of cultural Germans abroad and an idea of a German state which defines its people on racial grounds. The maps depict an imaginary of connectivity where the idea of empire transcends the territoriality of the nation-state.

The experience of connectivity in this case derives from the images and data depicted through the maps. By rhetorically employing colours, geographical projections, tables and other forms of information (including blank spaces), the publishers aim to create a spatial awareness on the viewer which might, or not, correlate with a current middle-class imaginary. The relevance of this observation is that the maps can either reinforce or create such imaginaries of connectivity by creatively deploying biopolitical technologies such as statistics and probabilities, to depict populations, territories, economic zones of influence and cultural regions.

The resulting visual imaginary of Germanness raised concerns in the international arena with regards to German future spatial aspirations. Foreign powers viewed with suspicion the way in which maps portrayed allegedly German spaces but refrained from formal complaints due to the private nature of the publishing house. Such suspicions, however, contribute towards revealing an experience of connectivity and disconnectivity with regards to cultural perceptions and constructions of space. In a context of international imperial competition, Germany was seen as a possible threat in relation to colonial territories and with regards to the European balance of power.

The maps, however, would not represent a unanimous spatial imaginary, be it in the form of Germanness, as a cultural depiction of space, or of Germandom, as an expression of an aspirational territorial expansion of the German state. They would depict different and sometimes not compatible spatial experiences within society. As products aimed at a private market, these maps could very well be interpreted as serving political, social, economic as well as cultural interests but also commercial ones. If feeding desires or fantasies for a greater Germany contributed to sales, it is well worth exploring the market dimension in order to better understand the experience of connectivity or disconnectivity that they promoted.

Finally, it is also worth considering the role of these maps for educational purposes. As state-of-the-art visual depictions of space, supported by apparently scientifically supported data, the images appear as factual truths ready for consumption. The experience of an uninformed observer will be different from that of an expert and the impact of an unmediated exposure to maps can frame the imaginary of connectivity for a time to come.

Imaginaries of Connectivity and the Creation of Empirical Spaces

The experiences of order, power and governance expressed through the different chapters in this book and the intellectual strategy of approaching imaginaries as empirical spaces where relationships between connectivity, governance and novelty can be explored, begs the question, however, of the binary logic on which the idea of connectivity/disconnectivity operates.

The relationship between connectivity/disconnectivity, where any form of connectivity refers to some form of disconnectivity and every disconnectivity reveals a formerly connected order, operates a binary distinction typical of metaphysical thinking. Aimed at facilitating order in a logic of argumentation by signifying oppositions that establish difference, binaries operate a role of stabilisers of meaning and frame thought within the spectrum of possibilities they allow (Plato 2005, 351–65: 102B–105D). For example, when posing something as a connectivity effect, engaging with such event requires a consideration of the disconnectivity out of which it emerged or that it created. If a connectivity effect reveals an order, it does so by relating to a possible disorder which can be approached as a difference or a change in the terms under which something was previously considered to be connected. A revolution, for example, would relate to a radical change in the terms under which the complexity of actors and interests constituting a social/political/economic/spiritual/intellectual collective connect and would reveal a particular disconnectivity characteristic of a previous order.

Binaries are, however, disruptable. Derrida, for example, showed how oppositions presented as foundational in metaphysical thinking such as presence/absence, inside/outside and friend/enemy can be subverted by deconstructing them. Deconstruction entails unmasking the traces of logic that stabilise the meaning of dichotomies (Derrida 2016). Subverting such logic requires an engagement with the epistemological formations on which they operate. As events, epistemological formations are always historical and as such leave traces through which they can be investigated (Veyne 1984). A careful historical epistemological analysis of these formations will reveal their precarious foundations, their unnecessary character and their evitability. The connectivity/disconnectivity opposition and the ways in which it is used in articulating discourses of order and governance and the constitution of novel spaces in modernity is revealing of not only a metaphysical mode of reasoning which supports a logic for ordering the real that limits the possibility for alternative thought but, most importantly, of a way of conceiving being in the world as connect-able. Connect-ability, in turn, reveals a form of agency and potential, which, framed through the binary, veils alternative ways of conceiving being in the world. The question that follows is, what would a way out of this particular metaphysical intellectual framing be? One possibility lies in problematising the relationship between experience and knowing that seems to have been solidified in modernity through discourses of scientific knowledge and method. This involves approaching imaginaries as creative empirical spaces.

Within the wider context of the problematic confluence between ontology and epistemology characteristic of Western, modern scientific reasoning (Stengers 2000), where the possibility of experience has been colonised and normativised through Enlightened understandings of reason (Agamben 2007a, 13–72), imaginaries depict the richness and multifarious dimensions of being. By thinking of imaginaries of connectivity as the experience of connecting, the aprioristic approach of observing phenomena as informed by theoretical presumptions is put into its epistemological perspective which reveals the subject who has sought to know but veils the excess of such a form of knowing. In simpler terms, a focus on the experience of connecting allows thinking about the relations that make order, power and governance possible in the contingency of events. This is not the simple move of the so-called 'practice turn' in the social and human sciences but a careful engagement with the excess of the politics of life expressed through culture, affect, aesthetics and also non-traditional sciences.

To think of connectivity as experience has an important implication. It challenges the traditional understanding of empirical sites. The empirical site is not that of the laboratory where controlled conditions are achieved and indeed necessary for the exploration of particular phenomena. It is not the space colonised by the evidence-based empiricism of the scientific method that has tamed the expression of the senses through graduations of intensity and typical kinds. The idea of an empirical site should be claimed back from the monopoly of a scientific epistemology which regulates what can be observed, by whom, in what way and for what purposes. A call for a sensitisation of the empirical is a claim for the possibility of observing expression beyond degree and kind and asking of it what the relations are out of which it emerges. By claiming back the empirical from scientific approaches to knowledge, the social and human sciences can move beyond the idea of an empirical site into that of an empirical space.

Empirical spaces are not locations of knowledge but their production. As produced spaces, they express the effects of the interaction of a plethora of elements where the nuances of being play a central role. Empirical spaces are to be approached as spaces from which to understand the particularities that constitute a connectivity event. Arguing that imaginaries make connectivities possible is not to say that there is a linear consequence between imaginaries and connectivity where imaginaries precede experience. It is to say instead that both imaginaries and connectivities can be understood as part of a single event where imaginaries can be explored to reveal what the connectivity effect is about.

Bibliography

Agamben, Giorgio. 2007a. *Infancy and History: On the Destruction of Experience*. Translated by Liz Heron. Annotated edition. London: Verso.

———. 2007b. *Profanations*. Translated by Jeff Fort. New York: Zone Books.

Baudrillard, Jean. 1994, *Simulacra and Simulation*. Translated by Sheila Faria Glaser. Ann Arbor: University of Michigan Press.

Blumenberg, Hans. 1985. *The Legitimacy of the Modern Age*. Translated by Robert M. Wallace. Cambridge, MA: MIT Press.

Chilvers, Ian, ed. 2009. *The Concise Oxford Dictionary of Art and Artists*. Fourth edition. Oxford: Oxford University Press.

Del Marmól, Camila. 2019. "Cultivating Disconnection: Imaginaries of Rurality in the Catalan Pyrenees." In *Imaginaries of Connectivity: The Creation of Novel Spaces of Governance*, edited by Luis Lobo-Guerrero, Suvi Alt, and Maarten Meijer, xx. Lanham, MD: Rowman & Littlefield International.

Derrida, Jacques. 2016. *Of Grammatology*. Translated by Gayatri Chakravorty Spivak. Fortieth Anniversary Edition. Baltimore: Johns Hopkins University Press.

Harman, Graham. 2016. *Dante's Broken Hammer*. London: Repeater Books.

Heidegger, Martin. 2011. 'The Origin of the Work of Art'. In *Basic Writings*, edited by David Farrell Krell, 83–140. London: Routledge.

Lobo-Guerrero, Luis. 2019. 'Novelty and the Creation of the New World in Sixteenth-Century Spain'. In *Imaginaries of Connectivity: The Creation of Novel Spaces of Governance*, edited by Luis Lobo-Guerrero, Suvi Alt and Maarten Meijer, xx. Lanham, MD: Rowman & Littlefield.

Palladino, Paolo. 2019. 'Organisms, Nodes and Networks'. In *Imaginaries of Connectivity: The Creation of Novel Spaces of Governance*, edited by Luis Lobo-Guerrero, Suvi Alt and Maarten Meijer, xx. Lanham, MD: Rowman & Littlefield.

Plato. 2005. 'Phaedo'. In *Euthyphro, Apology, Crito, Phaedo, Phaedrus*. Translated by Harold North Fowler, 193–403. Cambridge, MA: Harvard University Press.

Stengers, Isabelle. 2000. *Invention of Modern Science*. 1st edition. Minneapolis: University of Minnesota Press.

Veyne, Paul. 1984. *Writing History: Essay on Epistemology*. Translated by Mina Moore-Rinvolucri. Manchester: Manchester University Press.

Epilogue

Only Connect[1]

Peter Adey

At first I found it slightly odd to focus a collection like this on imaginaries of connectivity. It just feels so obvious, so ubiquitous but somehow so timely. As the editors note, connection is in many ways a watchword for our times. And it has been since plaudits of globalisation gave rise to so many of the metaphors of flux, flow, nomadism, interdependency, borderlessness which seem to imply limitless connectivity on a planetary scale. Connectivities such as these have also been perceived as disruptions to our dominant spatio-temporal ontological imaginaries: from territories, regions, locales, institutions, corporations, states as well as in more temporal frames, such as the paradigms, continuities, epochs, time periods, evolutions, revolutions, accelerations. In lots of ways then, connectivity seems to have been already taken on board by a whole raft of thinking and scholarship across the social sciences and humanities and in other ways too by engineers, ecologists, biological scientists, neurophysiologists – who have long thought in terms of various structures of connection, such as infrastructures, networks, systems, systems of systems, neural nets, the internet and an internet of things. Of course, we also know just how problematic some of these assumptions have been.

And yet, it is hard to avoid the burden of connectivity in everyday life, in our news, media and social media and our everyday objects – phones,

---

[1] I've unashamedly stolen the title of this Epilogue from the BBC Two series 'Only Connect', hosted by Victoria Coren Mitchell.

clothes, light bulbs. The quality of connectivity is of course a key determinant to many people's ability to sustain their social lives; maintain commitments; participate in work, access services, etc. At the same time, we're given warnings about the apparent proliferation of connecting things and devices which seem to connect us all too much and all of the time. Nineteenth-century sociologists and psychologists of course worried about this too in the whirlwind of industrial capitalism and conflict; some named it neurasthenia.[2] Today, connection is positively encouraged to almost all demographics but highly unevenly. Less so for children who we worry are overconnected, more so for busy professionals who are finding it very difficult to connect with meaningful relationships. Connectivity, we are told, is what will help us invent, be creative, find more clients, more friends, do more. It seems downright essential for elders who are becoming isolated and lonely by contradictory movements that see some disconnected from public life, in part, at least in the United Kingdom, from austerity that has reconfigured many connections to public services and even welfare through anonymous and electronic means. Indeed, what isn't more or less connected? What kind of relation does not rely upon a connection or disconnection in some way?

Rightly, the editors suggest that connectivity, and imaginaries of connectivity, could be given much more focus and more sustained historical and conceptual thought. The authors brought together in this collection take on this task in a set of inspiring, deep and original chapters which all have something different to say about connectivity and many other issues. Across this range, an onus is given to connectivity and its role within different orders of power and governance across time and space. Thus, most of the chapters in the volume focus on state imaginings, state tools and techniques of territorial and population management, influential political ideologies, maps, atlases, state theorists and influential academics naturalising their geopolitical imaginations. It is worth saying, however, that there is perhaps a predominance of state and semi-elite focus and less subaltern, marginalised perhaps indigenous and non-state actors. Instead, connectivity is understood through what Çapan and dos Reis call relatively privileged '"modes of reasoning" and ways of imagining time and space'. Perhaps the transhumant inter-European shepherding movements of sheep and other animals found in Palladino's chapter illustrate how some non-state networks and connectivities sit somewhere within a backdrop to this volume. One would wonder

---

2 David Harvey, *The Condition of Post-Modernity* (London: Wiley, 1992); Stephen Kern, *The Culture of Time and Space*, 1880–1918 (Cambridge, MA: Harvard University Press, 1983).

what imaginaries of connectivity would look like explored across other actors and empirical spaces?

In the rest of this epilogue, I want to pay tribute to the impulses and arguments made within this fascinating collection by trying to collate together some themes which could be taken further productively.

Mobility and Space

It is worth acknowledging that the modes of connectivity described in the book are performed by multiple kinds of mobility or mobilities. As some of the authors note, the scholarship from the interdisciplinary field of mobility studies provides some relevant context here[3] but also conceptual and critical fuel for the kind of movement being explored.

At the same time, what is really interesting from the perspective of a geographer is the importance of particular kinds of spatial containers that work with or against connectivity throughout the book. Maybe this is not surprising, as various authors from mobilities have shown, movement must always be thought of in terms of its motion through and across, and transforming of space and context, what Doreen Massey thought of in terms of a processual, extroverted sense of space.[4] Mobility, of course, has been a highly spatially inflected term, while many have shown how, throughout history, movement and connectivity necessarily push and pull different kinds of spatial terms, concepts and practices, with varying degrees of success.[5] Through the chapters then, connectivity and its imaginaries seem performed with various kinds of spatial framing or containment. For instance, Barry Ryan shows in his work on the 'will-to-zone' of state sovereignties on maritime space, different zones with varying affordances or capacities that overlay or crystallise maritime politics with differing forms of connective potential. Interestingly, finding the power in notions of the round or the sphere in maritime histories, Ryan shows how a zone provides a site of apparent boundedness and safety but also a vehicle from which the world is navigated. Moreover, we see how

---

3 See, of course, Tim Cresswell, *On the Move: Mobility in the Modern West* (New York: Routledge, 2006); John Urry, *Mobilities* (London: Polity, 2007); see also William Walter's recent work on what he has called 'viapolitics', which gives emphasis to the political significance of vehicles within different regimes of movement, such as the U.S. and UK deportation system. William Walters, 'Migration, Vehicles, and Politics: Three Theses on Viapolitics'. *European Journal of Social Theory* 18, no. 4 (2015): 469–88.

4 Doreen Massey, *For Space* (London: Sage, 2005).

5 Mimi Sheller, *Mobility Justice* (London: Verso, 2018).

zones or other forms of containment or enclosure work with connection and disconnection. On the one hand, they provide, for Ryan, capacities to secure and fend off, perhaps for states wishing to protect from bubonic plague. On the other, they help connect to valuable resources of taxation, fishing stocks, seabed hydrocarbons under the rights of sovereignty.

Ironically, then, *Imaginaries of Connectivity* actually see space of various kinds multiplying. Throughout the volume there are rural–urban regional differentiations; other kinds of scales from the body (not necessarily human) to the globe; European, colonial imperial ties; the space of landscape and landscape painting; place, borders and boundaries; topographic and topological spaces and networks.[6] Indeed, Sujin Eom's powerful exploration of the treaty port system is suggestive – through its careful and granular analysis – of a geography of connectivity composed of highly controlled and segregated spaces for inhabitation and movement. We see, here, then international connectivities, constituted and expressed in different spaces and scales which, through built form, help to channel or structure mobile bodies and practices. Earlier in the volume, Lobo-Guerrero shows that it is within the space of Spanish colonial exploration and conquest that the conditions of possibility for particular thinking about novelty was to come about. Connectivity as a space for novel thinking perhaps. In lots of senses then, *Imaginaries of Connectivity: The Creation of Novel Spaces of Governance* opens up some interesting points of dialogue across spatial thought, from IR and political philosophy through to human geography.

Proximities and Propinquities

The modes of connectivity through the book seem to demand a kind of proximity, the kind of 'compulsion to' that Deirdre Boden argued for. This becomes really interesting in the various forms of 'contact' explored throughout the book. This takes the form of contact zones where knowledge and customs, and concepts of sovereignty, are shared and transmitted; in Ariel Shangguan's chapter, for example, contact spaces such as borders and ports alongside other contacting practices and technologies are given focus. So I suppose my point is that what constitutes connectivity, and

---

6 See debates on the construction of scale: Sallie A. Marston, John Paul Jones III and Keith Woodward, 'Human Geography without Scale'. *Transactions of the Institute of British Geographers* 30, no. 4 (2005): 416–32.

imaginations of it, are multiple enactments of proximity between entities, places and even bodies.

For example, Huessey interestingly explores developments in facial recognition technologies in border zones or everyday life via rapidly advancing software, which potentially brings far higher levels of abstract scrutiny to the face which is scanned, recorded, measured and compared. In some senses it is *still* touched through what media theorist Lisa Parks has explored as a visual and technologically mediated form of 'close sensing'.[7] But it also goes about removing physical touch (perhaps like Ryan's maritime zonations) to an arm's length and precisely to remove the touch or proximity, often performed by the face, of an ethical relation between humans.[8] Conversely, Palladino explores a more intimate set of affective ties between people and animals in strange relations of connectivity, even if partly at the service of global capital. In a different way, Çapan and dos Reis explore the flickering presence of connections to colonial empire through a cartographic imagination and representational practices. While in Benjamin Tallis' chapter, it is a viewer perceiving a landscape painting.

In this sense, I think it is interesting how the authors see in these different kinds of presence and proximity a manner of connectivity performed through quite different modes of encounter, some passive, some engaged, some thoughtful and meditated, others affectively charged or technologically mediated.

Novelties

At the editors' and Luis Lobo-Guerrero's suggestion, we are invited to consider connectivity as a style of novelty. The book's chapters made me think about this in a number of ways. On the one hand, the rich historical grounding to several contributions helps us see that, of course, connectivity and its desire and concern to be connected or not, is not new or novel. Connectivity has a history, woven into the histories of empire through conquest, expansion and settler-colonialism – innately mobile and connecting if violent and suppressive practices. Ariel Sangguan shows how European and Asian political doctrines of sovereignty *and* connectivity came to infect each other. We see how a nineteenth-century Chinese notion of 天下 (tian xia), which

---

7 Lisa Parks, 'Points of Departure: The Culture of US Airport Screening', *Journal of Visual Culture* 6, no. 2 (2007): 183–200.

8 See Jenny Edkins. *Face Politics* (London: Routledge, 2015).

implied world connectivity through unity, government and the erasure of borders and the boundaries of nation-states which had epitomised the European Westphalian notion of an international system of state sovereignties, was reshaped by European diplomatic dialogue. In essence, a Chinese notion of complete unity presupposed total interconnectivity without boundaries, which came into contact with a competing imaginary of interconnected bounded entities of nation-states.

Furthermore, in seeing connectivity as a novel space of governance and for new forms of political thinking, the contributors to this volume also dedicate their writing to quite a novel range of forms and materials, from cameras and other material technologies, tourist guides and brochures, sheep, to popular representations, novels, landscape painting, atlases, maps. Even if, once again, these have often been the preserve of places to look for the state imagination, though perhaps not sheep(!), they also reflect a shifting attunement of IR and political geography, towards not only representations and practices but material objects, cultures and affects.[9]

Furthermore, perhaps in Tallis we see a push towards what the co-editors hint at in the introductory chapter, when they suggest that 'connectivity' could be engaged with as a form of experience, as experience. Tallis foregrounds the experience of the viewer/spectator with Friedrich's landscape of connectivity, bringing us closer to the ways in which connectivity makes and remakes not only a space of governance but also the subjects of it – with feeling and agency to resist and reinterpret. The reader then gratefully explores both Palladino and Camila del Mármol's exploration of disconnection through their ethnographic reflections and attunements, albeit in very different contexts.

The Allure of Connectivity

Finally, connectivity also seems present in the volume as a condition which is innately compelling and alluring – what Derek McCormack might refer to, following Graham Harman, as a crucial kind of allure for thinking and experimenting, drawing us in like a thread into something, novel or a space or set

---

9 Claudia Aradau, 'Security That Matters: Critical Infrastructure and Objects of Protection'. *Security Dialogue* 41, no. 5 (2010): 491–514; William Connolly. 'The "New Materialism" and the Fragility of Things'. *Millennium* 41, no. 3 (2013): 399–412; Katharine Meehan, Ian Graham Ronald Shaw and Sallie A. Marston, 'Political Geographies of the Object'. *Political Geography* 33 (2013): 1–10.

of relations.¹⁰ For Harman and by way of McCormack, what makes something alluring is not really its presence but rather how things or ideas and imaginaries like connectivity also remain, partly, withdrawn from us. There is a part of something which is somehow 'inaccessible to whatever perceives or apprehends it'.¹¹ In other words, connectivity as a mode of reasoning or government or political agency, as a condition of possibility for political thinking, is perhaps always also partially incomplete, fragmented, also (dis)connected and partially not ever really knowable but just out of reach.

Of course, connectivity animates the chapters of this book in different ways, but I think for most it is both an allure for thought and also an alluring potential over which (geo)political reasoning and practice desire and strive to make sense, of or to capture. For some it is a kind of infrastructure of life, residing at the thresholds of human experience; indeed for those concerned with infrastructures that constitute electronic connection, this is, a literal withdrawal beneath our feet. Connectivity may itself be invisible, ineffable or the single or multiple entity or things connected. It may be an impartial connection, perhaps of data, but not touch, perhaps of words, but not expression.

---

10 Derek McCormack, *Atmospheric Things: On the Allure of Elemental Envelopment* (Durham, NC: Duke University Press, 2018).

11 Ibid., 56.

Index

Abbey in the Oakwood, 161
actor-network theory, 4–5, 209, 225
Agamben, Giorgio, 207, 224
algorithmic warfare, 57–58
Alldeutscher Atlas, 134, 139–42, 144, 146–47
Alldeutscher Verband, 129, 133, 139, 147
all under heaven. *See* Tian Xia
altdeutsch, 165, 173
Alt Urgell, 177–78, 181–82, 184, 186–87, 189, 190
Amazon's Rekognition program, 40, 45–46, 53, 56, 59–60
Anderson, Benedict, 3, 41
Arendt, Hannah, 5, 22, 61
aroundedness. *See* maritime zones, constitutive properties of
assemblages, 4–5, 104–6, 209, 225
Auslandsdeutsche. See Germandom, imaginaries of
Auslandsdeutschtum. See Germandom, imaginaries of
Auswanderer. See Germandom, imaginaries of
AVATAR (Automated Virtual Agent for Truth Assessments in Real-Time), 48–49, 59–60

Bachelard, Gaston, 95–96
Benjamin, Walter, 60–61
Bergson, Henri, 17, 209
Berkowitz, Bruce, 42
biometric technology, 7, 42–43, 46–49, 52, 55–56, 220–21
biopower, 49–50
Blumenberg, Hans, 5, 57, 219
board of health, 75, 79
body, 200–204; and connectivity, 204–6, 209, 211–13; Deleuzian understandings of, 202–4, 210; and disconnectivity, 211, 213, 226; and materiality, 200–205, 208, 212–13; as sites of heritage and memory, 200, 202–4, 225
Boers, 127–29, 143, 147–48
border, 39, 41–42; border control systems, 40, 46–49; bordering practices, 39, 41, 51, 56–57, 59; and Chinese political imaginary, 111–17, 119–24, 229; creation of bordered space, 8, 42, 58; face as a border, 7, 46–48, 51, 54–56, 221
Bryant, Levi, 93
Bushes in the Snow, 154

cartography, as a technology of power, 8, 134–37, 139–41, 143, 146, 147, 229
Castoriadis, Cornelius, 3–5, 41
Catalan-Occitan nation, history of, 190–92
Catalan Pyrenees, 9, 117–81, 183, 187–89, 192–93, 200, 205, 212, 225
Cathar heritage. *See* Catalan-Occitan nation, history of
Chasseur in the Forest, The, 158, 161–62, 167
Chinatown, 7–8, 72, 76, 79–80, 82–84
Chinese migrants, in transpacific networks, 67–68, 74, 83–84; fear of, 68–69, 71, 78–83
Chinese translation of international law, 113–15, 117–18, 121
Cimatti, Felice, 210–11
colonial fantasies, 129–32
colonialism, 8; the German colonial movement, 130–33, 134, 147–48
Columbus, voyages, 13, 25–28
Common Agricultural Policy, 177
complexity theory, 4
Confucian worldview, 110, 120, 228
Congress of Vienna, 155, 159, 165
connectivity, 1–2, 9–10, 14–15, 39–41, 72, 106, 199–201, 235–36, 239–40; and affect, 39, 52–55, 61, 170–71, 206, 208, 226; allure of, 240–41; and biopolitics, 39, 49, 54–57, 229–30; connectivity and disconnectivity as metaphysical binary, 230–31; connectivity effect, 6, 137, 147, 220, 227, 231–32; digital connectivity, 39, 41–44, 45, 49, 53–55, 57; and experience, 2, 33–34, 39, 41, 220; in German imperial imaginaries, 130–32, 136–37, 147, 149; and Romantic aesthetics, 163–74, 226–27; in transpacific, 68–71, 74–75, 78–80, 82–84, 227–28
contact zone, 68, 75, 238

Convention for Prevention of Pollution of the Sea by Oil, 102
Cross in the Mountains, 156–58, 170

Daston, Lorraine, 17–19
da tong, 120, 122–23
De Acosta, José, 15, 25–26, 31–33
De Landa, Manuel, 92–93
De las Casas, Bartolomé, 15, 25–26, 28–31
Deleuze, Gilles, 15, 58, 200, 202, 204, 207, 209, 210, 212–13
Deutschbund, 133
Deutsche Erde, 134, 147
Deutscher Kolonial-Atlas, 127, 134–38, 140–41
Deutschsoziale Reformpartei, 133
Deutschtum, 127–28, 131, 136; *See also* Germandom, imaginaries of
digital surveillance, 7, 56, 221
Diplomatisch-Genealogische Jahrbuch, 140
disconnectivity, 177–79, 181, 185–86, 188, 192–93, 213, 224–26; as a precondition of connectivity, 211–13, 226
discovery, 5
disease, nineteenth-century the fear of, 67–69, 75
Dixon, Andrew Graham, 160–62, 171
Durkheim, Émile, 113, 181

Eigentümlichkeit, 169
empire: German imperialism, 8, 130, 132, 134, 141, 149; informal empire, Western rule in the Pacific, 73
empirical acts, 15, 22, 25, 27–28, 30–33
empirical dexterity, 15, 24–25, 30, 32–33, 223
empirical norms, 20
empirical space, 4–5, 15–16, 18, 22, 25, 31, 33–34, 41, 220, 230–32; *vs.* empirical site, 232
envisioned community, 172, 175

Index ~ 245

epistemic community, 14, 17; epistemic agents, 14
ethnonationalism, Germany, 8, 133–34, 149
experience, 2, 5–6, 8, 14, 17, 220–32, 240; human experience of space, 90–91, 96–98, 221–22; in medieval epistemologies, 18–19; in renascent European empiricism, 13, 20, 25, 28, 30–32, 33, 222–23; and romantic art, 167–68, 170–75, 226–27

face, 7 39–41, 58, 60–61; biopolitics of, 39–40, 221; as a border, 7, 46–48, 51, 54–56, 221; as confessional site, 55; face value, 52, 55, 59–60; facial recognition technology, 42–49, 50–51, 221; Janusian character, 7, 39–40, 42, 51–53, 55–57, 59–61, 221; as novelty, 60–61, 221; as a site/sight of connectivity, 7, 39–40, 42, 43–44, 47, 50–52, 54, 56–57, 220–21, 239; and time (pre-face, inter-face), 53–55
Forster, E. M., 200–201, 209, 213
Foucault, Michel, 15, 17, 42, 49–50, 54–56, 60, 91, 130
Friedrich, Caspar David, 8–9, 153–75, 226–27, 240

German Colonial Atlas. See Deutscher Kolonial-Atlas
Germandom, imaginaries of, 8, 128–29, 131–37, 139–41, 143, 147–49, 229–30; competing imaginaries of, 129, 131–32; making of the 'German people' 130, 135–36, 139, 147–49
German *Reich*, 130–31, 137, 139–41, 143, 148, 160
Gerstenhauer, Max Robert, 147–48
globality, 2, 7
Gosselin, Martin, 127–28
Gotha. See *Justus Perthes*

governance: orders of, 31, 219–20, 222–23, 227, 235; spaces of, 6–7, 14, 31, 33–34, 49–51, 53, 59–60, 147, 149, 155, 160, 163, 172–73, 175, 219–20, 240; subjects of governance in Romanticism, 155, 167–72, 175; zones of governance and the symbolic, 89–92, 97–98, 100–103, 105–6, 221–22
Great Enclosure, The, 172
Grosz, Elizabeth, 204–5, 208–10, 212–13
guo, 116–17. *See also* sovereignty, introduction to China
Guo Songtao, 117–18

Hacking, Ian, 130, 134–36
Hasse, Ernst, 147
Heidegger, Martin, 94–95, 211, 227
heritage discourses, 178–79, 184–85
historical epistemology, 16–17, 33, 231
historical ontology, 6

IARPA's Janus program, 40, 43–44, 56, 59–60
Iberian renaissance, 7, 15
iBorderCtrl, 47, 54, 59–60
imaginaries, 2–5, 14–15, 16–17, 33, 39, 57, 219; and biopolitics, 51–52, 54, 56–57, 229–30; Chinese political imaginaries (*see* Tian Xia); of connectivity, 4–7, 9, 14, 39, 41, 51–52, 58, 110, 115–16, 121, 124, 129, 132, 134, 139, 155, 159–60, 163, 166–68, 172–75, 219–23, 225, 227, 229–30, 232, 235–37; of disconnectivity, 9, 177–79, 186, 188, 192–93, 213, 226; as empirical space, 4–5, 15, 220, 230–31, 220, 230, 232, 237; geopolitical imaginaries, 144, 146; German colonial imaginaries, 129–31, 134, 136–37, 139, 141, 149; of Germandom (*see* Germandom, imaginaries of); as images of

(dis)connectivity, 6, 57, 181; of migration, 70–71, 78, 83; and novelty, 4, 19, 26, 33–34; of the real, 3–4, 6, 14, 39, 235; of real-time, 39, 41–42, 45–46, 52; of rurality, 177, 179, 182–86, 188–89, 193, 223–24
imagined communities, 3, 148–49, 154
immunity. See maritime zones, constitutive properties of
Incheon, 19th century, 68, 73–74, 76–77, 227–28
individual conscience, emergence of, 17–20, 23, 26–28
innovation, in renascent epistemology, 17, 20, 22–23, 222
instrumental readings of artworks, 154
international, introduction to China, 7, 110
international relations, study of, 4, 14–15, 106, 110–12, 124, 130, 222–23
international society, in Chinese political imaginary, 110, 118, 123
invention, interest for. See novelty, Maravall's conditions of possibility for

Japan Weekly Mail, 67–68, 74
Josa de Cadí, 190–91
Justus Perthes, 8, 127–29, 133–34, 138–40, 142–47, 148, 229

Kaiser Wilhelm II, 128
Kang Youwei, 119–24
kenning, 96–97, 103
Kiefer, Anselm, 162, 175
King Friedrich Wilhelm III of Prussia, 158, 170
Koerner, Joseph Leo, 154, 156, 160, 162–63, 165, 168–72, 175, 227
Kruger telegram, 128, 147
Kuhn, Thomas, 21

Lacan, Jacques, 8, 208
land kenning, 96–97, 99–100

landscape painting and imaginaries, 8–9, 155, 160, 163, 172–75; connectivity effect of, 163–70, 172, 173–74; and romanticism, 155, 157–59, 164, 167–69, 171–74
Langhans, Paul, 127–29, 133–37, 139–41, 143, 146–47, 149
Lebensraum, 132, 136, 143, 146
liberal-nationalism in Romantic Germany, 155, 163, 165–66, 167, 172, 174–75
Li Hongzhang, 115, 117
liquidity. See maritime zones, constitutive properties of
Lord Salisbury, 127–28
Lutheran revival, 158

Mackinder, Harold, 146
Magellan/Elcano's circumnavigation, 13, 25
Maravall, Jose Antonio, 7, 15–31, 33
Maritime Alps, 6, 9, 200, 202, 212, 225
Maritime sovereignty, debates in the, 17th–18th century, 99–101
maritime zones: capacities of, 94, 95, 98–99, 101–2, 104–6, 235; constitutive properties of, 8, 90, 92–96, 98–99, 101, 103, 104, 106, 222; contiguous zone, 102; exclusive economic zone, 102–3; human zones, and the imaginary, 89–90, 94–98, 105–6, 221; non-human zones, and the real, 90, 103–6, 222; search and rescue (SAR), 89–90, 102; zones of governance, and the symbolic, 89–92, 97–98, 100–103, 105–6, 221–22
Martin, W. A. P. See Chinese translation of international law
Mártir, Pedro, 15, 25–28, 31
marvellous, the: in medieval epistemologies, 19; in renascent epistemologies, 19–20, 26, 33, 223

medieval imaginary of knowledge: as based on tradition, 18; medieval empiricism, 18
Mitteleuropa, 135, 141, 143–47
mobility, 7, 235
mobility governance: in maritime zones, 91; and migration, 72, 80–82, 228
modernity, 5, 7, 9, 15, 220, 231; emergence of the figure of the modern man, 22, 28; modern *nomos* of the Earth, 99, 101
modes of reasoning, 3, 14, 18, 20, 30, 51, 129, 231, 236, 241
Monk by the Sea, The, 158, 161, 169–71
Moonrise Over the Sea, 165–66
moral economies, 17
mortality, 60, 200–201, 210–13, 224–26

naming, political ontology of, 206–8, 212
Nancy, Jean Luc, 200, 211, 213
Napoleonic subjugation of German lands, 158, 161
NATO, 89–90
Nazism and Caspar David Friedrich, 153–54, 159–63, 174–75, 227
network, 4–5, 7, 9, 44, 200–201, 205–6, 209, 211–13, 235
New World (creation of), 7, 24–25, 27
node, 9, 41, 200–201, 205, 209, 211–13
non-linear thinking, 4
North, Michael, 5, 18, 21
novelty, 5–6, 10, 14–15, 57, 60, 219–20, 238–41; Maravall's conditions of possibility for 15, 17, 22–23, 25, 28, 222–23; renascent problem of 13, 15–16, 18, 21–22, 24, 26–28, 30–31, 34, 222
NSDAP, 134

oikoumene. See Ptolemaic cosmology
On the Sailing Boat, 161
Opium War, 73, 110–11, 116–17, 118, 228

Index ~ 247

organism, 9, 199–202, 204, 206, 212–13, 225
originality, pretension of. *See* novelty, Maravall's conditions of possibility for
Oveja Xisqueta, 200, 205–7, 209, 212, 225

Pan-German League. *See Alldeutscher Verband*
Partsch, Joseph, 144, 146–47
Pecora Sambucana, 200, 202–6, 209, 212, 225
Petermanns Geographische Mitteilungen, 133
phenomenology of zonation, 93, 96–97, 104, 222
ports, in transpacific trading networks, 68–69, 73–74, 76–77, 79–80, 82
post-9/11 security discourse, 40–42, 221
post-humanism, 9
post-structuralism, 199, 212, 224
practices of zonation, 91, 93, 97; political affect of zoning, 93
problematisation, 5, 6, 52, 149, 154, 223–26, 231
properties *vs.* capacities, 92–93
proximity, enactments of, 238–39
Ptolemaic cosmology, 13, 25–26
public health journals, in, nineteenth-century pacific, 75

race, racism, 7–8; in Chinese thought, 118–19, 121–24; and disease discourse, 68–69, 71, 77, 79–80, 83; and urban space, 76–78, 83–84, 227–28
Ramdohr, Friedrich von, 156–57, 165, 170
Ramdohrstreit. *See* Ramdohr, Friedrich von
Ratzel, Friedrich, 132–33
real, the constitution of, 3–4, 6–7, 14, 28
Renaissance system of art classification, 156–58, 166, 168
romantic art and the activation of the viewer, 164, 166, 168–72, 226–27; Friedrich's techniques for activating viewers, 170, 226

Rückenfigur, 158, 162, 165, 170–71, 226
Ruins of Eldena in the Giant Mountains, 161
rural development strategies, 177–82, 199, 223
rural economic history of the Art Urgell, 186–88

San Francisco, nineteenth-century, 70–71, 74, 79–80
Schama, Simon, 160–62, 170
Schmitt, Carl, 69–70, 83, 99, 101
securitisation, 7, 52–53, 56
senses of the new, 17–19, 21, 28
Sloterdijk, Peter, 90–92, 94–96, 98, 104–5
Solitary Tree, The, 153, 171–72
sovereignty, introduction to China, 8, 110–11, 114–18, 120–22, 124, 228, 239–40
space: creation of, 6–7, 14, 139; European space, in German colonial imaginary, 130, 134, 136–37, 139, 143–44, 149; German colonial space, 135, 139, 143, 149; global space as a system of enclosures, 90–91; networked space, 7, 41, 44; non-European space, in German colonial imaginary, 130, 133–34, 136, 147–48, 149; rural space, 9, 178, 223; spaces of governance, 6–7, 14, 31, 33–34, 49–51, 53, 59–60, 147, 149, 155, 160, 163, 172–173, 175, 219–20, 240
Spinoza, Baruch, 3, 15, 53
state system: as an arrangement of macrozones, 91–92; spread to China, 110, 112–13; Westphalian state system as imaginary of connectivity, 110–12, 116, 119–21, 124
statistics, as a technology of power, 134–35, 140–41, 147–48, 229

strange, curiosity for. *See* novelty, Maravall's conditions of possibility for
subjects of governance, creation of, 155, 167–72, 175
surveillance: digital, 7, 56, 221; in, 19th century transpacific disease control, 69, 75, 81–83
systems analysis, 4, 235

Taylor, Charles, 3
temporality, 200, 209, 213
Tian Xia, 8, 109–12, 115–16, 119–20, 124, 228–29, 239–40; as a borderless world, 112, 116–17, 121, 124, 229; as imaginary of connectivity, 110–12, 228–29, 239–40
touch, 9, 61, 211, 225–27, 239; and border security, 53–54
tourism and rurality, 9, 177–82, 188, 190–93, 223–24; as concealing the history of the Art Urgell, 182–86, 188, 224; *vs.* imaginaries of connection, 188–93
treaty of Nanjing, 117–18
treaty port system, 68, 73–78, 81–83, 227–28, 238
trovas, 18–19
Turpentine-makers Museum, 184–85
Two Men Contemplating the Moon, 159, 165

umwelt, 8, 94–97, 104–5
United Nations Convention for the Law of the Sea, 102–3
urban forms, circulation of, 7, 69, 72, 76–78, 83–84

völkische Bewegung, 129, 132–34, 136, 139, 141, 144, 146–49
Von Hutten's Grave, 162, 173

Wanderer above the Sea of Fog, 160–61, 164, 171
Weltpolitik, 132, 136, 143
Western learning, 8, 113, 118–20
Wheaton, Henry. *See* Chinese translation of international law
world-landscape, art tradition of, 166
World maritime Organisation, 102
world system theory, 4

Xue Fucheng, 118–19

Yokohama, nineteenth-century, 67–68, 73–77, 79–80, 82, 227–28

Zhao Tingyang, 109, 111–12
zhu quan, 114–16. *See also* sovereignty, introduction to China
zones. *See* maritime zones

About the Editors and Contributors

Luis Lobo-Guerrero is Professor of History and Theory of International Relations at the University of Groningen where he chairs the department under this name. He is the author of *Insuring Security: Biopolitics, Security and Risk* (2011); *Insuring War: Sovereignty, Security and Risk* (2012); and *Insuring Life: Value, Security and Risk* (2016) as well as numerous articles in various journals and edited volumes.

Suvi Alt is Assistant Professor in International Relations at the University of Groningen. She holds a PhD in international relations from the University of Lapland and works on the areas of international political theory, biopolitics and critical perspectives on development and environmental politics. Her work has been published in *International Political Sociology*, *Millennium*, *Angelaki*, as well as in several edited volumes.

Maarten Meijer is a PhD student at the University of Groningen, where he finished his MA in modern history and international relations in 2018. His research operates on the intersection of ontological debates within continental philosophy, political theory, science and technology studies and environmental thought. His doctoral research focuses on the EU's geopolitics of soils, in which he studies the emerging relation between Europe and soils through scientific and policy practices.

Peter Adey is Professor of Human Geography at Royal Holloway University of London. His research interests are located at the intersections of space, mobility and security, and he is the author of several books including *Air* (2014); *Aerial Life: Mobilities, Spaces, Affects* (2010); and *Mobility* (2009).

Zeynep Gülsah Çapan is Lecturer at University of Erfurt. Her research agenda focuses on Eurocentrism of the field of IR, sociology and historiography of international relations and postcolonial and decolonial thought. She has been a visiting scholar at Copenhagen Business School and Cambridge University. She is author of *Re-Writing International Relations: History and Theory beyond Eurocentrism in Turkey* published in 2016. She has also published articles in *Third World Quarterly*, *Contexto Internacional* and *Review of International Studies* and contributed chapters to several edited volumes. Her recent publications are 'Writing International Relations from the Other Side of the Abyssal Line', *Review of International Studies*; and 'Enacting Internationals/Reproducing Eurocentrism', *Contexto Internacional*.

Sujin Eom is Postdoctoral Fellow at the Department of Geography at Dartmouth College. She is an urban and architectural historian whose research is anchored in a cross-regional and transdisciplinary inquiry into architecture and urbanism. Eom's research interests include global history of architecture, transnational urban history, gender and race, migration and diaspora studies, infrastructure and postcolonial theory. Eom's current research project explores the circulation of technologies of governing urban space during the Cold War. Eom holds a PhD in architecture from the University of California, Berkeley, with a Designated Emphasis in Global Metropolitan Studies.

Carina Huessy is an international relations researcher based in Berlin. Carina completed her bachelor's degree in international relations at Lancaster University (2007) and MA in international security at the University of Sussex (2012). Her research interests lie in the fields of politics, continental philosophy and critical theory. Having worked widely in a range of fields including social and healthcare work, and with formative work experience in the Palestinian Territories and India, these practical, real-life experiences strongly inform her academic work. Her love of writing includes poetry and prose, with the visual arts likewise providing keen inspiration; cycling, hiking and enjoying nature's wonders are her favourite activities.

Camila del Mármol holds a PhD in anthropology and works as Assistant Professor at the University of Barcelona. She has pursued ethnographic research in the Catalan Pyrenees focusing on the development of heritage processes. Her areas of interest and publications include the transformation of political and economic structures in rural areas and its impact on social perceptions and cultural meanings. She has also conducted research on intangible heritage and food heritage in Catalonia and Buenos Aires, Argentina. She is the author of *Pasados locales, políticas globales. Procesos de patrimonialización en un valle del Pirineo catalán* (2012) and co-editor of *The Making of Heritage: Seduction and Disenchantment* (2015).

Paolo Palladino is Professor of History and Theory in the Department of History at Lancaster University, UK. His field of expertise is the structure and evolution of biopolitical formations, particularly as these are articulated within biomedicine and agriculture. He has published three monographs and numerous essays on the subject. His latest research project in this field was enabled by the tenure of a Marie Sklodowska-Curie Individual Fellowship (Horizon 2020) (award no: 657750) in the Department of History and Theory of International Relations at the University of Groningen (Netherlands), where he holds a position as Honorary Research Fellow.

Filipe dos Reis is Assistant Professor at the University of Groningen. He holds a PhD in international relations at the University of Erfurt, where he also held a position as research associate ('Wissenschaftlicher Mitarbeiter') and has been a member at the interdisciplinary Center of Political Practices and Orders. His research focuses on international relations theories, global history and, in particular, the intersection of international relations and international law. With regard to the latter, he has expertise in the sociology of interdisciplinarity and the politics of jurisdiction in international law. He has been a visiting scholar at Bilgi University Istanbul, Bilkent University Ankara and the Vrije Universiteit Amsterdam. He has published in *New Perspectives* and contributed chapters to several edited volumes, including one in *The Power of Legality* (2016) and the *Oxford Handbook of the Theory of International Law* (2016).

Barry J. Ryan is Senior Lecturer in international relations at Keele University, after having lectured at the University of Limerick, Dublin City University and Lancaster University in the fields of international relations theory, security studies and conflict studies. He is a member of the editorial boards of *Capital and Class*, *Journal of the Indian Ocean Region* and *Regional Security* (University of Belgrade). His current research is concerned with spatial strategies of security and the maritime environment and the implications for IR theory of a critical turn towards the politics of sea.

Ariel Shangguan is Postdoctoral Fellow at the Schwarzman College at Tsinghua University. She holds a PhD in international politics at Newcastle University, UK. Her research interest mainly lies in the temporal-spatial conditionality of Western IR concepts and its translation into Chinese and Japanese discourses. She is a contributor to the book *Modern Japanese Political Thought and International Relations*, published in 2018.

Benjamin Tallis is Senior Researcher at the Institute of International Relations in Prague. He edits the academic journal *New Perspectives*, regularly appears in European media and advises a variety of European and North American governments. His research interests include European security; politics of border; critical geopolitics and political geography; politics of Central and Eastern Europe; post-communism and transition policy; foreign, security and neighbourhood policy and EU justice and home affairs policy; cultural policy (specifically architectural and material memory policy); critical pragmatism; and interpretive research methodology.

www.ingramcontent.com/pod-product-compliance
Lightning Source LLC
Chambersburg PA
CBHW070027010526
44117CB00011B/1740